"An absolutely compelling war memoir marked by the author's incredible strength of character and vulnerability."

—*Kirkus*, **starred review**

"A searing and moving memoir. . . . As she reflects on the many ways she brought the war home with her, King reveals the unique burdens borne by female veterans as they reintegrate into a society that seems oblivious to all they've been through. This is a harrowing and powerful book."

—*Publishers Weekly*

"Raw and unvarnished, as it must be, combat veteran Brooke King's memoir *War Flower* is a searing and unforgettable journey through death and dying, both at war and on the home front—as a child and as a mother, as a soldier and as a civilian. She somehow manages to braid several memoirs into one, offering several lenses into the battlefield of the mind, and the result is a book that has earned its place on the high shelf of American literature. While *War Flower* is set to 'the tuned pitch of human pain,' this is a book about survival. I've waited for this book for many years now, and yet, as I turn the last page, I'm stunned in the reading of it."

—**Brian Turner, author of** *My Life as a Foreign Country* **and** *Here, Bullet*

"Searing with unapologetic candor and grit—even during its surprising, fragmented moments of breathtaking, heartbreaking poeticism—Brooke King's *War Flower* sweeps aside all veils of illusion regarding the impact of trauma and moral injury on the human psyche, while also illuminating the disturbing cross-generational consequences of war. For those who have asked for years, *Where are the combat memoirs from women veterans?* Brace for impact."

—**Tracy Crow, coeditor of** *It's My Country Too: Women's Military Stories from the American Revolution to Afghanistan*

"In her memoir about a combat deployment to Iraq, army veteran Brooke King writes, 'Nothing good survives war.' I would beg to differ: King went to war, lived through months of unthinkable horrors, and returned with a very good book in her duffel bag. *War Flower* will leave no reader unmoved, no soul unscathed."

—**David Abrams, author of** *Brave Deeds* **and** *Fobbit*

"*War Flower* provides a different, but necessary perspective on modern war, and on war as a female soldier."

—Jade Anna Hughes, *From the Inside*

"Love, regret, sex, death, mistakes, forgiveness—it's real in the military and everywhere, and nothing is easy, but people contain a million things, and the beauty of writing is that the author decides what to keep, and what to let get away."

—*Military Spouse Book Review*

# WAR FLOWER

# WAR FLOWER

## MY LIFE AFTER IRAQ

BROOKE KING

Potomac Books
*An imprint of the University of Nebraska Press*

Acknowledgments for the use of copyrighted material
appear on page 255, which constitutes an extension of the
copyright page.

First Nebraska paperback printing: 2022

Library of Congress Cataloging-in-Publication Data
Names: King, Brooke, author.
Title: War flower: my life after Iraq / Brooke King.
Other titles: My life after combat in Iraq
Description: Lincoln, NE: Potomac Books, an imprint of
the University of Nebraska Press, [2019]
Identifiers: LCCN 2018028081
ISBN 9781640121188 (cloth: alk. paper)
ISBN 9781640125452 (paperback)
ISBN 9781640121812 (epub)
ISBN 9781640121829 (mobi)
ISBN 9781640121836 (pdf)
Subjects: LCSH: King, Brooke. | Iraq War, 2003–2011—
Personal narratives, American. | Iraq War, 2003–2011—
Veterans—United States—Biography. | Iraq War,
2003–2011—Campaigns. | United States. Army—Women—
Biography. | Women soldiers—United States—Biography. |
Pregnant women—United States—Biography. |
Post-traumatic stress disorder—Patients—United
States—Biography. | United States. Army—Women—
Social conditions. | Women in combat—United States.
Classification: LCC DS79.76 .K547 2019 | DDC
956.7044/342092 [B] –dc23 LC record available at
https://lccn.loc.gov/2018028081

Set in Questa by E. Cuddy.

*for Bowen and Zachary*

**war flower**—a term coined during Operation Iraqi Freedom (OIF) to describe a female soldier (usually enlisted) who has miraculously survived a mission and/or deployment without sustaining physical injuries.

# CONTENTS

# PROLOGUE

## Confessions

Before the court-martial began, I looked past the judge's bench toward the window where, outside, the rest of the world was going about its day. The sun came out, and the rain clouds that lingered all morning had shifted places in the sky. Streaks of water ran down the window, which had been opened to ventilate the room of its stifled air. Cars splashed by on the street outside, and from the witness chair I could see the sun reflecting rays of light on the puddles, but the sun would not last. Soon the clouds would return; outside and inside would be filled with darkness.

He sat behind the partition at a desk, next to his attorney, who was shuffling papers back and forth, reaching over every once in a while to look into his briefcase to make sure he hadn't forgotten anything. He was sitting there, waiting for me to look at him. He did not know that I had been briefed not to stare, not to smile, not to look anywhere in his direction, so he looked at me and waited for a small gesture that might never come.

The line of questioning began with a Bible, an oath of truth, and a hand held up.

The prosecution asked my name, if I was deployed, why I had come back early from deployment, and if I was married, and I answered all questions truthfully. My name was Private First Class Brooke Nicole King. I deployed to Iraq in August 2006. I had come back early from deployment due to pregnancy, and yes, I was married.

"Are you married to the accused, PFC King?"

"No, sir."

He fidgeted in his chair, straightening himself up at the sound of being labeled "the accused."

"Who is the father of that baby?"

"Captain Haislop."

"How do you know that?"

"Because . . ."

I couldn't bring myself to say it out loud, and before I had time to fabricate an answer that wouldn't lead to more lines of questioning, the defense attorney stood up.

"Objection. This calls for speculation, sir."

I looked down, too tempted to stare at him.

"Let me rephrase. Have you had sexual relations with the accused?"

"Yes."

I began to cry.

"I did."

I looked up and noticed a box of tissues on his desk.

I wiped my eyes, trying not to look at him through the motions of brushing the tears away from my cheek. He leaned toward his attorney and pointed at the box of tissues.

"Will the investigating officer allow me to rise and hand the box of tissues to PFC King?"

The prosecution walked over and took it before the defense could leave his seat. The tissues were placed in front of me, but I didn't pull any from the box.

"Are you able to continue, PFC King?"

I did not answer. I looked at every part of him but his face. His hands were folded in his lap. His uniform crisp and his boots cleaned up. His hair freshly cut. I couldn't stop looking. And I did it. I looked into his eyes.

He nodded his head and smiled.

"PFC King, may I remind you that you are under a no contact order and are here as part of an agreement to testify. May we continue?"

I nodded my head, but it was too late, I could not look away now.

"Okay. You mentioned just a bit earlier that the accused in this case is the father of the child?"

"Yes."

"Do you remember giving a statement on April 17th?"

"Yes."

"And during that statement you were asked who the father was. Do you remember your response?"

"No, I do not."

"You said, 'I decline to state.' Why'd you say that?"

I studied his face. My eyes traced the outline of his jaw, the round edges of his nose, the creases at the corner of his eyes.

"PFC King, I will not remind you again. You are under a no contact order and are not permitted to look at the accused."

I did not look away.

"I said that because of the fact that I did not at the time want to give them the name of the father."

He smiled at me.

"Did you know who the father was at the time?"

I smiled back.

"Yes."

The prosecution looked at me.

"PFC King, if you do not comply with the no contact order, you will be found in contempt of court. Do you understand?"

"Yes."

I looked at the prosecution.

"I understand."

"Who was the father?"

"Captain Haislop."

"But you did not want to tell at the time?"

"Yes."

"Even though you were under oath?"

"Yes."

He leaned forward in his chair. He had never heard this part before, the way I had tried to help him before all of this, and even now, I sat there defiant, still unwilling to give in to the prosecution's line of questioning.

He reached across the table, poured a cup of water, handed it to his attorney, and pointed to me. The defense attorney rose and handed it to the prosecution.

I took the water and tightened my hands around the cup where his had been moments ago.

"Can you state for the record if you have filed for divorce?"

"I have drawn the papers but not filed."

"Does the accused know your husband?"

"He knows *of* him."

"So the accused knows that you are married?"

"Yes."

I lowered my head and looked at the cup of water. I felt the plastic around the rim, dipped my finger into the water, and moved my padded fingertip over the lip in circular motions, but the cup would not emit a sound.

"And yet, though you're married, you entered into a sexual relationship with the accused?"

I was agitated. The wooden seat was hard, with no cushion to soften the plank.

"I left my husband because on more than one occasion he would throw me down stairs, beat me, slap me, and threaten to kill me."

He did not look at me. He couldn't bear this line of questioning. The window gave no light. In the near dark he fidgeted with his hands in his lap, rolling the ring I had given him around on his finger. He moved it up and down, then over the knuckle and back again as the line of questioning continued.

I felt my courage slipping along with my ability to speak of my estranged husband without loathing every sentence.

"Is it safe to say then, PFC King, the divorce had to do with his treatment of you?"

"Yes."

"But you have not filed yet?"

"No, I have not."

"So you are still married, carrying a child that is not your husband's?"

"Yes, but I love the father of my child. He loves me."

I said it unchecked, as I looked into his eyes. He was smiling at me. And though I was not permitted to say a word to him, I mouthed, "I love you."

It was the first time I had said it out loud.

# WAR FLOWER

# PART 1

## War Is a Machine

· · · · · ·

## Orders

There was no way of getting out of this one; I was fucked. I scaled each step knowing that in front of me a procession of soldiers were climbing up the staircase too, one that didn't lead to heaven but to a porthole on the side of a big metal bird that was painted a patriotic red, white, and blue. The American flag plastered on its wing waved as though it was flying in the wind, but the metal bird was still. The other soldiers gripped the railing tight with their black-gloved hands, but I didn't raise my head to look where I was going; part of me didn't want to know. I was out of place amid a sea of soldiers dressed in digital gray, soldiers who climbed in mindless unison ahead of and behind me. I watched the stairs as I ascended, the large pixilated gray backpack weighing heavily on my shoulders. I had to slump over to maintain my balance. We filed up the staircase one after another, our weapons in hand and our tactical vests attached, each one of us combat ready as we trudged up the steps. We knew all too well that we might be heading to our deaths, but I kept my head down in a desperate attempt to avoid what I already knew to be true: my fate was as uncertain as it was for the rest of these poor fuckers.

The plane would be overcrowded, the flight full of sweaty soldiers who had been standing on the tarmac long enough to be cooked well done. Though the air was still, the flag on the wing of the metal bird still waved, its stripes not long enough to cover the entire rear wing of the plane. I still carried my head down as I ascended the stairs, still stuck in a sea of digital gray. I still refused to touch the railing with my hand, even though I was struggling to maintain my balance. I heaved my head down and focused on each step that took me farther away from home, farther away from familiarity, farther away from safety.

None of the soldiers looked at each other, the solitary ascension of the inevitable, a short stop and a quick drop; some were not ready for the destination. I overheard one of the section sergeants say when he was waiting on the tarmac that only an idiot would think that this flight was a round-trip.

Each one of us filed up the stairs and into the plane, filling in the seats of the plane from the back to the front. The officers were in the front of the plane and the grunts were in the back, as usual, all of us crammed into that thing like a pack of sardines, all smashed and jammed together as tight as we could go, like shoving five pounds of shit into a two-pound bag. None of us could take off our gear because the overhead bin couldn't withstand the weight. The best we could do was take the helmet off, throw the rifle between our legs, and undo the Velcro that held the vest tightly together so that we could at least breathe and sleep semicomfortably on the six-hour flight to Kuwait International Airport. It took two and a half hours to load both Alpha and Bravo Company's soldiers onto the plane, 150 in all. We were the last of the battalion to leave.

Specialist Tina Kennedy looked over at me. "That tax-free October paycheck is going to look real nice in my bank account."

"That's what you're concerned about right now?"

She shrugged.

I looked around the cabin of the plane and noticed everyone getting comfortable. Tina was already pulling off her vest and laying her rifle on the floor beneath her feet. I wanted to do the same, except I knew that if I took off my vest, it was going to be a bitch to get back on, so I opted for just loosening it. Private Cheyanne Anderson, my battle buddy from basic training, was already asleep next to me on my left; Tina was starting to get comfortable on my right.

"No fucking way are you going to sleep before me," I said.

"You kept me up almost all of last night with your damn snoring. Fuck if I'm going let you cheat me out of the sleep I need now. You ever seen me sleep deprived enough to jam my sock down your throat?"

Tina looked at me inquisitively, as if to gauge whether or not I was capable of doing such a thing to her, but the crazy bulging eye stare that I was giving her was proof enough that it might be a good idea to let me sleep without waking me up until we got there.

"All right, you have until ten minutes after takeoff to fall asleep. After that you are on your own because I can be just as much of a bitch if I don't get my sleep either."

"Yeah, don't I know it."

She gave me her patented "fuck you" look, which made me laugh. The plane began to taxi down the runway, and as the flight attendant was telling us the usual spiel about safety, I decided to ad-lib my own version of her required routine safety instructions: "To buckle your safety belt, place the buckle over your lap and insert the flat part into the buckle. If you need assistance because you are too stupid to do it yourself, please don't hit the call button because if you can't figure out a kindergarten-level activity like this, you deserve to die. In case of a water evacuation, your seat may be used as a flotation device. Gently punch the person next to you, taking their flotation device as well as yours and use both of them as floaties in order to maximize your chances of surviving in the event of a water landing. If the plane should spiral into a fiery descent, the exits are located in the front, side, and rear of the cabin. Please find the nearest location to your seat, exit quickly and quietly while trampling anyone in your way since every single one of us is fucked. In the event that the cabin loses pressure, place the mask over your head to hide your scared face from the person next to you. If the person next to you is in need of assistance, please secure your mask first. After you have carefully secured your mask, point and laugh at them for being an idiot. If you are seated in an exit aisle, please take the card that is located in the front pocket of the seat in front of you and read the instructions very fucking carefully, so you don't kill everyone on the plane in the event of an emergency. Thank you for not paying attention to a word I've just said, and on behalf of the flight crew, we hope you enjoy your nonstop flight into a hostile combat zone."

Tina was laughing hysterically as the plane began to lift off the runway and make its ascent into the clouds. I looked out the nearby port window and watched as the runway and the air base faded away into a tiny speck; it was my last glance at what a peaceful country looked like. I turned to look over at Tina.

With a glare she said, "You have ten minutes."

I leaned my head on the headrest behind me and lowered my helmet over my eyebrows just enough so I could use my hair bun as a pillow. I put on my black Oakleys and closed my eyes, but what seemed like only minutes asleep had passed into hours.

The loud extension of the landing gear shook me awake. I nearly jumped out of my seat from the loud banging. I looked over at Tina. She was staring at me. I must have been talking in my sleep or something. She gave me a weird look and then shook her head. Over the loudspeaker the flight attendant was telling us to prepare for landing. Moments later the wheels would touch the ground. We would be in country, but this wasn't Iraq. No, it was much worse. Kuwait.

Tina chimed in as the flight attendant prepared the doors for arrival: "Thank you for flying Iraq Airlines. We hope you enjoyed your flight. Please take all belongings with you as you exit the aircraft. Items left on the aircraft, such as hopes and dreams, will be thrown away upon your exit. We do hope you remember when going into a hostile territory that you think of Iraq Airlines as your number-one choice when flying to your death. We know you have no choice, but on behalf of Iraq Airlines and the flight crew, we thank you for letting us overcharge your government for this shitty flight and hope you have a horrible stay in country."

Choking back a laugh as I sipped water from my canteen, I turned to look at Tina, who was holding her hand over her mouth like she was talking into the airplane intercom. She stood up and pulled her gear to her shoulders but fell back onto me. I put my canteen away and pushed her off me. Her gear weighed more than she did, but it didn't stop the red-headed, freckle-framed, buck-o-five twig of a battle buddy I had from swinging her 120-pound flak vest onto her back again. It was loaded to the teeth with ammunition, and the vest looked as though it would swallow her tiny frame whole. "Tiny Tina," as I called her, was one of the only female friends I had in the Bravo Company because I trusted her not to stab me in the back or throw me underneath the bus like all the other female soldiers. It was a girl thing that I could never understand; the kill-or-be-killed mentality that women in the military had for one another. Soon that wouldn't matter much to me, not in this place.

"Are you just going sit there and watch me struggle or are you going help a sister out?"

Realizing that I was just sitting there watching her struggle, I tried to help. In a cramped airplane seat Tina and I tried to stand and lift the vest onto her back.

"Damn, Brooke, just stick your ass in my face why don't you."

I turned my head to look at Anderson, who had her arms up in the air in a big Y shape, as if silently saying with her gesture, "What the fuck!"

"It's not the first time my ass has been in your face."

"Yeah, well, you better move your ass before I slap it."

I rolled my eyes and turned back around.

"Tina, why in the hell does your vest weigh more than mine? You're a 92 Alpha. Supply clerks sit behind a desk all day and push paper around. How much ammo do you really need?"

"You're a mechanic that fixes trucks all day. You think you need that much ammo too?"

"Touché."

As I tried to get her arm through one of the vest armholes, I grumbled out a retort to her argument. "Well, at least I might actually see combat, seeing as I'm on the recovery team."

"I wouldn't advertise that, Brooke. Sergeant Lippert's not exactly a nice guy."

As she finally folded the front flap over, attached the Velcro to the vest front, and sat down, I glanced over at Sergeant Lippert. He was sitting next to Sergeant Helm, across the way from us and up one aisle. His black Oakley sunglasses scanned the airplane until he turned his head and made eye contact with me.

"Sit the fuck down, Private!"

It was not exactly what I was expecting and the shocked look on my face made him laugh.

"Are you deaf, Private?"

Tina yanked the handle on the back of my vest and pulled me to my seat.

"Have you lost your fucking mind? I told you not to go advertising. Do yourself a favor, since it's your first deployment: keep your head down and your mouth shut. Don't volunteer for anything or draw attention to yourself, and that includes standing up on a plane that is full of sergeants who would love to chew a newbie like you a new ass."

Her advice sounded like something out of *Full Metal Jacket*. Sergeant Lippert looked like the Gunnery Sergeant Hartman type. I half expected him to come over and yell at me at the top of his lungs, eyes bulging out of his face, two inches from my head, screaming, "You had best unfuck yourself or I will unscrew your head and shit down your neck." I tried not to make eye contact with him again.

The plane was making its descent into Kuwait International Airport. As everyone prepared to land in full battle rattle, the soldiers shuffled their weight around trying to get comfortable in their seat, but no one spoke. The plane was silent. Tina was putting on her helmet, making sure to tuck her long red bangs behind each ear in an attempt to avoid helmet hair. I lowered my head in thought and straddled my M4.

The back wheels touched down, and from the runway you could see the vast desert that was Kuwait. A place in the middle of fucking nowhere and somewhere every soldier didn't want to be. As the plane taxied, Tina lowered her head and whispered, "Brooke, it's not as bad as you think. This is my second time around. Each time gets easier. I promise. I know that you're scared, but so was I my first deployment."

"That's easy for you to say. You have a cake job. I'm a mechanic with recovery training. It's not a matter of if I go outside the wire; it's a matter of when."

As she pulled on her tan military-issue combat aviator gloves, she peered at me. I sat there in my confined seat, still straddling my M4 with a newfound death grip. A long strand of my brown hair, not quite long enough to pull all the way back into my bun, kept falling in my face. I struggled to keep it out of my eyes, which were started to well up with tears. Tina could still make out that something was wrong with me beneath my reflective Oakley sunglasses. She placed her hand on my forearm.

"It'll be okay. We're in this thing together, battle."

I looked at her and smiled. When the port door opened, each soldier stood, filed into the aisle, and walked off the plane. I followed Tina. Walking into the doorway of the plane, a wall of heat hit me, almost like your body slamming up against a brick building; there was no give. I could see the ripples of blistering heat wafting off the tarmac. Below the staircase were three rows of fully air-conditioned buses, but all I could think about as I walked down the staircase was if I was going to survive this deployment in one piece.

The long, unsteady trudge down the stairs had dowsed me in sweat, soaking my crisp new "fresh from basic" ACUS. I followed the lined procession of soldiers walking toward the buses, but for a moment I looked out over the desert beyond the tarmac as the sun began setting in violent oranges and reds and realized in that moment that even though I was far from home, I could still enjoy the sunset.

"Private, get on the fucking bus."

Sergeant Lippert was behind me in the line and had been following me to the buses. My sudden pause and reflection had held up the line of soldiers. I turned around to see fifteen soldiers giving me the stink eye and Sergeant Lippert's black Oakleys staring me straight in the face.

"Well, Private. You officially just made my shit list. You better hope to God you ain't in my section."

From behind me I felt someone yank me away from Sergeant Lippert, who was chuckling a low, bellowing laugh at the "scared shitless" look on my face. I whipped my head around to notice that Tina had pulled me to safety.

"This is going to be a long deployment if I have to keep pulling you out of the fire."

With a blank stare on my face, Tina shook her head, rolled her eyes, and pushed me to the front of the line, where she had been before my second encounter with Sergeant Lippert.

I have to admit it: back then I had a knack for getting into trouble.

• • •

The heat coming off the land in Kuwait burned on your skin like a long day in the sun at the beach. The sweat poured down your back on your spinal column as it made its way to your belt line, gathering in a pool as it drenched your tan undershirt. The nights were cold, a reprieve from the heat, but they were longer and made it seems as though the weeks of not pushing north to Iraq were a scene from *Groundhog Day*, Bill Murray's stagnant face staring blankly off into space as he realizes the date on the newspaper is the same as it was the day before.

Our battalion began taking on equipment, hand-me-downs from the last brigade that was making its way back home. We were their relief, but with no orders to go any farther than Kuwait we sat in the desert for a month waiting until it was our turn to jump into the sandbox and get our boots weighed down by the war. I had tried to avoid Rob, my husband, while in Kuwait, sticking to groups, never letting us be alone together, but somehow he managed to get me alone the night before we were to finally push north. He begged for my forgiveness, for all the time spent bickering and fighting, but I had none in me to give. I had told him as much, but the emptiness in his eyes told me that though he was at fault for his behavior, his training and previous deployments had worn his soul thin enough to make his mind incapable of being human again. He had succumbed to so much and still had not been able to come out the same. I looked at him that night knowing that this might be the last time I would see him, that somehow I would be rid of him after all this was over. In the motor pool that night, I looked over vehicles, checked connexes, and double-checked manifests to make sure all of our equipment would make it to Baghdad. At night I watched the c-130s take off from the airstrip toward Iraq. Their evasive combat aerial maneuvers were made like the ducks and dives of a water fowl trying to avoid the barrel of a hunter's gun. I had watched this every night for a month. October had come and gone as we waited for orders that we thought would never come, but as I sat there watching them I thought about how fitting it was that tomorrow we were to be in the line of fire and how much courage I would need to summon for it.

· · · · · · · · · · · ·

## Operator Error

The Browning machine gun, caliber .50, m2, hb, is a belt-fed, recoil-operated, air-cooled, crew-served machine gun. The gun is capable of either single-shot delivery or automatic fire. It is used to support soldiers in both attack and defense, destroy lightly armored vehicles, and provide protection for motor movements. It weighs eighty-four pounds and has a barrel that is forty-five inches long. The maximum range of the .50 cal is 6,764 meters, but it is most effective at 1,800 meters.

I volunteered to train on the .50 cal in Kuwait. The range was hot, live-fire exercises. Sergeant Diaz, ncoic of the range, showed me how to lock and load the machine gun. I looked up at him.

"How do I aim it?"

He laughed. "You don't aim. You fire and fuck shit up."

Seemed easy enough.

He was showing me the parts of the weapon: the butter-fly trigger, the housing, how to switch out barrels and do the headspace and timing. I watched the distance as he spoke. A herd of camels had found its way onto our improvised shooting range. As they got closer, the firing stopped on the other ranges. Soldiers who had been lying in the prone position, legs canted off sideways, weapons on sandbags, stopped shooting and stood up. Sergeant Diaz came over and asked what the hell was going on. They pointed to the camels. He spouted off the maximum effective range of the M16 and M4 rifles and then assured them that they were too far in the distance to catch a bullet. Reluctantly the soldiers went back down in the prone position. The other sergeants on the range stood behind them and watched as the soldiers tried to get a grouping of three on their target board. Sometimes they bent down to point at what they were doing wrong, other times to hand them another magazine or critique their firing position. I watched as Sergeant Diaz came back over and loaded the .50 cal. He reminded me that the maximum effective range of a .50 cal machine gun was eighteen hundred meters and popped off the first couple of rounds. It exploded, *clat-clat-clat, clat-clat*. The rounds were sequencing in and spitting out as fast as Sergeant Diaz could make up his mind to pull the trigger. I looked off into the distance where Sergeant Diaz was shooting and watched as the camels fell one by one. He smiled. Target practice.

· · · · · · · · · · · · · ·

## Hurry Up and Wait

We sat in the shadows of our Humvees. Others stood or crouched but never lay on the sand. We stared out across the desert, or at each other, or at nothing at all and waited, simply waited.

Though it had only been a month since they told us that we were leaving, our troubles weighed down our gear. We did not talk to one another. Some of us thought of home, others of family. We pulled drag after drag off a smoke stick, hoping that by the end of this cigarette the orders would be cast and Kuwait would look like a dot connected by dashes on a map.

The younger soldiers paced back and forth, fidgeted, asked too many questions, and answered them before anyone could speak. The older soldiers, the ones who had been in the suck, they said nothing, looked into the distance, stood with a lax in their back leg, as if to say, I've seen hell and that is where they're sending us. The young didn't look at the old; their eyes stared down at the ground. They didn't want to know what hell looked like.

It was here that they said a man may find himself, gain the true measure of what it was to exist, but here was nowhere, a place in the desert set up and held, all of us roped in like cattle waiting for the slaughter. Here we ceased to exist as women or men. Here we were only the distant memory that our loved ones remembered. Here we were soldiers, and the remembering of training was of no consequence. Everything was now muscle memory, reactions, reflex, the texture of trigger pulls ingrained in fingertip feels and pressure points, the recall of radio 9 line medevac, call signs, and standard operating procedures.

And somewhere back home, someone was missing you already, and even though they could still smell your scent on the sheets, they gripped the pillow tight every night for comfort. Some soldiers started to talk, and it was then that they spoke of home, of families, of too many nights wasted. The longing started to creep in and someone quickly changed the subject. A deck of cards was produced with pictures of known Iraqi militants and leaders plastered on the faces. We played gin, spades, Texas Hold'em. We sang Lynyrd Skynyrd, rapped Dr. Dre, and shouted the lyrics to The Who's "Baba O'Riley." We talked shit about the newbie's ate-up rifle sling, pointed fingers and placed bets on how many NCOs would be going home to an empty house. We cleaned weapons, fixed trucks, talked more shit about the first sergeant's bitch of a wife. We waited, and waited, until the waiting became unbearable. We didn't want to go. We didn't want to die, but they said that another battalion would take our place, that it wouldn't be that long over in the box, that we might even get stationed somewhere safe, somewhere that didn't see combat. They said to desert was dishonor, to stay and fight was courageous, but the young were scared and the old were restless, gun happy, and ready. And when the orders came down to push north, we all stood up and shouted "Hooah" because we had chosen war and there was nothing more tempting than looking death in the face and saying, "Fuck you."

· · · · · · · · · · · ·

## Baghdad, Iraq

### 33°20' N, 44°30' E

I looked outside the open bay door of the c-130 and down the runway of Baghdad International Airport to where the end of the tarmac met the land, and I thought about my husband, Rob, and how relieved I was to be here, that I was no longer sharing the same roof with him anymore. He had been deployed to Ramadi, away from me. I thought about the last time I had seen him and shivered at the distorted memory of spousal abuse as it played back in my head.

It was never the fall down the stairs that hurt. It was the being dragged back up that was painful—the feeling of having to do the same night on repeat for the fifth or sixth time that month. It almost always started the same way: I would forget that I was his wife. On these nights I would get home first, take a shower, and start dinner before he got home from end of day formation. I'd drape my uniform over the front of the couch, getting everything ready for the next day, the 0500 wake-up call for morning formation and PT, which lasted just long enough for me to contemplate why I got up in the first place.

He would come home late. I tried flipping the veggies over in the skillet on low heat as often as I could, but I had gotten lost in a Nelson DeMille novel Nana had sent me last week in a care package. Rob walked into a house smelling of burned veggies—that was strike one. So consumed in the novel, I

War Is a Machine

hadn't noticed him coming through the front door—strike two. When he came for his usual hug, I kissed him on the cheek— the last straw for him. Grabbing the book from my hands, he threw it against the front window of our apartment. Startled, I looked up, but my glance was too familiar to him: the look of a defiant, independent woman needing to be tamed. He snatched me up from the sofa by my arm and half-dragged me into the kitchen.

"Can't even fucking cook vegetables."

He shoved me toward the stove, told me I was no good. Slammed up against the stove, I braced myself for the inevitable as I turned around. He would let into his rant on how he worked all day, I would spit back that I worked just as hard but wasn't bitching about it. And that's when it would come, the first slap in the face.

I had married early, barely nineteen when I said "I do" to a man I had known barely three months. I was young, stupid, and afraid of deploying to Iraq with no one to talk to but my family. So, I did it. I married Rob without thinking. There was something about him I couldn't shake, a mysteriousness about him that felt more like secure danger. It must have been his smile, but now I cannot remember why I truly decided to go against my family's judgments and frustrations about my match, but either way, I had done it. I married Rob. It wasn't the best decision to make right before deployment, but when you're young and dumb and facing war, anything looks like a good idea. I wanted someone to love me, someone to look out for me over there. For all his faults and misgivings, Rob loved me; he cared, and for my nineteen-year-old self, it was the only reassurance I needed, but that feeling didn't last long. Nearly a month after we married, after all the training for war had been completed, after we had settled down into our on-base apartment on the third floor, he began to change and so did I. I no longer wanted him because his love had turned sour, like milk that had sat out on the counter for a week or two. Our love for each other rotted and morphed into something that I'm sure now would be labeled as a volatile relationship, one I'm certain that we both created, but one that he took just a little too far.

I looked at him, disgusted that the gender bias was ready to fall from his lips, a full-throttled hatred for my kind, his masculine need to overpower the fact that even though we were the same rank in the army, he was in charge of this house. He grabbed my arm and yanked me toward him.

We had done this song and dance plenty of times before. My response was always the same, unyielding to his stance that he ruled the roost.

"Fuck you."

The contempt for his position in my life rolled off my tongue like Dante's seventh circle of hell, the violence on our lips patiently waiting for one of us to strike. His blow was hard and fast, across my cheek and nose, the blood slowly seeping out as I turned and spit in his face. With a handful of hair and a drag down the hall into the bedroom, I was thrown onto the bed and held down, his hands searching for the buttons in my jeans. A kick in the stomach kept him off as I scrambled for the door. A turn of fear had changed this fight into an all-out war, a fight to keep out of his reach, the first time his rage had turned to rape. He slammed me against the bed face down and fucked me from behind, his hand on the back of my head, shoving it into the feather down comforter. I cried into it, hoping the feathers would muffle my screams as he ripped the tissue between my ass and clit. My tears had become a puddle on the bed by the time he was finished; he shoved my head into the bed one last time before he got up and walked toward the kitchen. I got up, pulled my jeans up, but as I redid the top button and turned to leave, I caught a glimpse of myself in the full-length mirror on the wall. Clenching my hands, I walked into the kitchen. He stood there with a beer in his hand.

"Why do you make me do these things?" He looked at me and took a swig. "You know I don't want to, but you know you deserve it."

I started to plate the food I had prepared for him. As I went to hand it to him, he reached out, but I stopped short, drop-ping the plate on the floor.

He looked up at me; the glint of contempt in my eyes fueled his anger. He leaned up off the kitchen counter and moved toward me, but I had already grabbed the knife from the sink. He dared me not to do it, but I pointed the knife at him and swung, threatening that if he came closer to me I'd slit his throat.

"Fucking try me."

I swiped the knife at him as he came closer. He moved out of the way, but his counter move was better than mine. The knife was his now and I, powerless in his chokehold grip. I had remembered my training—arms straight up, slip down, and use force. I was free and making a break for the door, but the lock proved my downfall. Like I said, the fall down the flight of stairs didn't hurt until he started to drag me back up, my feet barely able to catch a step for footing. My screams echoed down the stairwell. Neighbors came out to look, but on a military base where domestic violence and fighting are common occurrences, my screams fell on the deaf ears of the men who came out to watch which woman was getting it that night. It was just luck—his mostly—that I didn't have a bro-ken bone, just bruises. He checked me over as I lay on the liv-ing room floor.

He threw a kitchen towel at me. "Clean yourself up; you're bleeding on the new rug."

When I first met Rob, he wasn't mean or nasty or even close to anything resembling who he was that day in our apartment. We met at a bus stop outside of Ledward Barracks in Schwein-furt, Germany. I sat there shoveling hot seasoned fries from the *Döner* vending cart, trying my best get my stomach to stop gurgling. As I shoveled another handful into my mouth, I heard him say, "Those look pretty good."

I smiled and looked over to see him, Rob. Standing there, large beret covering one eye, like an airborne paratrooper, briefcase in hand. Yes, he was carrying a briefcase. It was the first time I had ever seen anyone my age carry a briefcase, let alone a soldier. I thought it odd, but then again I dismissed it because, well, he was cute.

"You want one?"

"No, it's okay."

"I don't mind, really." I dangled the fries toward him, as if to tempt a nag to an apple. He walked over and grabbed one and quickly ate it. He was hungry. Damn. I knew I wasn't going to be able to eat them all, and so I asked him if he'd like to sit next to me and share them, hinting that I wouldn't be able to finish them all and really didn't mind sharing. He smiled, walked over, and sat on the bus stop bench with me and we began to talk. He was coy and funny, charming in a way that made you want to call him a dork but also made him endearing and lovable. I was smitten.

The conversation carried over to the bus and the slow, trudging walk back onto base to my company buildings. Yes, he walked me all the way to my company door like a gentleman. Now, I think he truly did it so he would know what battalion I was in so he could track me down. I thought him weird like that, but it didn't matter to me. I wanted to see him again and I did. Weeks turned into months of dating until he asked me to marry him, and like a doe-eyed young girl in love, I said yes in all my naiveté. It wasn't until we had been married and living together for a month that he started to turn, like cheese sitting in the fridge too long. Our relationship became stagnant and corrupted by the stress of deploying. He began to become enraged for no reason, at small things that I did, and soon I no longer wanted to be around him. I dreaded coming home every night after work. Our apartment began to feel like a jail, a place where he could trap me and do and say whatever he wanted. Several times I tried to talk to him, but it only made him worse, throwing things, yelling, and sometimes taking hold of me and tossing me against a wall.

Life as a military wife and soldier had decidedly not been like I had wanted it, and for a short time I happily counted down the days to deployment like a child would count down the days till Christmas morning. Being deployed meant not being with Rob every day; it meant I was one step closer to being rid of him for good, and it was that part of me that wanted him to die in Iraq. However evil it sounds to say, I wanted to be rid of him and I knew there was a chance that Iraq would do it for me.

The night we made it to Baghdad International Airport's runway, the lights flickered in slightly disjointed unison as the wheels on the metal bird were chocked and the cargo bay door lowered. Our 5-tons and LMTVs had made it up north before us. Several of them waited in the wings to transport us to the housing pad full of metal connexes made into living units: hooches that were more like prison cells with A/C units. The whole base looked like a rundown trailer park in the middle of Georgia or Missouri. We had been equipped with machines, weapons, and gear—the best the army could give us to help us survive. Our new ACU flak vests were given a facelift: extra padding around the shoulder. We called them bullshit wings. The rest of our gear was called full battle rattle: knee and elbow pads, flak vest with six magazine pouches loaded to the teeth with ammo, pistol holsters with Berettas cinched and buckled in place, gloves, eye protection, and a rifle. Our blood type was scrawled on the side of everything we wore—boots, helmet, the inside collar of our uniforms—anything to give us a one up on not dying. I scratched mine on the inside tongue of my boot with black Sharpie marker: O positive.

Our unit, 299 FSB, was a support battalion thrust into Baghdad proper to help First Cavalry carry out operations. AOR Baghdad swept through Route Irish, Highway 1, a corridor of violence, IEDs, and mortar fire. Camp Liberty was now my home, pad no. 14, the middle of the base next to Commo Hill. I threw my duffel down onto the ground outside of room 452A and looked around. No sign of a roommate yet, but I took no chances and told Tina, who was walking up behind me, that she had just inherited the role of my roommate. She smiled. I nodded, tossed her a key, opened the door, and stepped inside a room that smelled like a teenage boy's dirty gym sock. Throwing my gear and duffel on the bunk nearest the door, I flipped on the light, looked around at the empty wooden wall lockers and bare mattresses, then stepped outside to light a smoke and began walking down the corridor. It had only taken me an hour to acquire a mini fridge and microwave from a nearby battalion on their way out. "You can't take it with you," a soldier says to me. I hand him fifty bucks, the last of my paycheck for that month. Two trips from the soldier's hooch and I had secured some sort of worldly goods that resembled comfort, a consolation for the bullshit I would probably have to endure this deployment. Tina looked at me, amazed at my ability to turn our piece-of-shit hooch into a mini dorm room within just hours of hitting boots on ground. Full set of sheets, an afghan blanket, and a pillow; my new home was complete. Tina walked to her side of the room and pulled out pink satin sheets from her duffel bag. I shook my head. I was not a satin sheet, doily, and flowers kind of girl. Mechanic, machine gunner—that was what I was good at, that was my niche. I pulled out my copy of Hemingway's *The Sun Also Rises* and stepped outside onto my stoop. The night air was slightly cool with a breeze. The sound of soldiers walking on gravel and rocks, skipping them as they shuffled to and from the battalion headquarters drowned out any chance of silence. I cracked the spine open to my place marker, a page bent over at the edge. The words on the page were foreign. Brett is fussing over her drink being empty and Jake is trying hard to succumb to Brett's attempts at a good time, but the scene still was lost on me as the helicopter lifted off the helipad a couple hundred feet behind me, shaking the walls of my hooch and rattling the steps I sat on. I thought about Brett and the taste of champagne on my lips. The bubbling gurgle of it going down my throat sounded intoxicating and soon the book was like torture to read. I read the last line of Book I: "The door opened and I went up-stairs and went to bed." If only it were that simple in this place.

The next morning I sat in an uncomfortable desk chair steadying my M4 on its butt in between my legs, trying to get it to stand there without me having to hold it. The metal was hot to the touch. I didn't wear my gloves that day—a mistake.

A large projector flashed a blue screen onto the nearby wall. Sergeant Lippert walked in and sat beside me. Then the rest of the recovery team, Specialist Pierre and Sergeant Helm, walked in. A female sergeant from brigade pulled up the rear, shut the door, and started the debriefing with, "There's only one thing you need to know about bagging and tagging bodies in a war zone: don't fuck it up."

We were told every soldier gets a black bag and every piece flesh, bone, or body part not connected to a full body was to have its own separate bag. Pierre raised his hand and asked the reason why each body part needed its own bag. Sergeant Lippert cracked back at him with a "because I fucking said so." The female sergeant explained further, "Because there is no certainty that the leg lying near one body is actually that body's leg. It's not your job to figure that shit out. It's your job to clean it up. Got it?"

Pierre nodded. I grimaced. Sergeant Lippert and Sergeant Helm sat there unmoved. This wasn't their first rodeo.

A day later, or maybe it was a few days later, Sergeant Lippert and I stared at a Stryker burned up from an IED explosion. First Cav pulled security around us, cordoning off the area in a twenty-foot perimeter each way, blocking both sides of the road with their Humvees. The smoke was still wafting off the top hatch. Three bodies were inside—one burned, one beaten up by shrapnel, and one disemboweled. I began throwing up. The first time it landed on Sergeant Lippert's boots, the second, next to the HET trailer's hydraulic box, and the last in between the tires of the HET. I helped drag chains, called out when the Stryker hit midpoint of the HET semitruck trailer, and ratchet-strapped down loose debris, but the smell of iron lingered in the air, the smell of blood. We were only supposed to recover the wreck. The bodies, they were the hardest part.

The black body bags shifted their weight around in the cab of the semitruck as we maneuvered back through the base's concrete blockades. The plastic crinkled with every move of an arm or leg, a piece of flesh resting not quite perfectly in its place. I looked ahead at the road, watching as the HET navigated its front end toward the red clearing barrels outside the front gate. We came to a stop and I swung open my door and grabbed my M4, but the front sight caught on one of the bags, dragging it closer to me. I recoiled, hoping that by jiggling my rifle it would free the bag, but it was no use. The bag slid farther off the backseat and thudded to the floorboard. Sergeant Lippert looked over at me. He was outside the door, already yelling at me to climb into the back and put the bag back, but I didn't move. I just looked at the bag, the head of a soldier slumped down and mashed into the black abyss of that bag. Sergeant Lippert shouted at me, pointing to the bag. I looked at it, unmoved. I didn't want to touch the bag. I didn't want to know that it was the same soldier I had seen moments ago dead. Something about the blackness of the bag made me shudder, even now. The finality of the zipper being pulled closed and clasped shut, the tag labeled "KIA," with the body parts stacked in ink on its face; it was enough to send me into a panic. The sum total of this soldier's life wrapped up neatly in a black bag, as if by placing him there he was no longer part of this world but a dead thing needing to be buried and forgotten—much like what this war had become back in the States to those not directly connected to it. So I stared at the bag, frightened to touch it, frightened of everything it meant to be near it, and without me noticing, Sergeant Lippert climbed back into the cab and shoved me out of the way. Picking the bag up as though it were a priceless artifact found in some ancient Mesopotamian dig site, he gently placed his hand under the head, cradling it at the neck, and put the bag back onto the seat while I stared in shock, afraid to go near it, afraid of everything it stood for in this war.

• • •

Many years later I was in Seattle at a writers' conference, standing outside my hotel at night and smoking a cigarette as I stared at a homeless man lying in an alcove of a building across the street. It was cold outside. The clothes he was wearing did not protect him from the layer of mist that had started to come down. I watched as he walked over to a nearby trash can and rummaged through it. At first he picked out the cans, carefully walking over and placing them in small plastic grocery bags with the rest of his assorted aluminum hoard. Then he walked back, emptied the black trash bag's contents into the gutter, and walked back to his alcove. Turning it inside out, he lay back down, sliding his legs into the bag. He pulled it as close to his chest as he could and then went back to sleep curled up on the pavement, bearing his body down into the black trash bag as best he could. I looked on from across the street and wondered if this was his version of a good night's sleep.

. . . . . . . . . . . . . . . . .

## Embracing the Suck

"King, don't give them candy."

Sergeant Lippert shook his head in disappointment as I looked at the throng of children surrounding me, their hands up in the air, and all of them asking for a lollipop. "A little candy isn't going to hurt them," I said, as I handed out every Blow Pop I had in my cargo pants pocket. After the last one was gone, the children ran away, but they came back ten minutes later asking again for candy. They called me "mister." They couldn't tell I was a woman behind the sunglasses and all the gear I wore. For all they knew, I was the nicest male soldier they had ever seen.

"I don't have any more." I opened my cargo pants pocket and revealed to them that it was empty. "See, all gone."

A little boy no more than ten years old reached inside my pocket and felt around.

"No," I said, pulling his hand out. "Go." I gestured trying to shoo him away, but he wouldn't leave.

He stood there staring at me, as if by magic I would produce another lollipop just for him.

"What the fuck did I tell you? Never give those little fuckers candy." Sergeant Lippert pointed at the boy. "Now that little shit's going to follow you around."

"Well, how do you say 'go away' in Arabic?" I asked, but Sergeant Lippert said nothing. He just laughed and walked away.

Pushing the boy aside, I went about the mission, unhooking the ratchet straps from the eyelet hooks and tossing them up on the other side of the HET trailer. The little boy persisted, and every five minutes I had to stop, pull the boy's hand out of my closed cargo pocket, and push him away from me.

"Go, get out of here, damn it, and leave me alone." I pushed the boy again, but this time he tripped over himself and fell to the ground. "Get lost, kid, before you get me in trouble." I kicked some dirt at him.

It covered his face in a light gray cloud of dust. He wiped the dirt from his eyes with the front of his shirt and dusted his pants off at the knees. The dark brown sandals he wore on his feet had come off one of his heels. He slipped it back on and steadied himself as he stood up. I turned around and kept on removing the straps that held down the T-barriers on the HET trailer. Every so often I turned to look at the kid. He stood there staring at me with his hands at his side, like an Arabic statue, not moving, only blinking his small brown eyes as he watched me work. Women and men who lived in the nearby neighborhood walked past the outpost where we were unloading the barriers; they pointed and shook their heads at the concrete wall we were constructing to fortify the outside of the compound. Some would stop to look for a moment, but most kept moving for fear of being questioned by the security detail.

"What I tell you, King," Sergeant Lippert said. "Don't give those kids shit."

I glanced over at the boy. He was still standing there, staring at me from five feet away. I turned, leaned up against the trailer, and glanced up at Sergeant Lippert, who was at the tail end of the trailer unlatching the last of the ratchet straps. "Well, Sarge, how do I make him go away?"

Sergeant Lippert walked around the end of the trailer toward where I stood, pulled off his Oakleys, and looked me in the eyes. "That's how," he whispered, as he tapped his Oakleys on the butt of my rifle, which was dangling from my weapons clip on my combat vest.

"You're kidding," I said, as I looked at him, confused. "Tell me you're kidding, Sarge."

"You want him gone?"

"Yeah."

"Well . . . ," he said, "what are you waiting for?"

"Sarge, you're joking, right?"

Sergeant Lippert put his shades back on, looked at the boy, then at me, and shook his head. "Watch and learn, King." Sergeant Lippert walked toward the boy.

"Sarge, you can't possibly . . ." I inched forward. "I mean, shit. You can't do that."

Sergeant Lippert turned around. "You don't like it, turn your fucking head."

Sergeant Lippert stopped in front of the boy, pulled out his side pistol, pointed it at the kid's face, and said, "Rooh b'eed, motherfucker." The kid looked up at Sergeant Lippert, whose barrel was almost touching the tip of his nose, then at me. I moved in front of Sergeant Lippert's pistol.

"No." I pushed the barrel down. "You can't fucking do that." I turned around and looked at the kid. "Run." I pushed him away. "Run."

The boy took off running down the road until he disappeared around the corner. Sergeant Lippert and I watched until the boy was out of sight, then he turned around, holstered his pistol, and said, "You're welcome," as he walked around to the other side of the HET and began calling for a forklift to haul the barriers off the trailer.

He looked back at me as I stood there staring at where the kid had rounded the corner in a sprint. "King, what the fuck you waiting on, the second coming of Christ? Let's go."

I snapped out of it and walked toward where he stood at the front of the HET. As I was about to walk past him, Sergeant Lippert grabbed the handle of the back of my vest, put his mouth close to my ear, and whispered, "Next time I tell you not to fucking give the kids candy, don't fucking give them shit, you hear me?"

I nodded, looking forward at the forklift coming our way.

"Good," he said, as he shoved me forward.

Language was a barrier that didn't matter, and because it didn't matter, we didn't give a shit about the people. The only thing that mattered was our language and our way of doing things. We didn't know boundaries. We carried out the missions the way we saw fit, busting open doors, raiding houses, trashing rooms, desecrating prayer rugs, and kicking over shrines to Muhammad. The only respect we had was for each other and the American flag stitched onto the right shoulder of our uniform, and because of that the only communication we had with the local nationals came through brute force. But soon, after the first year in Iraq, we had no leads on enemy forces and we were forced to interrogate the locals, which always proved to be a challenge. Soldiers started to raid houses, dragging along a coalition forces interpreter to help get information about the area, but we couldn't trust the information or the locals. We never knew if they were giving us good intel or if they were setting us up for an attack. Because we couldn't trust them, we didn't care if they lived or died. Everyone was treated with hostility. We didn't know the customs of Islam or what traditions the locals held true to, and because of that, we didn't know the people or their way of life. We didn't know what to make of their daily life. Every move they made became suspicious activity. Staring at a group of soldiers meant they were plotting a suicide bombing, walking slowly next to the road meant they were trying to find the best place to plant an IED, and meandering around the outside of a house meant they were trying to gather information about troop movements. Goat herders who moved their flocks in the middle of the day across busy roads were presumed to be doing it intentionally, to block the roads. The machine gunners opened up fire on the herds, making any goat in the road .50 cal fodder. Even little children became widely accepted among the soldiers as TITS, or terrorists in training. Because we didn't know the Iraqi people and didn't care to, we "othered" them, forcing them into degrading positions by shoving their faces into the dirt and putting pistols to the men's groins. We defiled their houses by walking in with our shoes on, wiping the dirt from our boots on their prayer rugs. We rounded up the women and children and moved them into the bedroom while we beat and tortured the men in the living room, hoping to get information out of them. The men, women, and children of Iraq were no longer people. They were all terrorists.

In the first wave after the initial push into Iraq, brutality and ethnic othering became commonplace; pointing weapons at innocent children became standard and calling them derogatory names was just what we called them. The people of Iraq became known as sand niggers, mujes, towel heads, dune coons, hajjis, and camel jockeys. Iraq became known as the sandbox and bum fuck nowhere. Standard operating procedures no longer existed—we ran on general orders, and when they became too vague to use in combat, we disregarded them when shit hit the fan. Our armor became obsolete, and anything fabricated onto a vehicle became known as pulling a Frankenstein. Black Hawks became known as army lawn darts, and Humvees were dubbed IED detectors. If you weren't on the FOB, you were outside the wire. If you were lucky enough to pull a desk job, you were labeled a fobbit and made fun of because you were too chickenshit to fight. Some FOBs even had nicknames. LSA Anaconda became known as Bombaconda, and Camp Liberty became renowned for its one-lane road nicknamed Easy Street. What we wore every day out on mission became a burden. TA-50 was now called battle rattle. It was anywhere from fifty to a hundred fucking pounds of gear that consisted of a combat vest, the arm protectors that we called bullshit wings, a throat protector that only covered half your throat, a green Kevlar helmet with an ACU helmet cover that when knocked against another one was called turtle fucking, twelve magazines of ammo that attach to the front of your combat vest in six magazine pouches, elbow and knee pads that made it hard to run or move quickly without looking like a complete fucking idiot, gloves to keep your hands from burning against the metal of your weapon, eye protection for the sun and shrapnel, and sometimes a pistol with an extra magazine to accompany your M4 or M16 rifle, which was always nicknamed for an ex-lover.

OIF, or operation Iraqi fucking, turned into OEF, operation everyone's fucked.

Since the last bullshit war that U.S. soldiers were forced to fight in, war tactics had changed—the type of combat seen on the battlefields was different. No longer were we fighting in open spaces in the jungle, where everything blended in a hodgepodge of foliage. This time we were fighting in desert conditions surrounded by an urban environment, where buildings, alleyways, and corners all proved to be your enemy. The type of war had changed. Weapons used against us became more deadly. They were buried in the dirt with a pressure plate on top, inside the trunks of cars that would drive toward you at fast speeds before blowing up, in piles of trash on the side of the road, sewed into cadavers of people and carcasses of dogs, strapped around women and children, rigged to doors, and almost all of them were detonated remotely, from a cell phone. It seemed at times that even our weapons were being used against us, bought and purchased in the aftermath of the Cold War. Mortar rounds penetrated our bases, hitting our chow halls, hooches, communications towers, and motor pools.

We didn't know the war would take this long to fight. We didn't have a sense of time, and each passing day began to lessen our drive to keep going, and the war fervor that we once had when we first arrived boots on ground no longer existed. It disappeared along with all the other familiar things that gave us hope of surviving.

By the end of December 2006 the cold had hit the air in Baghdad, turning the saturated muddy ground into a crisp, crackled earth with a lightly frosted white topcoat. The cold, icy air ate at your uncovered nose, cheeks, and ears, turning them a soft shade of pink.

I sat hunched over a technical manual trying to figure out a shortcut to rewiring the wiring harness on the forklift I was suppose to work on tomorrow. It was the only thing I could do to keep myself distracted from the fact that I was still on the recovery team and under the leadership of Sergeant Lippert. I had finally figured out the wiring schematic when he walked through the closed flap of the tent hangar.

"They're going to kill that son of a bitch next week."

I looked up. "Kill who?"

"Saddam," he said, setting his rifle next to mine in the weapons rack. "The verdict's in; that motherfucker's going to die." He pulled the chair up next to me and sat down. "That asshole thought he could hide forever." He shook his head and laughed.

"Wait, what does this mean?"

Sergeant Lippert glanced at me. I looked down at the schematic and said, "I mean, does this mean the war's over—we can go home?"

"Hell no, Private, what made you think that?"

"Well, we came here to get that asshole and now that they're going to kill him. . . . I mean, it's lights out, end of story, case is closed. We can fucking go home now."

"It isn't that simple."

"What do you mean it isn't that simple? We got him. All the Iraqi court has to do is kill him and then we can go home. That sounds pretty fucking simple to me."

"We have to stay and help the country get back on its feet."

"Well, fuck that!" I shouted as I stood up. "We've been here long enough in this fucking country." I pointed my finger at the ground. "This is horse shit, Sarge, and you know it. Those fucking people don't want our help. They want us the fuck out of their country, and I'm happy to oblige."

"Watch it. There are still innocent people out there that need our help."

"Fuck that, Sarge." Realizing that I was crossing the line by yelling at Sergeant Lippert, I looked down at the ground. "I mean, we've done enough for these fucking A-rabs." I started to clench my fists. Too upset to stand, I sat back down. "We've done enough."

"Easy now." Sergeant Lippert stood up and started walking toward me. "You're working yourself up over nothing."

Sergeant Lippert put his hand on my shoulder. "This is bullshit, Sarge." I pushed his hand off my shoulder, stood up, and backed away from him toward the middle of the bay. "I should be able to go home now. I've done my duty."

"I have a wife and kids at home. You think I want to stay here? Fuck no, but there are times when you just have to suck it the fuck up and drive on, and riding out the rest of this deployment is one of those times. Now get your ass over here." He waved me over to where he was standing. "And calm the fuck down."

With tears in my eyes, I walked over to him. "This is bullshit, Sarge, and you know it."

"All right, King, all right."

"It's fucking bullshit," I said, sitting down in the chair. I looked up at him, tears spilling down my face.

"I know, King, I know," Sergeant Lippert said as he patted me on the back, grabbed his rifle, and walked toward the opening of the tent. He stopped short, grabbed his pack of smokes from his cargo pants pocket even though he didn't smoke, and said, "Come on, let's go."

I stood up, wiped the tears from my face with the sleeve of my ACU, picked up my rifle, and started walking out of the tent hangar with Sergeant Lippert. "I hope they fry that motherfucker tomorrow until he's charbroiled."

"They're going to hang him."

"That fucker deserves more than that."

As we walked past our HET, Sergeant Lippert laughed and said, "I'm not arguing with you on that one, King. I'm not arguing with you one bit."

For me it wasn't a matter of whether or not Saddam deserved it. It was a matter of survival, and if I was going to survive this war, I had to shut out my emotions, turn off my humanity, and get used to the thought of killing people, something that in the end would either ruin me or make me a better soldier.

• • •

We didn't know guilt or remorse. We didn't know how to turn off the kill switch. We didn't know the type of power that came with the weapons we wielded. We used them as a scare tactic, a way to induce fear in the Iraqi people. Pointing and jabbing the end of the muzzle at them, we shouted commands. "Stop or I'll shoot!" They always walked toward us, never stopping to question the words we shouted from behind machine guns. We fired warning shots off on either side of them, making them dance from one side to the other as they tried to move out of the path of each bullet. Most times the women would stop and raise their hands to the sky, shaking their palms up in the air to prove that they were unarmed, but we fired at them anyway. The children, who didn't know any better, still advanced our position. We shot at them again and again.

Some soldiers were nice to the children. Some were cruel.

Outside checkpoint 2, several miles from Camp Liberty, I watched the cruelty of a soldier who had been in theater too long, jaded by the war. He pointed his M4 at a boy walking down the street. The boy didn't stop but kept advancing, so the soldier shot his weapon to one side of the child. With each shot, the boy was moved closer and closer to the edge of the sidewalk. Heavy midday traffic lined the streets, cautiously passing the Bradley tanks that sat on each side of the roadway. Our convoy had stopped at the checkpoint to drop off supplies, water mostly. Leaning up against my Humvee fifteen feet away, I watched the soldier turn to his buddy and say, "I hope that kid gets far enough over, so we don't have to interrogate him." They both laughed, and then I watched in disbelief as the soldier fired again on the right side of a boy who was still walking down the street with a stick in one hand and a half-deflated soccer ball in the other. The boy jumped closer to the edge of the sidewalk, dropped the stick and the soccer ball, and stood still with his arms up. The soccer ball bounced twice and then rolled off the edge of the curb and into the road. The soldier turned to his buddy again and said, "Watch this. One more shot and we're in the clear." The soldier fired again and the boy hopped off the sidewalk and into the path of the busy street traffic. A delivery truck slammed into the boy, striking him in the back. I watched in horror from fifteen feet away, next to the Humvee, as the boy's body was hurled underneath the truck's undercarriage and dragged along by the exhaust manifold before it caught on the asphalt. His body tumbled toward the back of the truck until the back wheel finally ran over the boy's head and split it open like a pistachio shell, spattering brain matter and blood on the truck's mud flaps. The soccer ball rolled into the gutter as the truck came to a screeching halt on the roadway.

The soldier looked back at his battle buddy and said, "You know my mom taught me never to go into the street after my soccer ball."

For most of us, we didn't know how to feel in the moments when it mattered, whether to cry or smile, whether to be angry at the death of a fellow soldier or to be relieved that it wasn't you. We didn't know whether bravery was just stupidity in disguise or whether courage was just another form of fear. We didn't know what victory felt like or what self-sacrifice meant anymore. We didn't know the enemy or where to find them. We didn't know what was a bomb or what was just a pile of trash on the side of the road. We didn't know what our missions were for or why we were really fighting. We didn't know if it was for freedom, justice, or oil. On any given day outside the wire, we didn't know who would make it back or who would be hitching a one-way ticket on the black bag express. We didn't know the names of the streets or which roads led to nowhere. When shit hit the fan, sometimes we didn't know which direction to fire the bullets. We didn't know what honor or pride was or how we could find them. We didn't know the ties that connected our lives to each other, all of us dependent on the other to survive.

War Is a Machine

In the end the only thing we knew for certain was that we were all soldiers stuck in the same godforsaken country until the military let us leave or we died, whichever came first.

· · · · · · · · · ·

## Commo Hill

Camp Liberty was connected like a grid to Camp Victory and BIAP. Located near Saddam's palaces, the base had one main road that ran the length of the base. In the very middle of the base Commo Hill stood with four massive antenna towers looming, breaking up the beauty of a sunrise with their metal intrusions.

One of the largest bases constructed since the Vietnam War, Camp Liberty housed contractors, coalition forces, and U.S. troops. Northeast of the trash burns and fueling stations, Liberty looked like a city within a city. Large concrete walls with concertina wire kept the unwanted out and held us prisoner inside. On either side of the gates that sporadically punctured the perimeter, large two-story block towers stood tall, backed by M1 Abrams tanks and heavy artillery auxiliaries. Zigzag concrete blockades shielded the gates from full frontal attacks by VBIEDs, and streetlights lined the road for five hundred feet, almost like a homing beacon sent out to the enemy, a spotlight just begging to be bombarded with mortars. Inside the base there was a PX, a Burger King, and even a Green Beans coffee joint that, if you had time, was a watering hole for soldiers. Every once in a while there was a lull in the fighting and work went on as usual, the base functioning as it normally would had it been a time of peace. Sometimes the quiet lasted too long, and soon you would become complacent, forgetting that this was not a normal base, that we were in fact in the middle of a war zone. Almost once a month Commo Hill would get hit, the incoming mortar rounds blasting the antennas down the side of the hill. We knew whenever it happened because the lights on base went dark, the internet went down, and mandatory roll call would ensue, followed by a weapons check. Some days the mortar rounds coming into base were too close for comfort, the Iraqi insurgents finding the proper maximum effective range of their explosions, the best place to hit to do the most damage. On most days they were off. But on December 30, 2006, the day Saddam Hussein was executed, they hit their mark quite clearly, their aim that day better than it had been in weeks.

· · ·

It comes quickly—the sound of a mortar round as it crests the angle of hell and falls to the earth with a deathly whistle that is faint at first but becomes quieter than a whisper the closer it gets to you. They lock the position in, marking your location on a map, a place clearly thought out and triangulated flawlessly—the many weeks perfecting the trajectory of the round, the time it will take to make its target, and the blast radius it will create in rendering the target inert. It is a simple math equation meticulously planned to the exact moment when you are walking to a forklift just inside the motor pool wall. Cringing at the workload, you take an unsanctioned smoke break outside the motor pool before you start, but the cigarette isn't even lit before the mortar descends; its warning is a weak conversation in your ear as you question whether to run or stand still, but fight or flight doesn't register, only the need to hear the almost inaudible whistle. The sirens from the loudspeakers blare. "Warning: seek shelter. Incoming. Incoming." You turn and look at the first sergeant who is standing in the middle of the motor pool shouting for everyone to get to a bunker, but there are none near you. You are alone next to the front entrance of the motor pool. Soldiers in the bunker several hundred yards away are yelling for everyone to take cover, but you know there is no point. The round will hit you, if the man in charge of releasing the payload of mortars that day has double checked his math. The whistle becomes a whisper, and then silence. You don't move. It hits the hooches across the road from where you stand, and in an instant you become a Purple Heart candidate. But not today, because you are not a medal chaser. So shrapnel enters your leg, rips your flesh, and burns as it buries deep into your shin bone. At best you have a scar, at worst no leg. You are on the ground with no recollection of how you got there. Your head is pounding from where it hit the concrete barrier. You have a concussion or more likely a TBI. There is a searing pain in your leg. You don't want to look at it. You don't want to know if it's there or not. But you can't help yourself. You look. The leg is still there but is bleeding. You try to get up, but the leg cannot hold all of your weight, so you hobble to the bunker instead, everyone wondering what happened to you—why it took you so long to get to cover. You look at the ground and shrug your shoulder as you try to pretend that nothing is wrong with your shin. An hour later you are held up in the back of an LMTV with a first-aid kit from the cab of the truck, trying to pull out the tiniest piece of shrapnel from your shin with a shaky hand. There is blood seeping out of the wound, the gauze not nearly enough to stop the bleeding. You pour water over your hands, hoping they are sterile enough to do the job of tweezing the small piece of shrapnel out, but it is no use. The blood makes your hands slippery. Each tug on the metal brings shooting pain down your shin to your foot. You bite down on the collar of your uniform, hoping it will muffle the screams. It's no use in trying to pull it out. It won't budge. You leave it. Cover it up with gauze. Wrap a bandage around the wound. Pull down your pant leg and wash your blood off the bed of the truck with the rest of the water. The operating room is clean. You hop down out of the truck as best you can, holding onto the tailgate for support. You walk away. No one need know what happened. You don't want to go back to rear D, where all the rejects, new soldiers, and pregnant women go. You don't want everyone to think you're a pussy. You're a woman doing a man's job, so you suck it the fuck up because in the end you're no hero, you don't deserve a Purple Heart for this; you're just a casualty of a lucky shot, a mortar round aimed a little too perfectly that day.

There was no word from home yet. Many of us were wondering what they were seeing, how the war was portrayed back there. I stopped telling my family about the war when I made my monthly call to tell them that I was still alive. My cell phone calls to California were a 2:00 a.m. wake-up that my grandparents gladly accepted.

I called them the day Saddam Hussein was hanged, the day I had been injured. It had been a violent one; our base took more than its usual number of daily mortar attacks. VBIEDS at each gate. Daisy-chained explosives set at a guard tower along the back wall. Massive attacks throughout the city. The Paladin tanks of 1-82 Artillery were working overtime to keep the insurgents at bay.

I had time after end of day formation to call home. The groggy voice of Grandpa answering the phone, fumbling to put it on speaker so that Nana could hear, calmed me down; the sound of background noise, a reminder of home. I wanted to reach through the phone for a hug but said hello instead. The usual hello back was followed up by how was I doing, but then Nana asked me the only question I didn't want to answer: What I was doing over here? I couldn't bear to tell her that I was a number of things, worst of all a collector of bodies. I told her of trucks I worked on, friends I met, but never missions or attacks—never those. She asked me if anyone had died today. The static of the phone connection broke the silence on my end. I didn't tell her about Saddam or that fact that I had tried to take out a pea-sized piece of shrapnel from my shin, that it was still bleeding underneath my uniform, that my head was still pounding from my head hitting the concrete wall, or how I spent the better part of my afternoon after my injury out on mission. I cleared my throat and told her that I had heard a few soldiers had been killed in First Cav but that they were no one I knew. She told me of a news report she saw on the TV, a helicopter crash in Baghdad, civilians and soldiers, she said, with a shakiness in her voice. Six dead. Angry, because I knew the news report once again fucked up the facts, I told her that I knew how many civilians and soldiers died and the reason why the chopper was shot down. I told her to stop watching the news, that the liberal media may be telling her the count, but the facts were wrong and the order of events incomplete. She sighed into the phone but agreed. I asked about home. She proceeded to tell me about everyone in the family. My cousins were doing great. Erika was graduating high school soon, Emma was playing soccer goalie and doing well at it, Anthony had stopped playing football, but she avoided mention of Dad and my brother, John, so I asked about John. There was silence. I knew that something was wrong. I probed, but she said that she didn't want me to worry and I knew now that it was bad. I asked if he was dead. She replied no, but before I could demand that she tell me what was going on, sirens went off on base. I could hear the panic in her voice when she asked what the noise was. I told her I had to go, there was an incoming mortar attack happening. As I tried to get out the words "I love you," Commo Hill got hit, the phone went dead, and the base fell silent and black. The busy signal screeched from inside my pocket as I ran to the nearest bunker.

Phone calls home became less regular after that and then almost nonexistent. It made it easier to disconnect from the reality that back home everyone was going about their lives as though I were already dead. To me, calling only satisfied them that I was still alive, and yet I didn't call because I was callous; it was because part of me already felt dead. The war had a way of doing it to you if you saw too much, making it harder to pull back on your humanity and remember that not everyone is trying to kill you and that not everything will blow up. Phone calls made you complacent about that fact. They reminded you that you were at war and that this place was a far cry from anything that could remotely be called home. This was not home. This was a fresh new level of hell, and I had volunteered to walk through the fire.

· · · · · · ·
## Waiting

Private Dupree sat at the bus stop waiting for the hajji bus to come pick her up for work. She rolled the metal links from her dog tag chain in her mouth, contemplating the conversation she had had last night with her roommate, Specialist Hooper, about not being able to handle the deployment, the long months spent away from her family, her grandmother. Hooper only nodded to her, telling her that like anything hard in life, it's best to keep your head down and keep moving. Would she be able to endure the rest of the deployment? She didn't know, but the longer she sat there, the more she moved the metal back and forth, until the clanking sound of metallic disruption vibrated in her ears the way Tibetan tingsha meditation cymbals slap together to create a long, resonating sound reflective of a hungry ghost begging to be reborn again.

I wasn't there when the mortar round came into base and blew up the bus stop, wounding Private Dupree. I was in the convoy staging area listening to the NCOIC give a convoy brief. Sergeant Lippert stood there spitting brown tobacco on the ground in clumped streams while the new soldiers hurriedly scribbled down call signs, route info, checkpoint locations, and truck ordering. Other soldiers PMCS'd their trucks and checked tires, ratchet straps on the payloads, headlights, flashlights, and NVGs. Some stood around smoking Marlboro Reds, Parliaments, or Camel Lights. Others just stood there with their hands ruffed around the collar of their flak vest, waiting to roll out. The gunners checked their canisters of ammo, goggles, headsets, and piss cups. Some oiled down the bolt on their weapon, while others checked to make sure they had a case each of water, Rip It energy drinks, and shitty Otis Spunkmeyer muffins. When the convoy brief was done, the drivers started up their engines like Indy car drivers, checking and double-checking gauges, looking at the fuel levels, engine temp, battery life, and brakes. The radio hands conducted comm checks with battalion and the convoy commander. Across the base

Private Dupree was sitting at the bus stop waiting for her ride to work while I stood in the convoy staging area pulling drags of deep gray smoke from my unfiltered Lucky Strike and pretended to care about Sergeant Lippert's preconvoy prayer.

*Lord, keep us safe today . . .*

Throughout the base the sirens blared the warning to seek shelter, and it was then that the shells came hurtling into base. Inside a concrete bunker beyond the staging area, I was safe. In the distance a plume of smoke permeated the sky. Inside the trucks the sound of radio chatter buzzed and crackled, and it was then that I knew one of us had been injured. From my concreted spot I could see the main road on base and the Charlie Company doctors running half-dressed to their medevac Humvees. In a cloud of dust and kicked-up rocks, their wheels screeched out of the battalion headquarters parking lot and down the road toward the plume of smoke, which had turned from gray to black.

I didn't know Private Dupree very well. We had gone to basic training together, but she was in a different company than me. They say she sustained shrapnel wounds to her body and that is wasn't too bad. She would live. Either way, I sat with Specialist Hooper, one of her good friends, all night, waiting until she felt like talking. We sat there in silence.

• • •

When I was in middle school, I sometimes took the city bus home when Nana couldn't pick me up. I sat in the back of the bus, watched everyone file in and sit down, and then watched as they got up and left when it was their stop. It took two buses to get home, one of which I hopped on at Mission Gorge Road, the 113, but when I got on one day and walked to the back, I saw her, a ghost of my childhood—my sister, Courtney. You see, my parents had divorced when I was two, or was it three? The number always changed when I asked Dad.

The circumstance surrounding my parents' divorce went like this: Mom left for work one day and didn't come home for a year; she ran off with another man, who is now my stepdad,

Fred; distraught, my father made his first attempt at suicide; it didn't work; he got his shit together, worked two jobs and did night school to support my twin half sisters Ashley and Courtney, me, and my little brother, John; Nana and Grandpa helped out a lot; Dad asked Grandpa Blanton where Mom was, how he could find her, and if she would ever come back; he answered that it was complicated and involved; Dad decided since he didn't know when my mom was coming home, it was best to adopt my twin sisters; a week before the hearing, Mom came back, filed divorce papers, and told Dad what had happened; Dad tried suicide again; the court mandated that Mom take all four children, but she refused; Dad contested that he was more capable of taking care of John and me than Mom could ever be because, as he puts it still to this day, "She's a selfish conniving lying cunt who deserves to go to hell"; all of this is said by my dad with a smile; while the events after the final divorce hearing are vague and most of which will not be told to me until I turned sixteen, my understanding is that Mom refused to pay child support for John and me and then disappeared.

While all of this is somewhat like the typical divorce story, the next part is fucked up, even for my standards. Courtney noticed me on the bus, sat beside me, and asked what I was doing in San Diego in her part of the city. I told her that we lived off of Del Cerro Boulevard with Nana and Grandpa. She looked at me shocked. She relayed to me that she and Ashley were attending Patrick Henry High School up the road, that she is the next bus stop, and for me to follow her home. So I do. I waited hours for Mom to get home with Ashley, who had track practice that day. Courtney helped me with my homework and made me a cheese quesadilla with salsa, and we caught up on what we had missed in each other's lives. At twelve or thirteen, it wasn't much. Mom walked in the door, Ashley in tow behind her carrying groceries. Mom yelled for help, and when I came through the kitchen toward the living room, she dropped all of the groceries on the entryway tile. She asked what I was doing there, how I had found her, and when I relayed my story, she walked past me coldly, called my dad, and made me go sit on the brown leather couch in the living room. She didn't speak a word; she just stood there staring at me as though this little stunt was my dad's idea to fuck with her.

Dad came of course, they got into a fight, Dad dragged me home, and John and I started seeing Mom on the regular after that; it was no longer just phone calls on birthdays and Christmas. She could no longer hide from us now. My mother had been living a half mile away from me almost my whole life, and it wasn't until I saw Courtney on the bus that day that I knew how selfish my mother really was.

So there it is—the story of divorce no one wants to hear, that every person hopes won't happen to them, and the one every divorce child knows well. Of course my mother has gotten better since then. She's so proud of her little soldier who went off to war and fought bad guys. She loves me now that I'm grown up with children of my own. I had waited my whole life to have a relationship with my mother, and the irony was that it took me going to war for my mother to begin to love me again. It took an act of bravery and sacrifice on my part, the possibility of my death, in order for my mother to back into my life. Even now, when she tells me she loves me, I'm not quite sure she means it, but I say the empty "I love you" back, hoping one day that we will both be sincere when we say it.

I guess what bothered me about the whole divorce thing was that I never fully understood why my dad kept us. He was a total wreck, not fit to take care of himself, and yet I am thankful he didn't give up on us. Sure, he was a drunk, a druggie, and absentee some of the time, but he admitted his shortcomings. Like all good fathers, he was there when he needed to be, was present for the things that mattered, like soccer coaching, dancing in the kitchen to music that the neighbors across the street could hear, and challenging his kids. Although, now that I'm thinking about it, my dad's definition of challenging his child to do better was radically different than that of most traditional, conventional, or even seminormal parental units, but his way never seemed to bother me. Maybe it was because I was just like him or maybe it was because his parenting skills made everything fun. That was my dad, the fun parent.

I remember a game we used to play on the way home from school when I was elementary age. In fact Dad and I still play it to this day. Dad would turn on the radio to the rock station or put on a Grateful Dead cassette tape, and before the lyrics would start, he would ask me who the band was and the name of the song. If it was the Grateful Dead, he would ask me the name of the song, and when the singer started, he'd question me as to who was singing, Jerry, Bob, or Phil. Each time I got part of it wrong, he would swerve the car side to side until I got part or all of the answer correct. If I got it right off the bat without guessing, he would give me a huge smile that was usually accompanied by, "Right on, Brookerdoo." I guess it was his way of culturing me the only real way he knew how, but for me it was a game of chicken. Sometimes I would guess the wrong answer on purpose just to see how far he was willing to go, waiting to see how much he would keep up the charade before John pissed his pants from screaming in fear or I gave too many wrong answers that would have made us crash. Either way, my dad's version of parenting was fun, totally fucked up, but fun. So I guess the trick to real parenting is to be totally fucked up. That was easier for some parents than others, especially in a radically religious country like Iraq.

• • •

*He slit her throat.* Alonso had said it nonchalantly, as if it were common practice for fathers to kill their young. She pulled a drag from her cigarette, tilted her patrol cap down to her brow line, and lowered her head to look at the dirt. *I wanted to shoot him, but they wouldn't let me. I wanted to fuck his world up. Let that son of a bitch taste what metal felt like as it burrowed into his skin, but they wouldn't let me. It's not our fight, they said. He's not our problem. But what the fuck are we fighting for? What are we here to accomplish?* I looked at Alonso, waiting for her to tell me the rest of the story, but she never did. She gripped harder on the butt of the smoke between her fingers as they trembled—the anger still burning on her skin, branding her thoughts. We never talked about what happened to the girl again. *It was only a bottle of water. Why the fuck would someone kill their child over a bottle of water?*

# PART 2

Born for the Kill

. . . . . . . . . . . . . . . . .
## The Carbine Autopsy

Metal. Black. New, but not too new.

This was my rifle. There were many like it, but this one was mine.

It lay in pieces before me, disemboweled from butt to muzzle. I cleaned it with baby wipes, removed the dirt that filled its crevices. Q-tips saturated with oil cleansed it, taking away the years it hadn't been in my care.

The wafting stench of oxidized metal, rusty parts, and synthetic oils coagulated in the air, raising the odor level just to bearable. Sweat dripped down my temple as I labored on with the hard work, disassembling the guts—puzzle pieces I barely had recollection of how to correctly put back together. I was new—an apprentice to the labor of cleaning the body down and carefully removing delicate parts. My hands weren't made for such a delicate procedure as this— the task required gentle but firm hands. Mine were scarred, calloused, and rough—mechanic's hands. Had I been properly trained beforehand, such a task wouldn't be foreign, but I sat there anyway, the body splayed out before me, gutted of its innards, like a human corpse on an autopsy table. I examined the parts. The feel of each one in my hand raised my curiosity. What does each part do? I picked them up one by one. As if coated in some sort of sinew, they slipped and slid the more tightly I tried to grip them. Next I turned my attention to the body. It was cold, chilled by the air-conditioning that ran through the building. Its hard plastic parts were stamped with a serial number. Its rough neck was serrated with railing, edged so that the limbs could be easily switched out, changed for new parts or accessories added to create a better killing machine.

I began to put the pieces back in place, covering the skeleton. Each one resembled the manifestation of the living, each part working in unison for the greater good. It could've survived the war, but in my hands it will not achieve it. If I had left it, would it have decomposed, melted back into the earth, and become something new? Or would it have just simply ceased to be, a predicament for the next person who came across it?

I held it in my hands for a while before it was time to reassemble it. It must have had a birthplace, a name, people that cared for it before it was placed in my hands. It must have had a life before me, a story behind each scratch, ding, and dent, a special time when it had seen a different foreign battlefield and experienced the sting of war.

I put it back together on the table. It looked as though it were reanimated, clean and new, ready to be lifted and used, ready for me to manufacture death.

· · · · · · · · · · ·

## Friendly Fire

I was standing inside FOB Courage waiting for our truck's turn to download our concrete barrier payload. Pulling drags of my cigarette, I noticed First Cav's security detail mounting up. I turned to Sergeant Lippert, but he was already aware. He moved quickly from one end of the compound to the other, beelining for the convoy commander.

They were going to leave us here.

I stood there, my M4 loaded, attached to my weapons clip on my flak vest, pulling drags from my smoke when they told Sergeant Lippert there were hostiles in the area moving in on our position. The mission was supposed to be simple: drive barriers from Camp Liberty to FOB Courage, unload them, and drive back. Eavesdropping on the convoy commander's discussion with Sergeant Lippert, I heard the shakiness in his voice. There were a lot of insurgents, and this place was not nearly fortified enough for us to bunker down in and hold an offensive. The gun trucks rolled out, setting a perimeter outside the gate. Soldiers ran to the guard towers, manning their machine guns. The only tank in the compound, an Abrams, shifted its turret toward the outer wall. Sergeant Lippert turned to me and nodded. I knew what it meant—we continued mission. The crane operator, a civilian contractor, refused to keep working. Sergeant Lippert shoved him back into the cab. Night had fallen, and it was pitch black out, except for a few street lamps, when the first round came screaming into the base. We all ducked as it hit the building behind our trucks, scattering debris and cement dust onto us. I flinched and Sergeant Lippert hit me twice in the arm. "Two for flinching," he said. I rubbed my arm.

*Asshole.*

We looked back over at the crane, but it had stopped and the operator was gone. We spotted him running away. Sergeant Lippert yelled at him to get back to work, but it was no use. The operator ran for shelter in a nearby makeshift bunker. Sergeant Lippert threw his hands up, told me he'd be right back, and walked toward the bunker, but it was too late. Another round came in. No more bunker.

Crouched next to my flatbed HEMTT, the semitruck's wheels shielding me as best they could, I started to question what to do. Do I stay put, ride out the rest of the attack, or do I move forward? Across the way, Sergeant Lippert shouted for me to stay put. I knew that it was a mistake, but I did what I was told. Running with his rifle in hand, he shifted body weight from side to side as he sprinted to the cab of the crane. Inside he lifted and pulled levers, figuring out the system before he leaned out the cab door and shouted for us to keep working. The trucks rumbled to life again, each HEMTT now inching forward as Sergeant Lippert lifted and dragged each barrier from the beds of the trucks. In the distance I could hear gunfire, rounds being sequenced in and shot out with precision. There were no three-round bursts, only continuous suppressive fire. Each truck filed into the unloading area as more mortar rounds whizzed into the compound. Soldiers on the wall began laying down lead. I was trying to concentrate on ground guiding a truck out of the way of the crane, but the new sound of bullets ricocheting off metal nearby me made me jump. The ringing in my ears deafened the world around me. No longer were the engines of the trucks rumbling. All the sounds of war were put on mute by the adrenaline pulsating my heartbeat against my eardrums. I could see Sergeant Lippert yelling at me. Another round came flying over the wall. A cloud of dust was in front of me now. No sight. No sound.

I was no longer standing. I was on the ground on my back. I couldn't recall how I got there, but I could hardly breathe. My flak vest was shoved up near my throat, the plates inside constricting my airway. I scrambled to my feet, first checking for my weapon. It was still attached. I grabbed hold. My trigger finger instinctually found its home near the trigger well. I slammed my body against the HEMTT wheel, crouched, waiting for the enemy to come. I saw a figure running toward me. At first I was startled. A cloud of dust obstructed my view. I pointed my rifle at the unknown black figure moving toward me. As it got closer, the fear mounted in my chest until I was uncertain of what to do. I thought in my head, *Do not fucking die.* I pressed my finger gently against the trigger—a light squeeze that was gentle enough to take back or regret. The figure moved closer, and soon I was fighting the urge to pull the trigger. I slammed my head against the wheel as I tried to psyche myself up. I whispered to myself, "Do not fucking die," as I cinched my hands tight around the weapon's grip handle, trying to gain the courage to shoot. The slow motions of the figure's legs scrambling toward me in zigzag patterns, the body ducking and diving as though it were just as scared as I was, made it harder and harder to pull my finger out of the trigger well, but I did not pull the trigger, not out of fear but out of my unwillingness to fight. *Do something. Do not fucking die. Do not fucking die in this shithole.* I didn't want to be a killer, at least not yet, so I screamed loudly at the figure, pointing my weapon at it as it came closer.

My shouting sounded like disparity, the half-yelling of a girl who was not ready to become a killer. The cloud started to dissipate, but the figure was still coming toward me.

It was Sergeant Lippert.

He slid down toward my position, slapped his back up against the rim of the wheel, and turned to look at me. I was still pointing my weapon at him, finger still in the trigger well. He reeled back and pushed the barrel away from his throat. I was shaking. He shook me and I snapped back. My finger was no longer in the trigger well, but Sergeant Lippert was looking at me as though he didn't know what else to do in that moment but shout at me. I knew he was talking because I saw his mouth move, but I couldn't read lips, so his words were met with a scared blank stare. He pointed to his ear, then at mine.

Can I hear him?

I shook my head.

No.

He nodded and pointed two fingers at his eyes, then pointed up. I nodded. He raised himself up and looked over the flatbed but dropped back down. He pointed at me again and then at himself. I knew from training that I was supposed to follow him, cover his back as we ran, but I was still shaking, so I shook my head no. He grabbed hold of me at the shoulder straps of my flak vest and slammed me up against the wheel of the truck as he said something that I still could not hear. He let go and slapped the front of my helmet.

He mouthed a word: "Ready?"

I nodded even though I was not.

We were up and moving. I followed him as he ran three paces, stopped, and checked. We did this over and over again as we searched for the rest of the soldiers on mission with us from our battalion. Hobbs was by her driver's side door, hunkered down in a crouch. Myrick was next to her. They followed us. We moved to the next truck, where we found West and Slater. We gathered near a blown-out building. Now regrouped, we waited for a lull in the fighting, the shooting to cease, so we could finish our mission and get the hell out of Dodge. I winced when another mortar round came into the compound.

Sergeant Lippert punched me: two for flinching.

· · · · · · · · · · · · · · · ·

## Small Consolations

Before I unfolded it, brought it, and laid it out beside you, a blanket, shirt, bedspread, poncho liner, or nothing at all was draped over you. Before there was a heavy lifting and a sad remembering of who you were, there was violence and your death. Your body made a death rattle, a fellow soldier held your hand, and for a short moment you knew what it was to fear death as it climbed up your body.

The bag, splayed out next to your body, has held none before you. I unzipped the long metallic flap and folded it over, being careful not to touch the inside creases of the lining in your pool of blood. Fellow soldiers helped me gently raise you. I cradled your head while the other soldiers took their places to lift you, your arms crossed over your chest, but if that day had been different, if there had been only pieces, each one would have been delicately placed in different bags, parts of you that would never come back together again. Lifting with the knees and not the back, I placed you inside, into an abyss that was smoothed out from its edges by the contoured bulk of your wide shoulders and thighs. Once you were in, the top flap was slid over, the zipper dragged closed long and slow, like the sound of a childhood sweetheart gasping when she heard the news from a family friend in the checkout line at the Raley's that you had died. The gallon of milk in her hand bounced off the linoleum floor and into the other checkout line as she raised her hands to her mouth, unable to speak or hear the words "killed in action."

Once you were zipped inside, the soldiers lifted you up with black vinyl handles and carried you off, but do not worry, I was with you. You were not alone. I held your head as each soldier

Born for the Kill

shuffled their feet and took you from the ground to the waiting Humvee. I watched over you as the wheels on the Humvee spun toward base like the sequencing of .50 caliber bullets that enter into the chamber of a machine gun and blow out the barrel with forward velocity that tears through flesh, and bone, and metal alike. And though our journey was short, the spot where you lay inside the bag was only for you; my parting gift of loyalty and respect for your sacrifice was that the body bag carried only you.

· · · · · · ·

## Failings

It had been a while since I had thought about death or the fear of dying, but I was still scared of it. I buried it deep down, hid it from the others. I joked and laughed, shit-talked and made conversation, but deep down it was still there, the fear. It steadily came to the surface, rising slowly when an attack happened, when sirens went off at night while I was sleeping. The surge of fear, the uncertainty of my last minutes or seconds on the earth, and each time I began to question if this was what I wanted to be doing before I died. I looked around the room, or the motor pool, or convoy and noticed that I was not the only one frightened, but the mortars, bullets, and shaking walls stopped, if only for a short time. The panic subsided into a normal routine, and soon I was not aware of the fear anymore, just the racing pulse and thumping of my heartbeat in my ears. Some days I worried that I'd be shipped home in a metal coffin. Other times I lay awake at night wishing for death to come, for a mortar round to whistle into base and strike me down, maybe a stray bullet when out on convoy. I worried at times that I might mess up and get someone else killed. Soon I began holding the grip on my M4 tighter, cinching my knuckles down on the black plastic rails as I walked. I was becoming unpredictable in my courage, and it showed.

· · ·

When I was a child, I often wondered why my grandpa drank so much in the evening. We used to have a family understanding; we don't ask why he's drinking, we just let him do it. One drink—he's sociable, content. Two drinks—he's bitter and angry. Three drinks—he's silent and we don't bother him when he sits down to fall asleep in his chair. He drank the same thing every night—Johnny Walker Black Label with only two cubes of ice because three would water down the scotch. Gramps had been in the Vietnam War as a navigator on a plane. He never spoke of it. He said that it was just a war and he was not there long enough to recall any actions or fights, but I know now that he was lying.

I swirled the remnants of water around in a bottle, stared at the sky from the stoop outside my hooch, and looked up at the stars, which were barely visible. It had been a long night of counterattacks by the 1-82 Field Artillery unit. The clouds were smoke that strung out sideways, plumed at the top by another round whistling out of the base. I thought of home, of what liquor would feel like on the tongue, of what Gramps holds inside his chest that made him bring the scotch to his lips every night for comfort. I swished the water in my mouth and thought of scotch; two cubes of ice, three drinks, three drinks to fall asleep.

• • •

There were no mirrors in my room. No crosses. There were three pictures taped to my wall: one of me, my brother, John, and my dad; one of my friends and me drunk and stoned outside the house on Lancaster; and one of Nana and Grandpa hugging me. There was no alarm clock on my nightstand. There was a worn tan combat notebook filled with shitty poems, a green army watch, and a figurine of Buddy Christ smiling and pointing at me with his thumbs up as if he were Arthur Fonzarelli. There was a wall locker half full of gear and clothes. There was a bed with maroon sheets and a brown afghan blanket. There was a bed with wooden sides sticking up a half inch too high, making it feel more like a coffin. The bed was hard, the piece of wood underneath too firm, the mattress so thin that it might as well be another plank of wood. There wasn't laughter or happiness in the room because at night the walls rattled from the helos taking off, the air was stagnant from the A/C, and the sobs were too loud coming from my side of the room. I didn't sleep. I stared up at the ceiling, at the emptiness of the room, and wished that I was home lying in a bed that felt soft and plush and had more than one pillow, but I knew that it would be a while before I saw comfort and dreamed of something other than the war, so I lay there in my bed awake and thought of death.

· · · · · · · · · · ·

## Placing Bets

I held the barrel and housing of my .50 cal, nicknamed Big Bertha, high up on my shoulder and carried it toward the gun truck. Getting it up to the turret was the hard part, but as I looked down from the crow's nest, the gun already assembled, the ammo can attached, the rounds stowed and ready to go, an empty shell casing lodged under the butterfly trigger, the gun waiting to manufacture death, I looked over at Specialist Demaris, who was sitting in his truck, his black bandanna covering his pale white skin fade haircut. He signaled me for a smoke. I nodded and got down. Leaning on the barrier across from the convoy staging area, I watched Wach and Sergeant Tiesler talking shit, Harris and Lantrip laughing. Sergeant Lippert was walking around his truck, checking the tires. Captain Mauro was looking at an area map. Myrick was walking up and down the line nervously. I looked for the chaplain. He was giving out advice, prayers, and crosses. *God bless you* and *God bless you*. I pulled a drag from my cigarette. Fuck praying anymore. Prayers didn't keep you safe. I turned to Demaris and bet him a pack of smokes that we saw action on the convoy. He shook his head and walked away toward his truck. One last convoy briefing and we were ready to roll out. I put on my helmet, goggles, and comm headset. Demaris swiveled his turret and lifted his pack of smokes in the air. I gave him the thumbs up. We rolled out the back gate, swerving through the barrier blockades and down Route Irish and onto the blacktop; it was then that I knew for certain that his smokes were as good as mine.

· · · · · ·

## Ghosts

The young Iraqi girl stared back at me, her face covered over in black; only her eyes shown out from under the cloth. For years the girl I saw in the marketplace haunted me. I used to wonder what she saw. We were almost the same height, and though I had armor and a weapon, she stood there across the street from me staring at me as though she couldn't decide if I was a friend she'd once known long ago when she was child. We did not speak to one another, but I often wondered what I would have said to her, what she would have said to me. She stood beside her mother, who was waiting for water and aid from one of the soldiers who was handing out supplies from an LMTV truck bed. The girl's hands were clasped onto one another, her gaze direct. Her abaya and hijab covered her figure and her hair, only leaving the eyes for me to see. They were restraints from her religion, but they did not seem to bother her. She had lived that way as long as she could remember. She watched her mother carry out the same routine in the morning before she ever left the house: this is how you wrap the hijab around the head to cover the hair, she would say, pin it here underneath the throat and wrap the rest up and over the head. As a girl, she practiced it every day. Now a young adult, the girl had a hijab that was perfect, wrapped tightly and neatly around her head, the black shielding her from me. Her eyes peered at mine, locked in an understanding that this was her home, her street, the marketplace where her father sold spices, and though I was only there to make sure she received water and medical aid, I felt as though I were an intruder. I smiled at her, and it was then that she looked at my rifle. Two days from now the marketplace will be a pile of trash, rubble, and bodies. She will be dead. Her mother will cry out for her, not knowing in the chaos where she is, and the next time I look at her in the eyes, there will be no life in them. But I did not know that now. Right now, she stared back at me, as if to acknowledge that we were both trapped, that at some point one or both of us will die, and that for a short while we must continue living, if only to come to the understanding that the world consists of people waiting to die.

A few days later, after the market bombing, I saw Kyle Wotring, my first love, whom I thought I had long since forgotten. Perhaps I should have run to him and tried to touch him, like people do when they think they are seeing a mirage or a ghost. But with the knowledge that he was in the States, in the navy, and stationed in San Diego, I thought it couldn't possibly be him. Yet, I sat there across from him outside in the parking lot of the PX on Camp Liberty studying the features in his face, hoping to find a sign of misconception. His face was the same: square-boned jawline, pointed short nose, and piercing blue eyes. I stared longer and longer, the heat rippling off the ground, waving his figure. He looked at me, and I swore for a second he smiled. It couldn't have been him. I tried not to let myself think it. He walked toward me, and as a glimmer of hope crossed my face, he smiled again, and if this had been a mirage, the saunter in his step would have been swept away like dust flecks or sand being lifted up into the air, but he touched my arm, and I knew then that this was real.

He stood there in front of me, his smile playful as he stretched out his hand. I looked at him amazed. A moment ago I might have dreaded this moment, the realization that this might not be real, but there was a peaceful glint in the way his eyes met mine and it was as though the time apart, petty arguments, sad farewells, and moments of happiness blended together in an instant like water rippling off a brush as it touched the canvas. Neither one of us spoke, and for a split second I wondered if he thought the same as I, that this was some malicious prank, the universe converging to ruin our sanity by instilling false happiness in us.

The parking lot around us might as well have been empty, a desert, infinite, with no sound or shadow or person to interrupt, an intimate aloneness that between two lovers could spell out the word *sacred*. This man, the one I had once given my heart to, a piece of my soul, a prized section of my body—he carried it with him, and for some selfish reason I could not explain, I wanted it back. I needed him now.

As if by reflex, I stretched out my hand and touched his chest. The gesture was one of understanding that the body is living; the feel of his heartbeat against my palm reassured me again that this was real. The quick pulsations under my padded fingertips jolted my hand back, stopping it short of my own body. I feared if I reeled it back too far, I would lose the feeling entirely of what it was to touch him again. Was he a different man now? I didn't know, but I clung to the memory I had of him like a saw palm clinging to life as it gasps for air during a controlled burn. I did not know why he was there, smiling at me, how he came to be in this war; his job escapes me, even now. All the same, I wonder now while writing this if I picked up the phone, would he answer with the same tone and familiarity as he did that day when he said my name; surely he would. His voice, the smooth yet leathery deep-throated timbre that mixed together perfectly like Irish cream into coffee, swirling endlessly in a circle until it blended caramel brown and melted naturally on the palate as you slowly sipped it. Our conversation was short, a break in silence staggered by reverent smiles and questionable gazes. Small talk was not enough to say all the things I wanted to say to him. How I wished that we had more time together. I would have told him how wrong I felt for leaving him behind to go into the army and that, even now, as he stood in front of me, I still remembered the first time we kissed at sunset on a rock in Mission Gorge, how cheesy we had felt as teenagers for doing it, but how much I longed for it now. Simpler days and moments like those were all I clung to now to make me smile in this place. The conversation never went past catching up. Each glance and smile felt as though there was a silent conversation happening, one that told of everything we wanted to say but couldn't fashion into words. He told me he was there for only a short while, but it was long enough to tempt me into taking him inside me again, to breathe him in and exhale a piece of myself, a part that he took long ago, a part I desperately needed back, a part of me that I had let this war take.

I would never get the chance.

My crew walked out of the px, bags in tow, and for a brief moment I looked at Sergeant Lippert, a sort of begging with the eyes that comes from months in combat with the same person, of knowing when they need more time. He stopped short and nodded. I looked over at my first love, contemplating touching his chest again, but I didn't. I smiled at him and told him to be safe. I don't know if it was something in the way I looked at him or maybe the expression on my face that made him straighten up. I think it was then that he realized I might not make it back to San Diego alive. He grabbed my arm and pulled me close. I wrapped my arms around his muscular frame, my hands gripping tight to his uniform. We clung to each other and in that moment it was everything we were and might not get to be again, or maybe it was simply a gesture between two people, a silent farewell. It seemed as though he too would soon be gone, back out to the war, back to a life where I did not exist.

Soon I would be surrounded by nothing but ghosts.

· · · · · · · · · ·

## Abu Ghraib

Missions always seemed to vary in our battalion. Because we didn't have a clear understanding of our reason for being in country, our battalion had a habit of being tasked out with the shit jobs, the ones no one else in theater really wanted to do, like water supply runs to Abu Ghraib.

I was ground guiding a forklift with the last pallet of water off our HEMTT's flatbed, almost a successful supply run. Sergeant Lippert was driving and yelling at me to pay attention to the building in front of me, Abu Ghraib's unit headquarters— the main entrance to the prison just beyond the door up ahead to my left. For months now, when there were no recovery missions, Sergeant Lippert and I ran water missions up to the prison once a week, with loads at least ten pallets deep, each pallet carrying at least one hundred bottles of water.

It took us less than twenty minutes and we were finished, but while I was standing next to the HEMTT I noticed a soldier walking over to the first pallet. He grabbed a case of water and disappeared back into the building. There were no prisoners out that day. I wondered if it was because it was too hot in the sun or if the warden had taken away their yard time. I watched Sergeant Lippert trying to lower the last pallet onto the ground. He was having trouble with the forklift gears. I chuckled as I thought about a scene from *The Shawshank Redemption* where Andy Dufresne hasn't stepped out of his cell for morning head count and one of the guards is calling for him, but he's already escaped the prison, vanished overnight. I looked over at Sergeant Lippert, who was still struggling, and yelled, "Damn it, Dufresne, you're puttin' me behind! I got a schedule to keep!" Sergeant Lippert flipped me off and continued mission.

I turned around, looking at this place that I'd overheard some of the Cav scouts at the chow hall call the pit of hell. It was sparse and nondescript with its decorations; its ornaments of war usually were displayed for all to see, but I supposed that day they were hidden inside the building handcuffed and caged, no doubt being tortured for information they probably didn't know.

The outer walls, high and covered in barbed wire, were sporadically broken up with a guard tower. I looked up at the soldier standing watch with a rifle. His sheltered tower was covered in desert camo netting at the top. It dangled down a little on each corner edge. He walked from one side to the other. He must do it to keep from falling asleep. Guard duty—a job I did not envy. He noticed me staring at him and looked down at me. From behind his dark Wiley X sunglasses, I could not see the irises of his eyes. I could not see his nametape on his chest or his rank. He was covered. All I managed to make out was the American flag patch on his right shoulder, the sweat circles underneath his armpits, and the fact that he hadn't taken in any water in the whole ten minutes I stared at him. I knew from experience that while on duty, you're not allowed to leave your post for any reason unless relieved or ordered to do so. The dude had to have been baking in that tower, so I went to the cab of the truck, grabbed a bottle of water, and walked over to the tower. As I got closer, I could see he was sweating profusely. I yelled up to him, but he did not move from his post. I walked over to the edge of the tower where the ladder met the platform. I yelled up to him again. This time he walked over and looked down at me. I held up the water bottle. He shook his head no, but I knew he was thirsty. I knew he needed water. He was too proud. *Fucking men.* I shook my head, as I put the water bottle in my cargo pants pocket and climbed the ladder, hoping I was not breaking protocol and that this bit of humanity that I was feeling obliged to give would not get me into too much shit with his section sergeant. When I got to the top rung of the ladder climb, I knew instantly that I had made a mistake. My nose met the end of a rifle barrel. I apologized as many times as it took for me to pull the water bottle out of my pocket and place it on the floor of the tower. I started my climb down and made it to the bottom, but as I walked back over to the HEMTT and looked up at the tower, the soldier was opening the water bottle.

· · · · · ·

## James

I was leaning over a technical manual, hoping to find the answer as to why the backup lights on the cargo HEMTT wouldn't work, when Anderson walked up and asked me to go take a smoke break with her. Besides her, I was the only other female mechanic in Alpha Company, a feat in the eyes of the male soldiers. We walked to the smoke area just inside the motor pool walls when a Humvee pulled in, the occupants a former sergeant of mine and an officer. Called away from my smoke, Sergeant Lester introduced me to Capt. James Haislop. Anderson laughed at my helpless attempt to flirt with the handsome young captain. There was something about him I couldn't put my finger on. Maybe it was the way he looked at me as though he and I were the only ones around. Or maybe it was because finally, I had felt something for someone, something inside me that hadn't been there for a while, the feeling of being alive. Either way, I smiled, batted my eyelashes at him, and he stood there staring at me like a kid in a candy store, bewildered. A wave and a stumble, and the captain carried on toward his office. Sergeant Lester laughed at both of us, the ridiculousness that this place brought out in people. I laughed as well; I couldn't help it. After the moment passed, I went back to smoking with Anderson and thought about the captain.

The days wore on like this: filing work orders as completed, taking smoke breaks, lunch breaks, shitter breaks, and any other break so that we did not have to work in the sun. Down the pipeline, friends of mine knew the captain and, soon, where he worked. I visited on occasion, making myself a presence he couldn't forget, and soon it was more than obvious that the feeling was mutual, but there was Rob. In the back of my mind I knew what I was doing was wrong, that he was an officer and I was a married enlisted soldier, but war has a way of making you forget who you are, and soon after that first recovery mission, I had lost who I was completely. A numbness had taken over, the feeling of not giving a shit about much outside of your job and the soldiers in your section. The conversation with the captain had made me aware of that, and now all I wanted was to feel that again, so I started meeting him outside of work. At the chow hall, outside his hooch, at the smoking area next to battalion; I met him anywhere I could. All I wanted was a conversation and a friendly face, someone who didn't know me well enough to know that part of me was missing. A friendship formed but didn't last, and soon the darkness of the night that I used to fear became my friend. I used it to go see him.

The first time I fucked him, we only spoke of what our lives were like back home. Each night we were together brought me closer to someone who resembled me. I needed to feel like me again. The war was taking that away slowly, so I clung to James like an addict needing the next fix. I clung selfishly to these moments where I could forget the war and embrace passion and desire as though they were as necessary as air. And soon the war subsided in my mind, and each time I gave in, got my filler fix of drugs from my surrogate death dealer, the less I found I needed to fight back the urge to kill. I had found another sort of peace, and so the nights with him became something much more than sex, more than the need to forget the war; they became a piece of a dream, the hope for a normal life after all this death and killing, a day in my future that I might be able to will into reality. They became a life after this, a place where James and I would live happily ever after. We shared our dreams, aspirations for the future, and though I listened to him speak of his family in Florida, his upbringing, and countered with my own stories of growing up, I felt as though for once in this war I had connected to something alive, something that was tangible, that could grow into something better, so I allowed myself to fall in love with him, with the thought of what could be, and the possibility that I might have a shot at living after the war was over. He had given me that much.

• • •

"So why'd you do it?"

I looked up at him from where my face was buried into his pillow, shrugged my shoulders, and put my head back into the feather down indentation.

"Is that an 'I don't know' or a 'fuck you'?"

I knew eventually that this conversation was going to happen, the part where I'd have to open up about myself to James. So I told him something he didn't want to hear. "I'm married."

"I know."

"That doesn't bother you?"

"Not as much as you not answering my question."

"He used to beat me. One good backhand across the face. He always used his left."

James sat up a little in bed. "I was bored in college. Didn't have a clue what I wanted to do after I was finished, so I did ROTC instead. Figured I'd do at least that."

"He used to make sure the ring side was facing up." I lifted my left hand. "To make sure I knew his place in my life."

"You didn't fight back?"

"Of course I did, but a guy like that, he only knows one thing—how to hurt someone."

"Why didn't you report him?"

"It's a military base, a military couple; you think anyone would've given two shits if I came in complaining about my husband beating me?" I rolled over onto my back. "Every female soldier's got something to complain about. I didn't want to be one of them."

"You're not."

"To you I'm not, but to every other swinging dick, I am."

James looked at me, studied my face to see if I was lying. I knew the look of a skeptic. He thought I was full of shit, and most of the time I wished that I was.

"You going to stay with him?"

"My gramps was in the military. Navigation guy on a cargo plane or something like that. Nam."

"My dad was navy."

I crawled onto his chest. "You ever wonder if we'll be able to do this tomorrow?"

He moved a piece of hair away from my face. "I hope so, but you still haven't answered my question."

I crawled out of his bed, slid my PT shorts and shirt back on, slipped into my running shoes, and grabbed my weapon. James swung his body over the side of the bed and reached out for me, but I had moved away toward the door. Before I opened the door and left, I answered his question, but it wasn't the answer he wanted. I could see it in the way he looked back at me after I answered, a look of disenchantment.

"Drugs. I joined to get away from drugs."

· · · · · · · ·

## Dog Tags

Dog tags sway when you walk into the family house, fresh and new, minted and pressed, still warm where your name was printed, your religion pronounced, you blood type engraved, your serial number stamped. Down to their core, dog tags remind you that you've just signed your life away and are now the property of the United States Army. Dog tags slouch as you walk bent over from your friend's car to the house you grew up in, a last farewell with your ex-boyfriend Kyle and your best friends Tony, Dan, and Holly before you ship out. A wave and a stumble into the house, dog tags slam up against the wall of the hallway as you trudge to the bathroom. Dog tags slap against the toilet after a late night of downing too many types of liquor, that last shot of vodka you swore up and down wouldn't make you puke. Dog tags are silent as you sleep one last time in the house that you labeled on your emergency contact form as your permanent place of residence. Dog tags hide underneath your uniform at the airport the next day as Dad hugs and kisses you goodbye, tells you to be safe over there, while Nana sits in the front seat of the car crying and Grandpa stands by the driver's side door staring at you as he holds back tears. Dog tags swing in unison against one another as you board the plane and leave everything familiar—the orders printed, your names recited, and only a one-word response given when you asked where you were going: Iraq. Dog tags hang around your neck as you stand in formation at dawn in a place unfamiliar, waiting for marching orders, the sound of your heart beating against the tin metal. The rubber ring around your dog tags, the only thing that hides the panic you feel in your chest. Dog tags break the silence of the quiet morning, the clanging sound of each soldier coming to attention, the orderly unison of dog tags ringing out their impending doom. Here in this line is where dog tags find you equal, but here is where they separate you. Here is where they strip your pride and force you out of the line. Here is where dog tags come in handy as you ask the chaplain to sit and pray with you before you exit through the gate on mission. Here is where dog tags fight the urge to leave your body as your convoy takes enemy fire. Here is where dog tags bang against your combat vest as you bag and tag the body of a soldier you do not know. Dog tags yank you away from the smell of burned flesh. Here, next to a burned-out Humvee in the middle of the street, is where they are guarded and hidden from sight. Here, dog tags equip you for death, prepare you for the inevitability of war, but you didn't die today—today it is another soldier. Here is where dog tags are ripped off. Here is where you take one dog tag from him and put it in your pocket. Here is where dog tags give you no solace, as you and his fellow soldiers help you lift him into your truck. Here is where you hand the dog tag over to his commander when you return to the FOB. Dog tags clink in the shower as you try to rinse off the soldier's blood crusted on your hands and buried in your cuticles. Dog tags feel cold against your skin in the morning as you walk to the chow hall, hoping for the quiet and peace of a warm meal. Here in formation is where a set of dog tags once stood. Here is where dog tags still stand silently waiting for the next mission. Dog tags bring you relief when you are not named off the roster for another day out the gate, but tomorrow it will be your turn again. Here is where dog tags drip with sweat from the searing heat of the midday summer sun. Here is where dog tags cook your flesh if left exposed for too long in 120 degree F heat. Here in the crowded streets of Baghdad is where dog tags have placed you. Here is where the familiar sound of dog tags bumping and clanking is replaced by a local merchant yelling the fresh cuts of meat he's selling at his market stand and loud Arabic music blaring from a beat-up silver Mercedes Benz moseying down the street as if it weren't congested with wall-to-wall people. Here is where dog tags redefine you as a target inside and outside the gate. At the end of the day, when you have fought as hard as you can to do the job they trained you for, dog tags drag you down, their weight unbearable around your neck. Here, in your hooch, after formations and chow, when the night has come is, when dog tags don't mean shit. In here is where silent wars are fought, in the in-between hours when sleeping soldiers wake in fear. Here is where dog tags lie on the nightstand next to a green army watch. Here is where they separate and divide, placing reality in a box where compliance and devotion to the job do not exist. Here is where they are left while the rims around your eyelids fade slowly down to black. Here is where they watch you from their place next to your bed, hoping that one day the sleep you wish for will finally be called rest. Here is where dog tags don't matter until the next morning, when they are lifted up and returned to their rightful place. Here is where they learn the meaning of death. Here is where a girl is made into a woman and then slowly into a man. Here is where dog tags sit and wait, hoping that the humanity in you appears again. Here is where dog tags see the wayward daughters and sons of America fight on the front lines. Here is where they notice the landscape is not what it seems. Here is where they find that war is not fought by soldiers on both sides but by farmers, young boys who are confused in faith, and women who are forced to fight. Here is where you leave the semblance of the person you once were. Here, dog tags listen to you sob as you lose your will to live. Here is where dog tags are collected in blown-out vehicles where no faces or bodies remain. Here is where dog tags are the only thing that distinguishes one soldier from another. Here is where they are divvied up, one to your family, one to your unit. Here is where nothing is left for you but the name God gave you, the number the government rendered you, the religion your family instilled in you, and the metal that the army issued you. You wear dog tags around your neck until the day you die. But still, dog tags do not leave you. Here in this metal coffin is where dog tags identify you and bring you a step closer toward the mouth of a politician who knows nothing of your name but uses the number around your neck as a statistical reference to his ambiguous claim about the war he isn't supporting and the troops he doesn't know. Here is where dog tags sustain a memory, a lasting image of a soldier who once was a woman or a man. Here, on marked graves, among the rows of white headstones, is where dog tags no longer trouble the dead.

# PART 3

Somewhere in a Desert

## Now Entering Starvation

*On June 10, 2007, in the neighborhood of Fajr in Baghdad, Iraq, U.S. and Iraqi soldiers found twenty-four naked and abused boys, ages three to fifteen years old, in an orphanage, chained up in several dark, windowless rooms. A locked room fully stocked with food and clothing was found nearby.*

### Six Hours without Food

The paste of stale oatmeal mixed with dirt-brown water clings to his bones. The glucose giving him enough energy to sit upright after another night of restless sleep. Nassir's dazed eyes from the dimly lit room do not reveal to him that his captors, the men who run this place, are walking in to strip him of his clothes. The chains dangle from their hands, the jagged unhinged smile of anticipation clings to the men's cheeks before the children are beaten and shackled to the empty metal cribs. Naked and unsure, the other seven boys in the room look at each other but cannot translate the anger of their religion that slaps contempt for their existence across their backs as their food bowl drops from their hands and splatters the oatmeal mush onto the concrete floor. There will be no more bed. No more food. No more clothes to comfort their frames from the cold and damp of the room they are chained in. Nassir does not recognize the harsh taste of his tongue as it breaks open after the seventh hour. He begins to cry from hunger. The dull twinge in his stomach confirms that the door slammed shut will not open again for some time, his future translated into a language that only the ticking of time past can decipher.

The children do not ask when the food will come when a shadow crosses from underneath the doorway. Or cry out that they are hungry. They sob. Close their eyes. Remember the sound that jasmine wheat rolls make when the spine of the loaf is cracked open. The smell of saffron cutting the air that wrinkled the nose. Or the feel of holding the leg of their mother as she dressed the lamb for dinner. The boys do not ask after six hours when the sunlight drips into the horizon, the hallway light glinting under the metal door, offering the only hope that they will be set free. The boys, chained to cribs, are left, abandoned, forsaken.

### Twenty-Four Hours without Food

Try holding food in your mouth for as long as possible, savoring every granulated piece, the mushy texture resting on your soft pallet, the half-cooked oats squeezed between your teeth, stored for just one more hour before your will to satiate your stomach threatens your tongue, urging it to swallow what little life you have left buried in your cheeks. Imagine ketosis taking over, the depleting of your body. What little fat left gradually disappearing. Your intestines moving the food out of your body too quickly for your bloodstream to absorb it as you lie on a cold slab of stone. Imagine defecating close to your body to keep warm that night. The slow malformation of your stomach. Men's voices laughing through the peephole in the door when you slam into the metal crib and piss yourself because you have lost the strength to urinate away from where you sleep. Imagine slowly forgetting the definition for the word *freedom*.

### Seventy-Two Hours without Food

Your muscles are wasting away. Your cheeks are sunken. The door opens for the first time in days. Then men come in. Yell. Hit you with the metal buckle of their belt. Butt the cribs up against the walls, dragging you behind it, the chain cutting into your skin.

A woman walks by with a ripped-up, gold-sequined dress, fresh bruise in her eye socket, blood crisping the outside layer of her lips, the ghost of a woman made into a whore, a vessel for another child due to makes its way into this room. The brothel operates at a steady pace, the children raised for torture in the next room, the building breeding darkness, the forgotten remnants of what the war has done to this city. Nassir thinks of his mother, her offering to a suicide vest, of his father, now insane, who gave the men money to have Nassir taken away. Here, surrounded by his peers, Nassir rubs the faded chalk drawing he made of his mother the night he came to this place. It is his salvation from the present. The outline of her jaw smudged from his fingers tracing the hair he had quickly drawn on before his memory forgot how one suborned strand of hair always came loose from her hijab. He sleeps with her every night. His frail body hugging every line. Maybe tomorrow. Freedom.

### One Week without Food

This room. This dying chamber. It's an abyss of hate for these boys. It hasn't decided whether to kill them yet. The men are too occupied with their new toy, a fourteen-year-old girl they ripped from the streets before she could make it to school, her fate as uncertain in this building as the boys'. But this room invites Death to visit. It creeps along the ceiling edges, swings from the shadows, spitting molded, stagnant air around the cribs, the amalgamation of intrigue and wonder. It studies Nassir. He is the most vexing. It is amazed by the skin plunging in between bones, pressing the pigment thin of color, the tipped edges of knees and elbows that jut out, seducing the concrete with the hopes of blood. Sometimes repulsed by the defecation, it moves silently next to him, threading the chill over and under each vertebra as it watches from over his shoulder as Nassir's eyes close, his body curls, his abdomen distends, and his breathing slows enough for Death to be bored of him again. There are seven more boys that gasp for its attention.

There were twenty-four boys discovered in the orphanage—or only a handful, depending on if you believe the lie that the Iraqi health ministry told the world.

The soldier's boot scuffed the chalk drawing of Nassir's mother's face as he was cradled and lifted up out of his own feces. Outside, the light burned his eyes, but he was too weak to cover them. So the soldier shielded his face.

Hauled out of the building, the children were placed in white plastic patio chairs. Some naked. Some lucky enough to be clothed. IV bags. Juice boxes. Teddy bears. The lost children of Baghdad, the war's cargo, counted and loaded into ambulances. Their names were checked off one by one according to their need for medical aid. The worst saved for last.

Jamail—the charming

Gabir—the consoler/comforter

Ammar—the virtuous

Latif—the gentle/kind

Yasin—the thoughtful

Malik—the powerful

Hazim—the prophetic/wise

Nassir—the granter of freedom (the essence of war forced him to learn the meaning of his name).

*On Thursday June 21, 2007, Nassir died at Dar al-Hanan orphanage, eleven days after his rescue. He suffered from marasmus, a severe form of malnutrition and energy deficiency, characterized by loss of muscle mass, edema, and stomach bloating.*

·······
# Morning

The sun had barely risen in the east, but the crested lark sat atop concertina wire; its talons gripped between the razor edges. Looking back and forth, it chirped small echoing sounds of the morning. Dew had formed on the windows of the Humvees, the droplets running down in sporadic descent, collecting and forming larger streams like veins scattering inside a body. The crested lark chirped again as I ran past. My pace quickening, my uniform pants rubbing against my inner thigh. My breaths were short, huffing in and out. My boots, hitting the ground hard, scattered the dirt and rocks in my wake. The o-dark-thirty pounding on the door signaled the call to mount up on a recovery mission; the bodies were still warm, the blood not yet browned and coagulated on the ground. There was barely any light, but the streams break through the windshield, reflecting fragmented rays into the cab of the truck. The rifle was light in my hand as I set it next to my seat, but the empty body bags weighed down the backseat. There was no time for goodbyes, no prayer before we left.

We swung wide through the barrier blockades at the back gate, pushed forward onto the blacktop, the wheels of the HEMTT wrecker grinding the rocks to rubble, the sound of radio checks as we sped past the gun towers. The lark was surely gone by now. The strange and momentary silence of a simple morning broken by an IED blast.

The hole was big enough that the Humvee's front end was halfway submerged, its front grille ripped apart like wrapping paper, the sides of metal sticking up like claws curled up and scraping toward the cab of the truck. The engine was exposed, the pistons compressed, sunk into the heart of the compartment; its last breath was the huffing rattle and hiss of oil spewing from a hose that used to connect to the body. The windshield was cracked, splintered from the right side toward the middle, like spider webbing shaken free from a brisk wind. There were no mirrors, only shards of glass that, when looked down at, cast the reflection of horror back at you, the look of shock, repulsion, and hate as you lifted a severed arm that had been cut off at the elbow, a wedding band still attached to the ring finger. It went into the bag.

This was where the mourning began in Iraq.

· · · · · · · · ·

## James (#2)

My head snapped back when he pressed down too hard. The synaptic misfires of my brain reeled as he moved in circular swirls with his padded fingertips. The movements were slow and methodical but still as precise and formulated as the muscle memory recall of clearing a double feed of a rifle jam—cock the pin back, drop the magazine, clear the bullet, slide the bolt forward. My knees bowed out, bent, and released toward the fitted sheet, making room for his wide shoulders as he moved slowly past my hips. A grip on the pillow with my teeth allowed no words to pass from my lips, a stifled moan into the feathers was all he heard before my thighs gripped tight around the nape of his neck, my fingers searching for his high and tight, a place to hold onto that was not bare skin, but rather a handhold for what was about to come. An arch of my back, a shiver, and tighter grip on his head, and he knew that he had released what little tension I had left in my body to give. He moved his way upward and before I could catch my breath and take in the moment, he was finished. We were lying there in the bed, and it was then that I notice how sweaty we were and that even though we were in Iraq, this was a different sort of dying.

· · · · · · · · · · · · · · · · · ·

## The Only Stars I've Seen

The Paladin tanks of First Cavalry, Eight-Second Field Artillery, had been firing shell rounds for an hour, creating a low-lying fog around the base from the barrel smoke of their guns. Their constant firing echoed like thunder and the flash bangs from their turret barrels reflected off the smoke like lightning. The war-generated storm that had engulfed our base reflecting the mirage of a foreign battleground from history's past. Atop the back wall of our base, our brigade colors flew true in the slight wind that had picked up. It had made the battle sounds of firing guns less persistent, as the artillery unit battled not only the wind but the incoming barrage of mortar rounds that were starting to land inside our concrete barrier–lined base.

It had been a few months since my near-death experience with the mortar round, but I still couldn't sleep; the residual pain in my healing shin and the noise outside kept me awake. I'd climbed to the top of my tin-roofed hooch, and as darkness fell I sat there thinking about what every soldier far from any familiarity would think about—home. I thought back to Kyle and the last night I spent in his pickup, his hand trying to find a space on my leg—how he finally settled on my knee, firmly holding it with his sweaty palm. I remembered wishing that he had found a place for his hand closer than my knee. I thought back about what I could've said in the silence of that cab or what I could've done, but I knew only a good fuck and an "I love you" would have made him wait for me. I looked out beyond the concrete walls lined with razor-edged concertina wire and realized how stupid I'd been to leave home and come to this hellhole. All I wanted now was Kyle's loaded "I love you's" and the warmth of his suggestive hand on my knee.

The outgoing fire had ceased. The smoke from the barrels was too thick, making vision nearly impossible. From my perch, sitting in the rusted lawn chair I had acquired earlier from the smart-mouthed medic who lived behind me, I watched as the smoke slowly rose into the air. I'd been trying to fall asleep when the outgoing fire started, but I now found myself looking up at the night sky, waiting for the outgoing guns to start up again. It was the only sound of war I looked forward to.

Whenever the cannon cockers of Eighty-Second Field Artillery began outgoing fire, it was tradition for Tina and me to watch the outgoing shells. The artillery unit had missions only when the sky was completely clear. Normally it was covered with smog, sandstorms, or clouds. Tina and I missed the clear skies of our homes in California—dark nights full of twinkling stars and crisp, cool night air that could suck the breath out of you if you didn't wear enough layers. Of course it was dangerous to be outside because of the return fire, but we braved it. It was the closest we could get to seeing the night sky, a taste of home. I had gotten the bright idea one night to sit on top of the roof of our hooch while incoming mortar rounds were whistling into the perimeter of the base, but it only took one time for Tina and me to be sent scrambling from incoming mortar fire for her to say that she was never going up there again. But those nights were few in number. Most times I sat for hours by myself on the roof looking up at the stars. When Tina joined me, I'd sit down on the stoop with her, swapping funny stories or talking about our families, and sometimes we just sat without saying anything, just looking up at the clear night sky, listening to the incoming and outgoing fire.

Tonight Tina had been called into company headquarters for the first shift of radio duty, and so I was left alone to watch the night sky by myself. The military field chair I had acquired from outside of First Sergeant Hawk's hooch stood beside me empty, as I sat in the white plastic chair I stole from a Charlie Company medic for mouthing off to me in the showers the night before. The smoke was beginning to lift, but I guess not fast enough for the Eight-Second's gun bunnies because they began to shoot flares up into the night sky, staining it with red streaks of bright light. The flares' light gave away my position, and Sergeant Lippert, who happened to be passing by, looked up and found me sitting on the roof.

"King," he shouted up, "just what the fuck do you think you're doing?"

The sound of his hard voice shouting up to me made me jump. Soldiers were not allowed on their roofs because of safety issues, something Tina and I ignored at least once a week. We had managed thus far not to get caught.

Somewhere in a Desert

"Hey," I said, clearing my throat, trying to come up with a bullshit explanation that he knew was going to be a lie. "I just wanted to get a look at the action that's going on by the back gate."

He glared at me in disbelief. Normally soldiers didn't intentionally put themselves in harm's way, but that didn't matter much to me anymore. He kept staring up at me. I knew he was contemplating whether or not my excuse for being on the roof warranted his attention. A couple of seconds had gone by before he looked like he'd come to the conclusion that I was up to no good.

He yelled at me and pointed to the ground, "Get the fuck down from there. It's one in the morning. You don't need to see anything but the back of your eyelids."

I leaned forward in my seat and peered down at him. "Not to be a smart-ass or anything," I said, as I gestured down at him, "but you're not exactly slamming back zzz either."

I was still sitting in my seat atop the roof when Sergeant Lippert stomped closer, with a heaviness to his stride like he was putting out a fire with each step. He didn't looked pissed off, but his stiff and quick gate suggested he was none too thrilled at my remark. In a few seconds he was next to my front door and I was stuck on the roof, cornered. For a couple of seconds he disappeared and then reappeared again.

"Hey, King, how the hell did you get up there?"

I leaned out of my chair, cringing as if he was already within arm's length of me with his hand stretched out trying to snatch me up. "You're not going kick my ass or anything, are you?"

"No, now tell me how you got up there or I am going to kick your ass."

For a split second I contemplated whether or not he was bluffing about kicking my ass, but looking down ten feet at him next to my front door, I realized that either way I was fucked. I sighed and said, "All you do is scale the side of the concrete bunker by sticking your feet in the metal rings on the sides. Then when you're on top of the bunker, swing a leg up onto the roof."

He started up, his combat boots slipping on the bunker wall. "It's easy, once you get the hang of it," I said, as I watched him struggle up the side. He looked like a dog trying to scale a chain-link fence to get to a cat. It took him three tries before he finally got to the bunker roof, and next thing I knew he was sitting next to me in First Sergeant Hawk's chair.

"This chair looks familiar."

"Really?" I said, looking away from Sergeant Lippert, who was inspecting the chair. "It's Specialist Kennedy's."

Trying to shift Sergeant Lippert's attention from the familiarity of the first sergeant's lounge chair, I quickly changed the subject.

"So," I said with a nonchalant smile, "what brings you up here?"

"I wanted to see if your bullshit excuse about being able to see the action was true. But from what I can see, you have a pretty good view of the back gate."

"Yeah, well," I paused. "That bit about the artillery wasn't exactly true."

We both looked at the back wall; the gun bunnies had reloaded the guns and were getting into position inside the turret. The fog from the guns had started to lift and the night sky was visible again—the stars breaking through the haze in patches.

"I thought so," Sergeant Lippert said, as he shifted his weight in the chair to look at me. "So what the fuck are you really doing up here?"

"Don't laugh, okay?"

"Private, tell me what the fuck's going on or I'm going drag you down from here," he said, pointing to the ground, "and smoke the shit out of you."

"Okay, okay." I took a deep breath. I knew he wasn't going to believe me, but telling him the truth was better than doing pushups until I couldn't feel my arms. "Specialist Kennedy and I come up here when the artillery is going off because it's the only time you can see the stars at night." I pointed up to the sky. "That's what we do up here."

As I spoke, he looked up, then back at me, and then back at the sky as if to study if I was fucking with him or not. For a minute I watched him, his head tilted back, quietly looking up.

"You know," he said, his voice dropping a little, "if you sit on the deck of my parents' house back in Austin, Texas, you can see a whole sea of stars. So many stars, you can't even begin to count them." He leaned back in the chair, arching his neck so he could get a better view. "I used to love sitting out there on summer nights with my kids. I used to point out the constellations. The kids would point at other stars, trying to make them into different things." He was smiling with his hands on his chest. "Jeanie, my youngest one, she loves horses. She'd swear up and down that Orion's Belt was really a horse." He laughed and glanced at me. "You couldn't tell her anything," he said, shaking his head, "stubborn, just like you."

I looked over at him. He didn't say anything for a minute but sat there quietly squinting up. I could tell he was thinking about the same thing Tina and I thought about when we came up on the roof to look at the stars—home. Though he was probably thinking about more memories of his wife and kids, I was thinking about my dad and where he lived now in Colorado. He always used to tell me about this lake, Turquoise Lake, where he would go camp out underneath the big Colorado sky. I wanted to be there now.

I turned and looked back up at the sky and said, "You know what's great about the stars?"

"No, but I'm sure you're going tell me," he said, as a smirk cracked across his face.

"Constellations never move, only the earth does, so no matter where you are in the world, your loved ones are staring at the same sky as you are right now. It's like looking up at a little piece of home."

For a while, Sergeant Lippert sat there staring up at the sky. Then he looked at me and nodded before he got up from the rickety chair and started scaling back down to the ground.

"You okay?" I asked, as I watched him move down the side of the bunker and then disappear out of sight.

Below me, the gravel shifted and rustled. I stuck my head out over the edge of the roof to make sure he'd made it down all right. After a moment he reappeared below, brushing off some dirt from his ACU top. He shouted up to me, "King, don't fucking stay up there all night, you hear me?"

I smirked. "You got it, Sarge."

I watched him walk down the aisle of hooches. He'd just disappeared around the last hooch on the corner when I heard Tina call to me. I chuckled at Tina's skinny, gangly legs striding out of sync as she walked toward our hooch, flinging gravel behind her.

I called her name as she got closer to the door. She looked up. I smiled.

"No way in hell."

"C'mon, I got you a chair."

Slinging her M16 over her shoulder and scaling up the side of the bunker, she shouted, "We better not get in trouble for this!"

I decided not to tell her about Sergeant Lippert or the fact that I had thrown her under the bus a little bit. As she made her way onto the roof of the bunker and then onto the roof of our hooch, I said, "You'll be fine."

"Where'd the chairs come from?"

Smiling coyly at her, I said, "You really want to know?"

With one eyebrow raised, Tina said, "Ah, something tells me no. I heard over the radio that the outgoing fire is going to start any minute now."

"Did you happen to grab any munchies?"

She plopped down in First Sergeant Hawk's chair, set her M16 next to her, opened both cargo pockets of her ACU pants, and pulled out two bags of Hot Cheetos. She handed me one of the bags.

"Thanks, battle."

"Anytime," Tina said, smiling.

Opening our bags of Cheetos, we leaned back in our chairs. We peered up at the clear night sky as we waited for the outgoing fire to start up again, both content to sit and gaze at the stars all night. Again my mind wandered home. I missed the routine sounds of familiarity, the slamming of the front door, Grandpa yelling, "Don't slam the door!" The low chuckle Nana used to make every time I purposely slammed it so I could hear Grandpa holler at me from wherever he was in the house. I missed Dad's loud music, the crackled sound of the stereo blaring Grateful Dead that echoed in the driveway like an amphitheater. I missed how Dad burst in the door every night, yelling with a crescendo in his greeting, "Hello!" I thought about the last time I'd called home just to hear their voices. I'd only gotten the answering machine, the sound of Nana's voice, "Hello, you've reached the Kings. We're not home right now, but if you leave a name, number, and a brief message, we'll get back to you as soon as possible. Thank you and have a beautiful day."

I closed my eyes, trying to see the faces I knew so well. But the memory was blurred. I clenched my teeth in anger. I needed home right now.

"Do you think it's too late to call the West Coast?"

Underneath her patrol cap, Tina was trying to figure out the time difference as though it were a calculus equation. Using a Cheeto and an invisible chalkboard, Tina leaned out of her chair, counting the hours with her Cheeto, trying to deduce the correct answer. Nodding her head in agreement at her calculations, she turned in her chair and said, "I think it's only five in the afternoon in California."

I lifted up my ACU sleeve and looked at my watch. It was one in the morning. Nana was always my first choice. Counting nine hours back from my time, I realized that it was only four in the afternoon California time.

"Tina, you suck at counting."

"What?" she said, raising one hand in the air, a Cheeto caught in between her index finger and thumb.

"It's four in the afternoon, not five."

Throwing me a cocky look, Tina's green eyes stared at me, daring me to challenge her again. "No, Brooke, it's five."

"No, it's not," I said, shaking my head. "You count back nine hours from our time. It's one in the morning here, which means it's four in the afternoon in Cali."

With a furrowed brow, Tina threw a Cheeto at me. "Whatever."

It bounced off my forearm and onto the tin roof. "Waster," I said, leaning over and tossing it into my mouth.

I decided to give a phone call a shot, hoping to reach Nana. It was Thursday, which meant that she'd be home from her stint at Saint Therese's, where she sat in the chapel every Thursday for an hour to pray. As I pulled out my phone—a red Motorola Razor, the only perk of being stationed so close to the Green Zone in Baghdad—I contemplated what to tell Nana. I couldn't tell her that I was having a hard time being in Iraq and that I was seeing way more combat than I antici-pated. You just didn't say those things to Nana. She was a gen-tle and sensitive Old Italian grandma who got what she called "worrying stomachaches." Ever since she'd had her bleeding ulcer two years back, I had tried not to worry her about my army stuff. She was having a hard enough time with the fact that I'd been deployed.

I dialed my home phone number, hoping that Nana would pick up. I let it ring twice but then closed the top of the cell phone and hung up. It felt wrong to call home, but I needed to hear her voice. Her gentle but frail voice always reassured me that everything, no matter how bad, was going to be okay. I opened the phone back up and dialed again. I sat waiting, looking up at the stars, thinking of my bedroom back home. For my seventh birthday I had begged my dad to buy me a packet of plastic stars that I could stick on my ceiling. Grandpa had said no, but Dad ignored him and bought them anyway. The night of my birthday my dad woke me up at midnight to give me my gift: the ceiling above my head covered with stars and even a glow-in-the-dark full moon. He had snuck up to my room and put them up while I was sleeping. Of course Grandpa was mad, but by the time I was in high school I had bought enough stars to cover the whole ceiling, so I had the constellations inside my bedroom. I looked up at the night sky and thought of my room with all the twinkling stars plas-tered to my blue ceiling as I sat there waiting for someone to pick up the phone at home, but it rang four times before going straight to the answering machine. Nana's voice—a resonating crackled sound that echoed through the receiver I held to my ear. Tears welled in the corner of my eyes. From the other end I listened to the background noise of the greeting—the living room TV turned on, the sound of someone shuffling past in the kitchen, the distant sound of Molly, my Alaskan malamute, barking at the back door. As the greeting came to an end, Nana's voice grew louder as she said to have a beautiful day. The usual cadence of silence passed before I was prompted by the answering machine beep to leave my message. In a shaky crackled voice I said, "Hi, Nana. I couldn't sleep and just wanted to hear the sound of a familiar voice. I guess you're still at the church, probably praying for me not to die here. I guess I'll call tomorrow or something. I, ah . . ." I tried to rush the rest of my message before I totally lost it. "I miss you and love you. Talk to you later, bye."

I slapped the phone shut and shoved it back into my pocket. I was a total wreck. I threw my hands over my face and bent forward, resting my head on my knees.

Looking up from her bag of chips, Tina asked, "You okay?"

I turned my head toward Tina, wiped my tears onto my uniform, and said, "Ah, no. I think I successfully just left the worst message a granddaughter, who is at war, could've left on the family answering machine."

Leaned back in the chair with her legs crossed, Tina canted her head toward me, raised her eyebrows, and nodded her head in agreement as she said, "Yeah, that was pretty bad."

Chuckling, I wiped snot from the back of my hand onto my black PT shorts and said, "Oh gee, thanks, Tina."

"Eat a Cheeto." Tina handed me the one in her hand. "It'll make you feel better."

Shoving the Cheeto into my mouth, I let the hot flavor of the chip dissolve in my mouth, hoping that it would take away the longing for home that I felt, but it wasn't making my homesickness go away fast enough. I started shoving them in one after another until my mouth felt like I had just shoved ten habaneros inside of it, but I still didn't feel any better. I didn't feel anything but the need for the normality of home.

"Ease up on the Cheetos, Brooke." Tina put a hand on my arm, preventing me from putting another Cheeto in my mouth. "You're throwing those things back like some anorexic chick who hasn't eaten in days."

"Fuck you," I said, spattering half-chewed debris from my full mouth.

Tina just shook her head at me, eased her hand off my arm, pulled another chip from her bag, turned to me, raised one of her Cheetos in the air, and said, "To home."

I leaned over out of my chair, put my arm on her shoulder, raised a Cheeto, and with my mouth still stuffed full, I echoed her toast, "To home."

A loud booming sound rippled through the air like a shock wave. The outgoing fire had begun again, but it didn't bother me. I was thinking of my bedroom, of home.

· · · · ·

## Jahir

He stood above me on a building while holding an AK-47. He shot at me. He missed. I do not know the young Iraqi boy who died. He fell or jumped off the roof, swan dived down to the ground, and thudded on impact. Everyone called him Muj. Another terrorist down, who knows how many to go. Sergeant Lippert joked, told me to scrawl a dash on my helmet: First Confirmed Kill. I stared at the boy instead because I didn't know who had killed him. I still don't know. Some of those details from my deployment, the missions, the everyday routines, some of the people I was with, have been swept away in my memory, blurred and unclear backlash from my TBI.

What I do remember was that the PSD team pulled security. Sergeant Lippert put a dip in. I crouched next to the body in the sun. Six bullet holes. Broken limbs. Blood coagulating in the dirt. Lividity. Body rigor. No shade except on the sidewalk near the building. The sun was coming down the building in minutes, giving the body a stench. Bloating of the organs. The boy's face was intact. His eyes wide open, looking up at the sky. His mouth gaped. Part of a tooth lodged in his tongue. A necklace around his neck. Chest exposed. Flesh resting on his abdomen, torn from bullet impact. I stared at him, imprinting his death into my mind, a place in the hurt locker for him, a place next to my humanity or what was left of it.

I began to tear up, and it was then that Sergeant Lippert slapped me on the shoulder. Time to go.

· · · · · · · · · · · · · · · · ·

## Rest and Relaxation

It was barely the middle of the deployment when they asked me in early January if I'd like to go on R&R. I looked at Sergeant Lippert with a blank stare. Rest and relaxation. I think I nodded my head, or did I just say "sure"? Either way, I left the war to go with Rob. It was the least I could do, a last farewell before I divorced him. I didn't want to be one of those wives from war—the ones who run off with someone while the man's away—but I was away too, so the line was blurred and I agreed to go to Bloomsburg, Pennsylvania, with him for reasons of guilt or shame or maybe to see if the war had changed him somehow. I turned in my weapon and hopped a flight to Pennsylvania.

In JFK Airport I was stopped by a man who asked me if I was coming or going. I answered neither. I was on leave. He thanked me for my service while I stared at the tile floor. I nodded my head and walked quickly to the bar. When I sat down, the bartender asked me what I wanted. Johnny Walker Black straight, two ice cubes. It went down hard and fast, and soon I was asking for another. I looked up at the TV. The war was playing on muted silence, showing the recent bombings near the Green Zone, commentary scrolling across the bottom of the screen, the voices of officials on war, a retired general spouting insight on the best way to keep the insurgents at bay, but no one was watching the screen. They did not see the images of women crying over children, soldiers shouting orders in the hushed silence of bomb blasts and crowded streets now littered with lifeless bodies. They did not watch as the locals gathered up their dead, picking them off of the ground like a child reaching for the comfort of a favorite blanket. They did not watch me as I poured another drink down my throat in the hope that the next one would stop the phantom tingling in my fingers from trigger pulls, that my constant scans of the room would convince me it was safe to feel more normal, and that the asshole who was slapping his hand on the rail of the bar would realize that I was jumping out of fear because the noise was vibrating down toward where I stood. All this revolved around me at the bar as the bartender poured me another drink, told me that they were all on the house as I stood there in my army combat uniform swaying, the war playing on mute above my head.

I was half drunk while staring at Rob, who greeted me at my gate when the plane landed in Pennsylvania. I did not kiss him. I gave him a hug, and it was then that everyone around us started to clap, whistle, and cheer. I hated it. I hated the attention, and when I stopped fake-hugging Rob, I tried to break away quickly and walk toward baggage claim, but they gathered around me, shook my hand, patted me on the back, and told me welcome home. I was not home. I was in Bloomsburg, Pennsylvania, spending my R&R with a man I no longer loved, letting people touch me who had no idea that every pat on the back was like torture to my adrenal glands, and sensing that every time I raised my right arm to shake another hand, my uniform still smelled of charred flesh.

Rob insisted on us going to a house party the day I landed in Pennsylvania. I agreed only because there was free booze and because I didn't want to be anywhere private with Rob. We walked into a house that smelled of cigarettes. The floor was sticky from spilled liquor. I walked past the throngs of people, shoulders square as I scanned the room. Rob looked left as I looked right. Both of us on edge. We made it to the kitchen, the keg sitting in a red Walmart special tub. It was almost empty. Rob got his drink and wandered off. I stood at the keg trying to pump it and pour at the same time. A guy came up to me, asked me if I needed help. I give him my stupid face. He smiled and pumped the keg until my drink cup was full. The music banged loudly against the walls, thumping downbeats into the floor, rattling the floorboards. Rob was in another room flirting with a girl about my age. She wore a U of P sweater and tight white jeans. I looked over at the guy who helped me and smiled. He introduced himself, said he was in a band, the lead singer of Pan.a.ce.a, whoever they were. He went on about how they had just come from a gig, how this was their friend's house, and how I looked pretty in my Ramones shirt and zip-up black hoodie. For a moment I thought about walking away but decided that any conversation with anyone was better than being around Rob. He flirted with me, asked me my name, but I just smiled and asked for another beer and if he could show me to the bathroom. The tile of the bathroom was stained yellow around the edges, the sink too high up to sit on, so I stood. He wrapped his arms around me, kissed my neck, and told me that he might be too drunk to do this. I held the back of his head, tried to like him touching the small of my back, the smell of whiskey and beer on his breath, but by the time he worked up the nerve to undo my jeans, someone banging on the door startled me. He told me not to worry about it, told them to hold on, but I was scared, Rob was somewhere outside, and the bathroom was starting to feel smaller. He told me not to worry, that it's some drunk asshole, but the banging got louder, my heartbeat heavier and faster, and soon I bolted out the door of the bathroom, down the hallway, out the front door, and toward the sidewalk. Rob came out, asked me if I was okay, and I told him I was in the bathroom with a guy. He wasn't mad. Nodded his head and asked if I wanted to go home, and when the guy came out to find me, Rob turned and said, "She just got back from Iraq. She's my wife. She's fine." The guy looked at me hunched over at the waist hyperventilating and said that I didn't look fine. He came down, tried to calm me, but Rob wouldn't let him near. And as Rob grabbed me and hustled me down the sidewalk, his hand wrapped tight around my arm, he whispered, "You had better get your shit in check. This is not your home. This is my home." But I couldn't and he knew it, so we found ways to keep me busy; spending my hard-earned blood money was one of them.

There was only one good mall in Bloomsburg, and even now, while I sit here looking on Google Maps to figure out which of the two malls was one the one we went to, I cannot for the life of me remember the name, but I do remember sitting in the food court with bags of clothes, trinkets, and a box containing samurai swords that, for some reason when I saw them in a shitty dollar store, I had to buy. I leaned over and opened the box, pulling out one of the swords. I unsheathed one of the katana blades. On the hilt was an inscription that I would later come to understand was the trademark of the sword maker. I lifted the sword up, looking at the handle wrapped in blue cloth, the curvature of the blade, and thought about a samurai warrior carrying it into battle, the feel of coming close enough in combat to pierce the flesh of your enemy with the edge of the blade. I knew my sword was a replica, not sharp enough to slice a piece of paper in half with one swipe, but I imagined that this shinsakuto could carry weight with its appearance alone. For a while I contemplated bringing it back to Iraq with me, carrying it around like a warrior given special permission to slice the enemy where he lay, but then I remembered—I don't know my enemy, I am a woman, and this blade was not even sharp enough to cut a steak. Rob walked up and loudly asked me what the hell I was doing. I looked up. Everyone in the food court was staring at me. I was standing with the blade pointed in strike position at a ficus, the ficus with several shattered limbs, drooped over and limp, shredded leaves scattered on the floor. I stayed the blade back into the sheath and put it back in the box. Rob knew that I was some sort of fucked up war flower, that this mundane public area was no place for me. He knew that soon I would be returning to a place that felt more like home than this place would ever feel. We stood up to leave, but someone behind me banged their tray against the garbage can and I dropped to the floor, a piece of french fry smashes in to my hair, spilled soda presses against my skin and leaves a sticky residue on my forearm. Rob yelled at me to get up, that I was embarrassing him, that I was making a fool of myself, but the heat in my chest rose, my heart rate pulsed blood into my arteries, and the scabbed-over truth that the war was still with me broke the air of silence when I screamed at him that there were more coming, to get down. Rob reached for me, tried to drag me up from the floor, shook me, and yelled at me that we were not in Iraq. The crowd was still watching. He grabbed my face, pointed it at the people, showed me that we were not there, that I was home, but I did not feel at home, and for a moment, the heat in my chest was unbearable, the tightness of fear and fighting crashing against each other as every breath came out ridged and unmatched with its fury.

Later I was told by Rob's mother that he carried me out of the food court over his shoulder as I screamed. And now, as I am sitting here, all I really remember of that day was how the sword's blade was not sharp enough to cut through the ficus leaves in a single swipe.

In the in-between hours I sat awake in bed in Rob's mother's house, which was too quiet. I looked over at Rob sleeping and thought about how we hadn't made love since I came. I didn't want to be in the same room with him let alone touch him. So I sat up most of the night thinking about Iraq. Somewhere back in Iraq that very same day, an insurgent was doing his morning prayer, kneeling on the rug, chanting, eyes closed as he recites the lines recalled from memory. And after he is finished, he will rise, walk out of his house, get in his car, and drive down the road toward our company's convoy. Private McDonald, who is sitting in my gunner's seat, will look ahead on the road and see the car moving toward him. He will call it in, ask for permission to fire a warning shot, and take aim. The bullet will hit the side of the vehicle, but the car will keep coming. He will fire another and another until he hits the radiator grille. But the car will keep coming, the man inside unfazed by the shattering of metal sprayed up from the hood. McDonald will let another bullet go from my .50 cal. It will hit its mark, and though McDonald will tell me when I return from R&R that the headspace and timing are off on my machine gun, that he wasn't cleared to kill the man, only deter the vehicle from getting close to the convoy, I will see the relief in his eyes—the certainty of knowing that the bullet saved him from dying that day. He will tell me that it was his first kill shot. I will nod. He'll say that he has trouble sleeping now, that he is just a mechanic, not a machine gunner. I will tell him that I too was once just a mechanic, but not anymore. I will tell him all of this, but for now, I was lying in bed awake in Pennsylvania thinking about Iraq and getting back to the noise of war.

Two weeks go by quickly and I drowned most of them in booze, but some I passed in silence sitting on the banks of the Susquehanna River watching the chunks of ice slide downstream and catch on each other. Most of that time I spent alone. But the day I was to leave, I sat with Rob on the bank and told him that I was leaving him, that this was not the life I wanted, that he was not what I wanted. He argued with my decision, told me that it was just because of the war, that I was confused, that I should wait until the dust settled and the deployment was over, but I could not wait. I told him that I'd drawn the papers, and as soon as the words left my lips, I felt the chill of the air finally brush my skin cold. He stood up and started shouting that I was his, that he would tell me when I could go, but I pulled out my dog tags and told him that I was never his, that I was bought with a ten-grand signing bonus and the job I wanted, that I was owned long before he knew me, and that I would be the property of the U.S. government until I died or got out, whichever came first. He shook his head, the tears forming in his eyes, the anger on the tip of his tongue, the urge to hit me in his balled-up fist that clenched my dog tags, wanting to rip them free from my neck and beat me with them. But he didn't hit me. He didn't say a thing.

Somewhere in a Desert

He spit in my face and walked over the hill, past his mother's house, and out of my life completely. For a moment I felt what it was like to be relieved, unburdened. I walked back to the house and put on the same uniform I came in, the smell of flesh rotting within the fibers of digital gray. Soon enough I would hear the unified rotation of single blades thundering over my hooch, see the plumes of smoke as they separated the sky in vertical streaks, feel the heat from the metal on my machine gun as it radiated through my aviator gloves, heed the resonating warning sound of the bolt catching and clacking forward, understand once again what the weight of a soldier felt like in a body bag, and by the time I would reach the armory and retrieve my M4, I would remember what the noise of war sounded like again and ignore the notion of home.

And yet there was a strange stillness to the war when I returned, as if nothing had moved since I left, but everything was still in motion. The mortar rounds. The Paladin tanks. The bullets. The body bags stacked next to one another in a row. The crescendo of violence upturned by IED blast points emblazed in scorch marks in the road. But the machine gun felt heavy in my hands, my fingers forgetting the pulling pressure of triggers, the letting loose of bullets. Beyond the wire one day our convoy went past a known hostile village on Route Irish and I forgot to nametape defilade. I froze. Sergeant Gomez pulled at my pant leg, yanking me down into the Humvee. For a moment I forgot where I was, the goggles around my eyes fogged, the chinstrap too tight around my face, the flak vest too constricting for my chest. Inside my comm headset, I heard the word *shoot*, but I didn't pull the trigger. I was locked inside myself, wondering what I was doing here, and contemplated the urge to remember home, but a slap on the leg reminded me that I was in Iraq and that this was where home was now.

After another mission, with the same result, I was permanently pulled from machine gunner, moved to Alpha Company, and given the option of working in the motor pool or recovery. I chose recovery. I chose death in a different form. I was back with Sergeant Lippert, and soon the missions become mini funerals, bringing back what was left in pieces and parts, an unjustifiable end to the means of war destruction. Weeks carry on into a month, and the body count kept rising. Our mission was to bring them back, but as I pored over a piece of flesh, a chunk of arm, my hand shook the pen marks on the description tags, ones that I wished read: *I'm sorry, I didn't know you before this* or *I will try to find all of you*. Each bag was stacked in the back of the truck, brought back to base, and given to Mortuary Affairs. I watched as they carried them into the building. I saw the looks on the tired faces of the soldiers who sighed from having to put yet another name down on a clipboard. Sergeant Lippert told me that this one would be number thirty this month. He slapped me on the back. I flinched. He punched me twice in the arm, told me that the war wasn't over yet, that we had months to go before this place was a pushpin on a map that we could say we visited once, but I watched the door of the building close, the finality of the metal handle snapping shut on the frame, and gripped my M4 tightly. It wasn't long after being back with Sergeant Lippert on recovery, maybe a week at most, that Alpha Company moved me in between being a mechanic and doing recovery, but truth be told, I never wanted to go on another recovery mission again. I think Sergeant Lippert knew it because the number of recovery missions I went on became far fewer and my time in the motor pool more frequent, which was fine. Slowly, as the deployment worn into February, I no longer was called out for recovery missions. I was tasked out elsewhere. I had, in a sense, become a utility soldier, one that could be moved around, used for everything from turning wrenches to operating vehicles that moved connexes. I was still useful to the battalion, so I was moved from squad to squad, company to company, passed around like a wartime Vietnamese whore.

It's how I survived; I kept moving. Day in and day out I paced myself with the rhythm of battle drums banging on around me. If I became complacent, the steady percussion of explosions crescendoing outward into a symphonic overture just outside the FOB's concrete walls made me realize that it was time once again for me to keep moving. A bomb had gone off somewhere in the city. A plume of smoke permeating the horizon with vertical streaks of black, a car explosion this time, but I kept walking. One foot in front of the other, my boots slapped the ground as my pace quickened. I walked faster and faster, my rifle in my hands, my momentum jostling my vest side to side, my helmet, too big, strapped down at the chin, pressed down on my black Oakleys, hair falling out of my bun, the collar of my uniform scratching at the back of my neck. One of my knee pads was sliding down toward my shin, the other riding up toward my thigh. And as I ran, all the buildings began to look like blurs, the smoke like clouds, the people, the soldiers like ghosts, the palm and eucalyptus trees like foreign creatures reaching out to snare and entangle me in vines. The road was once just dirt and mud, the grass long and overgrown. And then it came, the past war creeping back in, and soon Iraq was Vietnam all over again. My M4 was now an M16A1. My helmet green. My boonie hat now had a peace sign scrawled on the side in black ink. My hair was short and there was no need to be clean and kempt. My digital gray was now olive drab. But the helos still came in, and the past was now the horrible present, the wounded an unfathomable number. There was no enemy that we could see. We did not know why we were fighting. We could not see what tomorrow brought with its sunrise, but we felt it coming, like the heat that swelled off the land at midday. There were no words or cigarettes that comforted those who left for patrol. There was a look, a nod, and pace to their walk, a shuffling of boots that kept them moving forward in the hopes that this war wouldn't be like the last. And yet . . .

· · · · · · · · ·

## James (#3)

After we had talked about family and life, about God and what we wanted to do after the army, we stopped speaking altogether. There were no more stories of childhood or growing up left between us that could break the silence of the room, so we watched movies instead or listened to music, anything to keep away the silence of our own static breath clinging to life in this place.

I climbed through his window. It was late in the evening, almost midnight, when I returned from the motor pool, a last-minute wiring job on a HEMTT flatbed that I was tasked out to help with so that another barrier mission could leave on time that night. All I could think about the whole time was a hug from James. It had been a long day in the motor pool trying to help the mechanics of Alpha Company clear their work orders. When I walked to the showers that night, no one was around. I was alone. I took a shower alone. I got dressed alone and walked to James's hooch alone. When I crawled through the window and saw James waiting for me, his smile was a comfort telling me that, in this room, I was no longer alone. He was here. The half-glazed look on my face made him realize that it had been a long night. His smile disappeared. I sat my weapon down at the foot of his bed. I stood there and, for a moment, contemplated leaving. He grabbed my hand and pulled me toward him and cupped my face with his hands. I looked into his eyes. The tears came. The first time I had let him see me weak. I crumpled into him and bawled as he held me tight and told me that whatever it was, whatever I had been through, it was okay now, that he was here, that I was alive, that everything was as it should be.

He made love to me, but I only went through the motions, staring at the ceiling as he finished and kissed my forehead. Before he went to bed, he looked at me, told me he loved me. I smiled politely but knew I was far from being able to tell him that I loved him, far from a place where it was possible for me to love him the way he needed me to. After a moment of silence, I said it back to him, hoping that with my saying it back he would be content enough to go to sleep. He smiled and rolled over, but I lay there watching the orange fluorescent light outside his window flicker on and off until dawn approached through the cracked windowpane and slithered up the bed toward where he lay. I turned and looked at him asleep. Peaceful and calm, he looked content with life, with me. I envied him. I rose gently from the bed, slipping out of the sheets sideways. I dressed and grabbed my weapon but looked back at him sleeping in the bed.

I could love him.

...

It was the end of February. I was late coming back into base. He was worried. I heard it in his voice as I stood outside his bedroom window. It was dark. The streetlight, no longer working, left the alleyway littered with long black shadows. I whispered that I hadn't taken a shower, but I knew he didn't mind. I told him that I didn't want to stay, but he insisted, showed me the food he'd brought me from the DFAC, and I couldn't help but smile. I joked that he really did love me and that he shouldn't. He did his best Scarlett O'Hara, batting his eyelashes and waving his hand like a fan, and he sassed back with an "I do declare" before I handed him my rifle. In through the window now, I stood in his room. He flicked the desk lamp on and stared at me. I wondered what he was looking at. He sat me down in the chair next to his bed and handed me the Styrofoam plate of food. I was not hungry, but I appeased him by choking down some of the salad and half a grilled cheese. He asked me if I was okay, but I couldn't answer because I didn't know if I was okay, so I shrugged. He nodded, picked the plate up from my lap, and set it down on the desk. He pulled me up from the chair and wrapped his arms around me, gently making forgiveness for something that was clearly not his fault, so I did not hug him back. I couldn't. He whispered into my ear that it would be okay, and it was then that I lost my balance, an invisible weight pushing down on my shoulders. My knees buckled. I surrendered and slowly sank to the floor. He knelt down next to me and asked me to look him in the eye. I couldn't. He asked me to stand, but my legs didn't seem to move. He lifted me and set me on the bed. One after another, he removed each piece of my clothing until each undone Velcro, zipper, and button had stripped me down to nothing. I sat on the edge of his bed naked as he rummaged around in his wall locker and produced a PT shirt and shorts for me to wear. He helped me dress and laid me down on the bed. It wasn't until the next morning when I woke that I realized I had slept in the bed alone. He took the floor. Next to the door was my dirty uniform. I walked over and picked it up. The blouse was punctuated with black char marks. I can't remember now what it was that I had been doing before I went to his room, but the blouse I remember. I dropped the uniform back down onto the floor and walked over to his place on it and lay down beside him, wrapping my arms around his ribcage, pulling the weight of his love toward my chest. I had realized that night how bad I was at pretending I was fine. I wasn't fooling anyone, least of all James. And what was even worse about James trying to help me was that I didn't think I was worthy of his help or his love. But of all of the people in the world, only he could save me, only he could keep the skin from collapsing.

· · · · · · ·

## Wishes

The children didn't crowd around me like they used to, but they still called after me with "mister, mister" as I walked away. I didn't take my black Oakley glasses off anymore, even in the chow hall. I didn't carry my M4 at the ready. It was heavy now, a burden to lug around. I put a rifle sling on it and carried it on my back. James and I barely talked anymore. My journal had too many empty pages. I hadn't cracked the spine in more than a month. Even if I had been able to bring myself to write, the words would come out heavy-handed and displaced on the page.

But there were things that hadn't stopped.

The convoys kept coming in and going out the gate. The medevac Humvees still barreled down the main road, sirens blaring. The helicopters still lifted off the pad behind my hooch every night at half-hour intervals. I still went to see James. He was my one comfort. I lay awake, still stared out the window at the sky until dawn came and I had to leave. I still dressed for formation and rolled out on a recovery mission to pick up blown-out trucks, and I did this every day without fail because it was what I was programmed to do; it was what they had trained me for; it was the only reason I was here. Fuck everything else they tell you about war. It's all about training and how you fit perfectly into that military machine that produces death and destruction because that's all they knew how to do. It's all I knew how to do, too; they had made sure of that.

• • •

I sat outside my hooch most nights smoking cigarettes, wishing it was anything that would make me feel a euphoric high, something to counter the dissonance that was slowly building up inside me. I wished for many other things. The will to pick up my pen and write again. Little Debbie Oatmeal Creme Pies or Sugar Daddy pops. My dignity. A place to lay my head that wasn't accompanied by the sounds of helicopters and sirens, the clacking of a bolt sliding back and a bullet entering the chamber. A semblance of who I used to be or maybe someone else entirely different.

Sometimes I wished for far less pleasant things. For my aim to be on point that day. The urge to stay awake. My Hemingway book to be used as a doorstop. Another canister of bullets for that motherfucker shooting at me. The need to stop carrying a cross around my neck. The fear of dying to go away. Not living past tomorrow. Or at least, to run out of body bags. For that soldier to eat a bullet instead of me. Soon I would stop wishing, but on most nights I dragged that smoke long and hard, wishing for all those things and more.

• • •

In the DFAC I sat down to a table with a full plate of food, and though I was tired, dirty, and didn't feel like eating, I tried to enjoy the first sit-down hot meal I had had in several months. The steak was boiled—not char-broiled, boiled. The mashed potatoes were gritty and the green beans tasted like rubber. The soda from the fountain was almost out of sugar syrup, making my drink taste more like fucked-up ginger ale than Pepsi. On the walls big-screen TVs broadcast CNN, some shitty cooking show, and an episode of *Seinfeld*. I looked down at my meal and then up at the cooking show, watching as a woman sliced onions and put them into a pan with butter. I could hear the sizzle as she slid them from the cutting board into the pan. On another screen Jerry was yelling at Kramer and Elaine was sitting on the couch staring at the two with a cruel scowl of disappointment on her face. CNN was running some nightly news about the war in Iraq. I stopped watching the TV and focused my attention on my soft serve ice cream that I had layered with chocolate syrup and sprinkles. There was no way they could fuck up ice cream. I picked up my spoon and took a bite, and for a moment I was content enough to look back up at the TV with the cooking show. The onions were caramelizing.

. . . . . . . . . . . .

## Show and Tell

One of the guys from the Personal Security Detachment team was showing off pictures from his camera while we sat in the motor pool smoke area. It was passed around. Anderson handed it to me. I looked down at the picture. It was Firdos Square. The statue of Saddam was not there. The picture showed only a pillar with green bronzed feet and half a leg adorning the top. A piece of the pillar was missing from the center. Weeds had grown around the cracks and creases at the base, and what was left of the fountain bottom was chipped and cracked. Around the outside edge of the base graffiti posters plastered with propaganda were scrawled in black lettering, plastered in rows of four, nearly covering the bottom. There was no statue, no bronze dictator in the picture to signify that this was where, three years ago, Americans had torn down the statue of Saddam, trying to symbolize his removal from power. But it was only a symbol. Saddam was still at large when the statue came down, and his son Uday was still trying to bomb his way out of Baghdad. Years later I looked at the picture on a small LCD screen, seeing what looked like the soldier posing in front of where the statue used to be. He pointed out everything about the square in the background of the picture—the large round Grecian pillars that surrounded the circular epicenter, the large mosque-like building, the hajji who wouldn't stop staring at them, and the soldier's shit-eating grin, but I looked at the photo, told him it was cool, and passed the camera back to him. But what the soldier didn't point out from the photo was how the statue was in fact still there. Remnants of Saddam's legs still clung to the top of the pillar in defiance of our presence. Inside the fountain, at the bottom, stagnant algae-filled brown water had pooled next to one of the cracks at the base, leftovers from the rainy season. Decay had set in there in the foreground, and yet the pillar still stood there surrounded by the city and its people. Cars no doubt passed it daily, but did the people remember when the statue had stood at the top? Did they think about a time when they only had to fear one government in their country and not half a dozen? Did they shake their heads and wish for those days again? Or did they simply pass it as though it were just another eyesore in their city filled with wartime destruction?

. . . . . . . . . . . . . . . . . . . . . . . .

## MEMORANDUM FOR RECORD

SUBJECT: Mandatory Safety Briefing for All Incoming Females in Adherence to Joint Task Operations While in Theater

It is the recommendation of the U.S. Army in accordance with the Joint Task Force that all female soldiers adhere to the following Standard Operating Procedures for AOR Baghdad.

• • •

*They will tell you that you won't see combat.*

Separate your uniforms from your whites, put in different bags. Buy tampons only on Tuesdays when the stateside shipments come in. Don't wear mascara on convoy. Better yet, don't wear makeup at all. If you get to take a warm shower, wash your hair first; the warm water won't last long. Don't go to the latrine by yourself. Don't dye your hair. Hang up your uniforms; turn your boots upside down. When buying new sheets, don't buy white.

*They say you won't see combat.*

Always bring a hijab when on convoys. When frisking a local national woman, wear thick gloves; some hide razor blades in their garments. Always be polite and accept local food. The wheat rolls are best with the chai tea. Never shake with the left hand. Stay away from the left. Don't speak to local men. Always carry a knife. When on base, walk like a man so the male soldiers think you're gay. Don't ask for help from the hajjis or the infantrymen or the Cav scouts; they all like fucking with women. Don't leave your neck exposed while manning the machine gun; the bullet casings will fall down your vest and burn your skin.

*You will see combat; it's not like the movies.*

This is how to load a magazine into your weapon while being shot at. This is how to clear it. This is how to stack the bullets. This is just how it's done. Don't forget your knife; keep it in your boot and not your belt loop; trust me, don't ask. This is how to take a piss while on convoy.

*This is not a joke.*

Keep tampons in your grenade pouch for bullet wounds. This is how to bag and tag bodies. Make sure to drink plenty of water; make sure it's only bottled water. Don't let them see you weak. This is how to say "yes" when what you really mean is "fuck you." Never give the local national kids candy. Don't even think of fucking an infantry dude. Don't fuck a married man. Better yet, don't fuck anyone. Keep your list of close female soldier friends short. Don't take shit from anyone lower ranking than you, especially if it's a man. Take a shower every day; crotch rot is real. Yes, you can use baby wipes; no, don't use just water. This is how to ask for help. When using a port-o-shitter, squat or hover, never sit. Lift with your knees when stacking sandbags. On second thought, don't piss on convoys—you're not a man. This is how to avoid male soldiers. Don't ever lie on a mound of sand.

*You will see combat.*

Do not get shot. This is how to not get caught. Do not fucking die. Braid your hair into a bun; don't just put it up. Do not get blown up. This is how to treat a male soldier; this is how they'll treat you. This is how to shoot while running. Do not fucking die. This is how to listen for mortars. This is what it sounds like. This is what they won't teach you. This is what you have to learn.

THIS *is how to be a woman in a combat zone.*

· · · · · · · · ·

## James (#4)

He leaned out of the window of his hooch, his military ring in his hand. I stood there stunned, unable to understand the words he had said.

"Marry me."

I asked him if that was a question or a statement. He laughed, but I was still confused. It had been only a few weeks since I told him that I loved him and actually meant the words. In full battle rattle I stood there in between hooches in an alleyway, waiting for him to clarify, but I heard my name being called by Sergeant Lippert, who was looking for me. Another barrier mission to bum fuck nowhere that I didn't want to go on, but as I heard the convoy trucks rumbling to life, I knew that I had go.

He asked me this time.

"Will you marry me?"

I looked back at the convoy and said that I had to go. He begged for an answer, but all I could say was that I had to leave. He repeated his question louder as I walked away, but I kept walking. Half falling out his window, he shouted the question again.

"Will you marry me?"

I turned to look at him. I loved him, but I was still married to another, not yet legally allowed to answer him, and yet I did.

"Yes."

He smiled and motioned for me to come back. There wasn't time to come back for the ring. I told him to hold onto it. He belted his "I love you" loud enough that it echoed out to the convoy staging area. I couldn't say it back. I was too far out in the open. Someone might've heard me, but I smiled and nodded a silent "I love you."

· · · · · · · · · · · ·

## One-Way Ticket

I could not stop throwing up.

· · ·

They all lay stacked next to each other on my nightstand. They all read positive. They all spelled trouble for me, but I could not stop smiling. My ticket out of here. My freedom from bullets, body bags, and barrier missions. It was the beginning of April. James had been gone for two weeks. His time in service was up; his positive piss test for cocaine and a two-star general who told James to get the fuck out of his army had made sure of that. I could hear him giggling through the phone. He was in Kuwait waiting for his flight to Germany. I smiled as he said that he was excited. I knew what was waiting for me when I returned to rear detachment, but it was too late. There was a knock at the door. First Sergeant. He asked me point blank if I had anything to tell him, and with a smile on my face I told him I was pregnant. He nodded his head, said okay, and walked away.

The next few days were spent writing sworn statements and answering questions by a battalion headquarters butter bar that could barely say my name without stumbling over his words let alone ask me the hardball questions like who was the father. I denied everything, except for my one-way ticket back to Germany, back to rear detachment.

I was transferred to HHC, located near the brigade headquarters, so that the brigade could keep tabs on my comings and goings. I was ordered by the company commander to report to the CASH, take a pregnancy test to confirm my status, and go back to my hooch. I was to be confined to my hooch until I was summoned or whenever they figured out what to do with me. Eventually they sent me back to the motor pool, stuck me behind a desk, and made me push paperwork until they could get me out of country. It took them until June.

. . . . . . . . . . . . . . . . . . . . . . . . .

## Redeployment Packing Checklist

Pack your army combat uniforms first. Military roll. Cram the black under armor sports bras, the tan undershirts, and the lucky convoy socks around the bottom inside edges of your green army-issue duffel bag. Tuck the laminated photo into the bag, but don't look at it. You don't want to look at it. It's the picture that you held every day since your first recovery mission in the sandbox after three soldiers burned alive when their Stryker rolled over a pressure-plate IED. Your brother's smirk and your father's wide grin, the picture taken before you left for the war, all three of you standing in front of the house, each one of you pretending that nothing will change when you get back from Iraq. It helps you fall asleep at night. You can't help yourself; you unpack the photo to look at it once more. The corner edges are falling apart. The girl in the photo used to be you, but that's not the face you see in the mirror anymore.

Pack your camo-covered army Bible. The pages have to be rubber-banded shut, otherwise it opens to Psalm 23. Pack the tan Rite in the Rain combat notebook, another sort of bible: the name and rank of every soldier you ever placed into a black body bag are written on its pages. Poems. Letters to your father that you never mailed. Pack the maroon prayer rug you stole while raiding a house in Sadr City. Unpack the prayer rug. Kneel on it while you pack the empty M4 magazines, the pistol holster, ammo pouches, and desert combat boots. Pick up your aviator gloves, the feel of manning the .50 cal machine gun on convoy. Pick up the shell casing from your "first confirmed kill." One of six M2 rounds fired into a fifteen-year-old boy's chest. He was shooting an AK-47 at you. You shouldn't have the shell casing. You shouldn't have the gloves. Women aren't supposed to see combat. Pack it all into the duffel.

Pack the hours spent in a concrete bunker waiting for mortar rounds to stop whistling into base. Pack the hate and the anger. Pack the fear. Pack the shame and disenchantment for a job done too well. Pack the back-to-back months spent going out on convoy without a day off. Pack your Combat Lifesaver bag, your hajji killing license, and the rest of your dignity. Pack them all next to the army core values and the bullshit promise your government made to protect innocent civilians. Pack your worn copy of Hemingway's *The Sun Also Rises*. Pack the tattered American flag you picked up off the ground outside Abu Ghraib. Pack the *fucks* and the *goddamns* tightly next to *it should've been me*. Pack the green duffel until there isn't room for anything else. Fold over the top flaps. Shut it up tight. Lock it. Heave it onto your back. Carry it all home.

# PART 4

Frag Out

# Schweinfurt, Germany

There was a no contact order, a plea agreement, an Article 15, a sonogram with two fetuses on it, and an engagement ring on my finger.

• • •

We saw each other anyway. We lived in the same house in Iphofen, Germany. We went to every doctor visit together. The two fetuses were boys. James was so happy he was crying. Dad was elated, Nana was laughing in excitement, and James's parents did not even know I existed. I hated it. I wanted them to know that I was here, that I loved their son, and that we were going to be together not because I was pregnant but because we were meant to be together. But the court-martial, the pregnancy, the not knowing me long enough made James reluctant to mention me to his parents. Hell, he waited until I was back in Germany to tell me that he was being forced to leave the army because he had pissed hot for cocaine, but then again there were a lot of things that James didn't tell me. When I got back to Germany, I worried that he was having doubts about our relationship, that he thought he had made a mistake getting me pregnant, but I knew that he would do the right thing and marry me; it was the way he was raised—a Southern Baptist good ol' boy from Florida. Maybe in the beginning, deep down, he truly loved me, but I know now that our happily ever after was manufactured and that our sort of love was not meant to last a lifetime. It wasn't built on a foundation sturdy enough. It was built on the idea of love, survival, the need to not feel alone. The stability, intimacy, and personal depth that a marriage should be founded on were not present in the marriage we were building when I returned to Germany, but I was twenty-one and so blinded by the happiness that I had craved for so long that not much mattered about my distant future. I was enamored with the idea of playing house because it helped me focus on something other than Iraq, if only for a brief moment.

. . .

I don't know why I did it, but everywhere I went, I looked for signs of World War II. Germany was filled with them. I guess I wanted to make sense of what it was to feel the sting of loss, to survive war, and keep living. To connect with the world again instead of feeling lost.

On the way to the apothecary shop to buy prenatal vitamins, I walked past an old building shuffled back from the street. Though it had been a month since I had returned from Iraq, I still remembered what bullet holes looked like in concrete walls. Atop the building, a swastika was still visible, the center of it scratched out but the impression of its symbol still stamped firmly into the stone. When I asked the pharmacist about the building, she replied in a thick German accent that some things were best left in the past, that Americans had no right to ask of it anymore. I pressed her for an answer as to where I might find information about it. She shook her head, told me that it was just like an American to demand answers to something I had no right to know. I reminded her gently that if it wasn't for our involvement in the war, Hitler would have surely ruined the rest of Europe. She gave me a dirty look, told me to leave, but to this day, I do not know why I told her I would not leave without an answer. I knew I had no right to keep pushing for it, but I did. She came out from behind the counter, walked to the window, pointed at the building, and told me that it used to be a general's house, that Schweinfurt was Nazi occupied during the war, that most of her family was killed when the ball-bearing factory was bombed by U.S. planes, and that if I wanted any more information, I should go look it up on the internet. I told her thank you, but she had already walked away. She did not hear the forgiveness in my voice.

• • •

At least once a week, sometimes more, I stood outside the chapel on Ledward Barracks at a memorial service for a fallen soldier, listened to the trumpet sound "Taps," and lent my ears to the tuned pitch of human pain.

• • •

Dichotomy is described in botany as the branching of a plant, with each of a plant's branches splitting into two or more limbs. The war seemed to me a dichotomy of humanity, each religion, culture, race, country branching out in different directions, all unable to stop, all unwilling to concede to the inevitability of war, that we are all linked in a downward spiral, like a starling plunging to the earth only realizing its fate seconds before impact.

• • •

A soldier is driving in his car on base. He is done with work. The day is coming to a close, but the sound of a trumpet over the loudspeakers stops him. He puts the car into park, shoving the gearshift toward the radio. He unbuckles his seat belt. Opens the car door. He steps out. Beret in hand, he fixes it atop his head, covering his high and tight. He steps to one side and renders a rigid salute, his right hand snapping to place at his brow line. He is facing the American flag that is now slowly sinking to the ground in slow, melodic timing. The song is almost over, but everywhere on base it blares from loudspeakers, this small part of the world stopping to render a salute, stand still, and pay their respects to the flag. The soldier is still standing outside his car when the song is finished, and other soldiers around him, they are stopped too. Each one facing the flag, each one stopping their world for a flag and the idea of flags; for the remembrance of what the flag means, stands for, brings with it when it shows itself on installation flagpoles, in front of houses, at ball games, and funerals. The soldier stops for the flag to remember all this and more.

Somewhere in Baghdad, at about the same time, Amir is driving his car or maybe a delivery truck when the *adhān* sounds. The speakers are broken, so the muezzin with a megaphone in his hand stands at the top of the mosque shouting the adhān, and though the muezzin has a cold and cannot keep his cough at bay, he continues the prayer call. There are no instruments to accompany him. He is but a man of Muhammad, and he does this three times a day to remind his people. Amir stops the vehicle. Grabs his prayer rug. Turns toward Mecca. He makes his intention as he kneels on the edge of the rug. The sun is setting, the adhān screeching roughly through the megaphone, the muezzin coughing. The world around Amir is still, the truck is running, and the slow steady huffing of the muffler burns hot and loud in Amir's ear, but the muezzin begins:

> *Allaahu Akbar. Allaahu Akbar. Allaahu Akbar. Allaahu Akbar.*
> *Ash-hadu an-lā ilāha illā allāh*
> *Ash-hadu anna Muhammadan-Rasulullāh*
> *Ash-hadu anna Alīyan walī-ullāh*
> *Hayya ʿala ṣ-ṣalāt*
> *Hayya ʿala ʾl-falāh*
> *Hayya ʿala khayr al ʿamal*
> *Allāhu akbar*
> *Lā ilāha illā-Allāh*

He says every line twice, each with the same intonation. The twelve melodic passages are slow and tonal at best, the muezzin's voice barely audible over the grumbling coughs that spurt through the megaphone. While listening to the adhān, Amir repeats the same words silently, except when the muezzin says *hayya ʿala ṣ-ṣalāh* and *hayya ʿala l-falāh*, Amir quietly says *lā hawla wa lā quwata illā billāh*.

After the adhān is over, Amir recites the *dua*. The call to prayer is almost over, but Amir's back is rigid as he bows toward the ground, his head touching the rug's outer edges, his eyes closed, his mind on the prayer, a thousand years of religion pressed between the words, his lips are the fastener of their meaning, and those around him know that Amir is a believer of the faith and all the history that it carries; the prayer has reminded him of that.

· · · · · · · · · · · · · · · · ·

## The House in Iphofen

There was a stillness to the air. A stagnant, pungent odor that crept into the bed next to me, lying in between James and me while he slept and I lay awake. I tricked my body into thinking there was a panic switch that would wake me up if the nightmares became too severe, but the pep talk only lasted a short while, and soon, after barely two hours of sleep, I was awake again, staring up at an eggshell-colored ceiling with crumpled waves of plaster. The fetuses moved inside my stomach, making the restlessness worse. Barefooted, I walked down the tiled floor toward the living room. Empty and barren of anything but black leather couches that clung to your skin like a dark abyss, furnishing only the remembrance of what it was like to seek comfort in a house that had promise to be a home, I stood at the window that met the porch instead. I contemplated smoking one of James's cigarettes, thought about Iraq, and pondered whether it was too cold out to go for a walk, but I chose instead to sit on the rug with a puzzle of Neuschwanstein Castle. I looked at the puzzle pieces, each one more perplexing than the last; none of the edges seemed to fit, and soon my frustration at my inability to sleep was cast upon the puzzle pieces before me. One piece was too short, the edge around it wide and thick, the corners ridged. Piece after piece infuriated me. I started mashing the pieces into place, trying to make the puzzle come together, but no matter how hard I tried, none of the pieces fit, the picture incomplete, the overall goal hopeless. Soon I found myself back in bed, fed up with the puzzle, fed up with sleeping, the small flat-screen TV on, and a show turned on that we had started to watch on DVD, *Prison Break*.

•••

The fan rotated back and forth, flipping the sheet up against my face with each rotation. Inside the bedroom James lay awake watching TV while I slept, a lazy Saturday night. In my sleep I dreamed of Iraq. The after action reports, the rifle cleanings, the mortar fires, the bombs bursting in agony upon impact— the dream took them all in, sucked them under, drove them free. My body lay there twitching, forcing muscle contractions produced by muscle memory recalling how the limbs move and muscle burns as the body is forced backward from a blast. I dreamed of preconvoy meetings, of reloading magazines and ammo cans, of burning through a pack of cigarettes while waiting for the flames to subside on the Humvee so that the bodies inside might stop screaming. I dreamed of the feeling of vomit rising in the throat as the stench of bodies, burning trash, and feces broke the smell of my own body odor. In the room my legs began to move too quickly. I accidentally kicked James. He got up and went into the kitchen, but I was sleeping. I did not see him leave. I dreamed of radio silence, NVGs, barrier blockades, and the feeling of breaking flesh as a bullet opened the skin like a finger poking through plastic-wrapped meat in the grocery store. I rolled onto my side, my arms flailing as I tried to wrap them around an invisible body bag, to grip a nonexistent rifle. I dreamed of golden, glinted sand trapped in the corner edges of my Oakleys, of boots laced too tight around the toes, of the feeling in my stomach when I knew that something was not right about this road. The twitches became violent shakes, and moaning was turning into soft screams. I dreamed of shouted orders through in-truck comm systems, of standard operating procedures forgotten by screams and all the fucking blood, of shaky hands trying to dress wounds that could not be mended, of the sinking feeling of death creeping up your leg to your spine when the tire rolls over a divot in the road, the one you did not see a moment ago. I awoke upright in bed screaming. I had scared James, who was in the kitchen making a sandwich. He ran in, asked what was wrong. I told him that one of the babies hooked his foot in my ribcage, that I'd be fine, but I was drenched in sweat, my mouth barely able to bring the words to my lips, my breathing unsteady. I lied to him. He knew but did not say a word, put his hand on my swollen belly, smiled, and said it would be okay. He lied to me. I lay back down on the bed and said, "I know."

· · · · · · · · · ·

## Waiting (#2)

It was not past ten in the evening when I started to count the minutes like seconds. Every set of headlights passing down the street began to refract through the glass of the front door like the ones that were expected in the driveway. I stood a while at the kitchen sink, soapy water in the one side, the dishes filling it, and when the lights passed, I hurriedly dunked my hands into the water, scrubbing a glass or fork, making myself busy enough to show that it didn't matter that he was gone. If I'd had courage enough to drink while pregnant, the bourbon on the top of the refrigerator would have sufficed to go down as smooth as water, each pour as easily executed as the last, the ice barely melted before the next drink was poured. But I was afraid of drinking, of smoking, of waiting at home by myself, the anticipation of loneliness creeping through the blinds like an intruder forcing himself through the darkness of a sleeping house. When the lights kept moving down the street, I walked to the window, looked out at the silence of the street, the lamp-post with the flickering orange light reminding me of the one outside of James's hooch in Iraq. It buzzed on and off, casting shadows on the cars, making them dance across the pavement and up the driveway. Then I walked into the living room, looked out the window. Off the porch the vineyard in the distance spiraled shadows of grapevines stretching through the darkness, the stillness of the roots climbing through the night, the grapes expanding and bulging with excess water from the mist that was coming down in soft billows. I wondered how James was fairing on the winding back roads, if the tires on our Audi were worn enough to make him spin off into a ditch or a rock wall; Germany is lined with them in the countryside. Bavaria's small villages are marked only with small town centers and long walls that stretched just enough outside the limits of the town to be called annoying by an American driver who is used to no barriers of any kind on the sides of the roads. The roundabouts flagged both sides of the villages, and on days when it was quiet James would go around them, skirting the tires, breaking hard lefts and rights so as to make me scream at him, begging him to slow down. I had not survived Iraq to be killed by his stupidity. I looked out the window now and wondered if he had veered off into one of the walls, taken the roundabout too fast. I poured myself a glass of water, dreaming of what bourbon would taste like on my lips, wishing that I had even a drop to help me sleep. I remembered Grandpa's three-drink rule and wondered if three would hurt the fetuses, if three would help me sleep, ease the restlessness, and calm my mind enough to stop thinking of James.

When he told me that some of his friends from his old unit had gotten back from Iraq, I knew what he was trying to ask for but couldn't bring himself to say. We had agreed on a set time home, midnight. But as I stood at the window in the living room and glanced over at the clock that now read eleven, my heart jarred loose from the confines of my chest, the water uneasily consumed as though it were a shot of Jäger, the licorice concoction forcing its way down my throat like razors dragging my esophagus open. Soon I found myself standing in the office with no recollection of making my way through the door. The wooden wall locker was open. The uniforms— BDU, DCU, and ACU—all lined up, pressed, his and hers dangling next to each other. Boots lined the bottom. Patrol caps stood ridged on the top shelf next to the berets, one captain, one PFC, a picture of us from Iraq plastered to the door. Dress greens held up next to dress blues, the mangled coagulation of military camouflage melting together like a modern interpretation of a Picasso painting splashed with rank, gleaming silver insignias, subdued black combat action badges, and unit patches. The abandoned traipsing of letters, financial statements, and orders stacked among the chaos on the desk behind me. The laptop open but turned off. A Big Red One calendar fixed to the wall, the month showing June of last year, a year too late. I walked to the living room: the clock, 11:20. I pulled out my mobile, dialed his number, paused over the green call button like a young boy looking at his first nude mag, rubbing the edges as though each groove was more important than the last, staring down at the green phone icon as if it were St. Peter standing at the gates ready to bring good news or bad. The house, half empty when I moved in, was now cluttered with the assortment of both our lives mashed together in a frantic attempt to create something outside of the war. I looked at it all. James's *Star Wars* Legos jumbled on shelves next to my anthologies of British literary works; his Xbox holding up Poe, and Hemingway, and Plath. I went back into the kitchen again, looked outside at the lights splashing white reflections on the wet road. I put on my coat and walked outside, hoping that a short walk would consume time wasted waiting inside an empty house. I walked up to where the vineyard gates met the road and back. I stepped back inside, hung my coat up, and looked at the clock. Only ten minutes had been wasted. I filled my glass with water and sat down on the coffee table in the living room, stared at the clock, tried to dial the number once more, but found the button more disturbing. I thought of the infinite things that could be wrong, might be happening, all things out of my control, and soon the rush of panic turned to anger, a bitter jealousy that ate at my concern. As a child, I was the oldest, never receiving more than I should; I balked at my brother's ability to get everything he wanted and more. Oftentimes I would try to ask for more but would be met with the understanding that asking too much of a good thing is hurtful to the person giving it. So I never complained, never asked more than I should. Staring at the empty living room, the darkness of the space, my hesitancy to dial the number fueled my jealousy, the bitter pregnant woman patiently waiting at home for her mate. I contemplated throwing the glass of water against the wall but knew that I would be the only one to clean it up. I got up and walked to the kitchen, leaving the empty glass on the table. Through the filmed mist collecting on the pane of glass, I looked out at sets of headlights hurriedly moving through the streets, coming home from late-night parties or work. Each set that passed reflected shapes around the rims, each one different, and I imagined that the next set could be James, but Peugeots, BMWs, and Land Rovers passed, all square-shaped lights with no cylindrical scope to their making. After a while the traffic would die down, the street silent again except for the distant sounds of a dog barking and the slow, steady dripping of collected water coming off the downspout of the gutters. I stared at the phone concerned that by not calling I was being a bad fiancée. I looked at the numbers, confused by the green call button. From somewhere far off, I heard tires screeching, an engine revving too high in one gear. I sat waiting, mentally preparing my speech, the contemplation of how angry I was coupled with concern. As the headlights came around the corner and veered into the driveway, I stood up and walked out onto the landing. James got out of his car and shuffled toward me. I asked how the meet-up had gone as we walked through the front door. He mumbled an unintelligible answer that it was okay but how they seemed to be weird to him when he mentioned us. I rubbed his back and told them that not everyone would understand why we did it, not everyone would be on our side. I thought back to my anger, the misunderstanding of his tardiness, but he wasn't late. I asked why he didn't call me on his way home, that I had been worried about him driving after drinking. He walked up to me and kissed my forehead; the smell of beer saturated the air between us with a lingering yeast smell that ate at my nose hairs. As we walked into the living room and James plopped down onto the black couch, I stood next to the coffee table; arms crossed, I reminded him that he said he would be home by midnight. He leaned his head to the side and glanced at the clock on the wall and told me it was not even midnight yet, that he wasn't late. I reminded him that he didn't call me on the way home. He lifted his phone out of his pocket. The phone was dead; the battery had long since extinguished his ability to receive calls. I asked why he didn't charge it. He said he didn't know it was dead. He got up and walked to the kitchen, got himself a Dr Pepper, and walked back to the couch, plopping down harder than before. He asked if I was angry at him. I switched stances, uncrossing my arms and resting them on my pregnant stomach. I nodded my head yes, told him that he should've called, that he should've charged his phone, that I was up late waiting on him because I was worried he was going to do something stupid, like crash the Audi. He leaned away from the couch, told me I worried too much, that it was just the pregnancy hormones making me crazy. At the mention of me being crazy, I picked up my empty glass from the table and threw it at the wall. He jumped off the couch and yelled at me for breaking a glass. Called me crazy. I turned and walked down the hall, told him to go fuck himself, to sleep on the couch, and to clean up the mess because a crazy lady shouldn't be trusted with broken glass; I might kill myself with it.

· · · · · · · · · ·

## Battle Scars

I stood naked in front of the mirror examining my pregnant belly, the lines that creased the form at my hips, the fullness of my breasts that had become fuller, more pronounced since last week. I rubbed my stomach, pushing it in, trying to remember what it was like to have a flat tummy. I stretched the skin tight at my hips, hoping that the stretch marks wouldn't be that noticeable by the time I was done being pregnant. Fat chance. I looked down the mirror at my feet, my legs, which I couldn't see any other way, and noticed that they looked swollen, and then I noticed it—the scar on my shin. I hadn't looked at it before, but now it stuck out of my body like an unruly branch poking out of the hedgerow. I imagined one of my children years from now rubbing it, asking where it came from, the coarseness of their fingernails roughing the already scarred skin as they accidentally scratched it. It had happened so long ago that I had almost forgotten that it existed at all. The small thumbnail scar was browned around the edges, darkened by the time it spent rubbing against my uniform, being banged up against the stoop staircase outside my hooch, on lips of truck doors, and inside edges of protruding metal seating in a Humvee. Each bang or scrape would reopen the wound quicker than it took to heal. I had tried to cover it with bandages, gauze strips taped on that peeled away from movement, but the result was always the same: scar tissue busted and bleeding. I looked at it now and thought back to the piece of shrapnel that I had tried to pull out. Each time the wound was reopened, I tried my hand at pulling the piece out, but every effort was made with the same result: shooting pain up my leg and the inability to cut it out of my shin. Now I looked down at it, contemplating whether I could get it out, if it was radioactive, if it would hurt the babies to have something like that in my body. I thought about going to the clinic, letting them know it was still in there, but as quickly as all the thoughts raced through my head, they left when James walked into the bathroom and saw me standing there naked. I hurriedly walked out of the room, leaving my pile of clothes on the floor. Now dressed in a nightgown, I sat on the bed thinking of the scar I could not see. James walked in, asked why I dressed so soon, and began pulling off my nightie. I stood up in front of him naked, looking at him as he studied the formed curves on my body, the overarching of my stomach, the lines that crested over my hips, the thick and unflinching thighs that gave way to swollen calves, and ankles, and feet. Naked I stood there and watched him reason to the fact that my body was deformed, lumpy in the middle, round around the edges, soft and malleable in the arms and breasts. This was no longer the woman I was, but some tender mothering figure unhardened by war, weakened through the pulling and stretching of skin, more vulnerable in the middle than before, and soon

Frag Out

James smiled, moved the hair away from my face, and began to kiss my body. When he reached my legs, I shifted, pulling away from him, but he grabbed firm at my knee, raised my right leg, and kissed the scar on my shin. He looked up at me and said that this was his favorite place on my body. When I asked him why, he did not respond, but I knew the answer. Of all the places on my body that had turned to mush as the months went by in my pregnancy, the scar held firm, the center unbroken by change.

## For a Short Time We Had Peace

You held the rifle for months at a time, the weight sometimes unbearable, the sling cinching it around your neck, the thing that bound the war to your breast. You walked with it proudly at first, carrying it to the chow hall, on missions, displaying it like a war trophy. After a while, you tightened your grip on it, holding firm to the belief that it is your best friend, without it you would be dead. The rails made grooves in your palms, digging deeper calluses into your lifeline that has now split sideways, one veering too dangerously to the line that said the number of children you would have and how many husbands you would go through. The thing around your neck bore down on you as you used it to clear buildings, stop cars from coming toward your convoy, and get children to leave you alone when pulling security. After more time had passed, the weight began to bear down on your soul, dragging it through the dirt. You no longer cleaned it; dust collected in the grooves, trigger well, and bolt. You were told to clean it, make sure it worked, but there was no part of you that wanted to hold it any longer. It swung as you slung it over your back, no longer carrying it at the ready. You had started to become a danger to yourself and others; soldiers no longer wanted to ride in convoy with you, the stages of maddening crossing your face like a distant shadow of light haunting the corner edges of your mouth; the stale look of long days pushed the bags under your eyes deeper into your skull. At times when the maddening was finite, in the spaces in between waking, you played the scene out in your head; the memory stretched out before you. You remembered Iraq, the rifle in your hand, and what blood looked like when it was mixed with dirt.

The convoy was stopped. The boy in front of you was bleeding out, a sucking chest wound, and the seal of death lingering on his lips. He looked up at you, but you could not bring yourself to look into his eyes. The six bullet holes in his chest were beyond help. There was no medic in the convoy, and I was the only one with Combat Lifesaver training. I did not kneel or try. I did not move or give last rites. I stood there looking away as the blood seeped into the dirt, turning it into a pool of brown mush that, when stepped on, stuck to your boots. It was getting dark. The convoy was ready to leave. Sergeant Lippert told me that there was nothing I could've done, that it was for the best, that it could've been me. None of it comforted. Too long I walked with the kill switch on, checking, breaking, and moving through war with unfathomable accuracy, stepping into death with speed and assurance, guiding me forward with a cocky, well-assessed lease on life. The boy was dead. I was alive, but the urge to kill was off, replaced entirely by a panic switch that made me reach for a rifle in the middle of the night, the one that was not there but still bound the war to my breast, cinching it down tight around my neck.

And yet, going to war was like being alive; after my deployment, I couldn't tell the difference between the two; I couldn't live any other way. I had gotten married before the war so that I wouldn't be alone, so that I would have something to look forward to coming home to, but that faded with every blow across the nose that he gave me, and soon the thought of being married sickened me. I forced myself to hate being married and love the war instead. At first I loved the missions, the fighting, the mortar attacks, the uncertainty and adrenaline of not knowing which day would be your last; I even came to love the bullets, the death rattle a body makes before it chokes on living, the feel of the air ripping apart as a rocket or grenade blasts the buildings to rubble and rock. I loved the violence, the blood, the way muscle tore open and frayed at the edges from shrapnel. This was my life, the very reason I was at war, the reason why I volunteered. But all these things were a trap that I found myself caught up in, the moments of fear, panic, tiredness, and the countless nights of not sleeping because of ambushes or attacks or worse, sleep. It moved me forward, the feel of the weapon in my hand, the pull of the trigger, the bang it made, where so much depended upon the sight and angle of kill. I loved the emptiness of it all, the way I was cut off from everything, how the world around me became a snow globe encircled with T barriers, barbed wire, and machine guns on towers. I loved how each day our missions brought me face to face with not living, how everything on invisible front lines brought me at odds with living. So it never occurred to me in the moments when I lived them that these were lulls in the fighting, that the point when I should've died, it was the soldier next to me or the hajji across the street who did. On recovery missions some of the bodies made me vomit, pull away from the stench, but never moved me enough to care about the war around me. Each body, leg ripped off, severed arm, smashed skull with brain matter spewing on the street like a kicked-over stew pot—none of that did it for me. It only pushed me further into the suck, raising the stakes for the next day. If I'm going to be honest, war is hateful, hard, and menacing to humankind. It takes no pleasure in killing you, but it will kill you all the same, and for the soldier who does not love it back, it will take you quickly and painfully. That is why I walked around with blank stares, a canvas of white, haunted by the fact that to survive is to love war. I piled death upon my shoulders, carried the weight in my chest because to love something so completely is to forget that you are good at anything else but that. This was what war did, defeat or win. I carried on because when it was over, it didn't matter that I loved it; it only mattered that I survived.

## Tin Box Battalion

The flag lowered, sinking down to white-gloved hands that were already saturated with sweat from standing in the late afternoon sun. The rope whipped against the pole, slamming the rings against the metal, the sound of shell casings dropping from a machine gun onto the roof of a Humvee.

I stood there among a sea of black, stuffed tight into a green army dress uniform, the waist of my pants too tight to be considered comfortable. My ungloved hand was pressed against my head in salute, the rigid lines of my fingers tracing the outside edges of my right eyebrow. The trumpet began to play "Taps," the slow, steady sound ringing through the base as the flag sank down to the ground. The wife and infant son sat in the chapel, the doors open, the music carrying through to the front near the pulpit, where a pair of boots stood next to an upside down rifle, a helmet adorning the top. The music kept playing, each note long and steady, the slow motion of a body rippling from a bullet, explosive, shrapnel impact, the tearing away of flesh and bone, limbs and gear, the flight of the body's uncertain landing on the ground, met with the collision of air casting the sad melody of the trumpet as I stood there holding back the tears that were blurring my vision. An envisioned look at the Vietnam wall, a man's palm pressed against the names and an invisible soldier holding him up, a job his legs could not do for him on that day. The tune continues at the grave of the Unknown Soldier, the soldier standing guard, his rifle at salute, the song echoing down the corridors of white, marked gravestones, the price of freedom some would say. But I stood there, unflinching, as the flag was folded, carried inside the chapel, and presented to the woman, now widowed. I didn't flinch when the first volley went off, or the second. The third, all seven men standing there, guns at the ready, aimed. The final nail in the coffin, the third volley. Many couldn't stand the gunfire, most flinching through the whole procession, others unable to keep composure at the sounding of "Taps." I stood there, tears down my face as I watched the soldiers one by one follow suit. Another name was engraved in the stone in front of brigade headquarters to remind me what the cost of war included. But I did not deserve the song, the salute, or the flag. I did not commit my life to stone.

· · · · · · · · · · · · · · · · · · · · · · · ·

## State Your Name for the Record

We settled on names after weeks of turning over pages, sitting at dinner asking, What about Luke? Or Jonathan? Or something tied to our heritage, Declan or Amish? Or a relative's name? Asa Alva? Salvatore? In the end James got one first name, Zachary, and I got the other, Bowen. Their middle names were simple: the twin archangels of God, Michael and Gabriel. We determined that whoever came out first was Bowen Gabriel, the second Zachary Michael. We did it just in case James was not there for the birth, just in case I was not conscious when they came out. We named them together, just in case.

· · ·

The Article 15 for misconduct had stripped me of everything—my money, my rank, and all of my wartime medals, but I did not care because I was no longer at war. I was out-processing from the military, taking a Chapter 8 discharge for pregnancy because I did not have a family care plan in place in order to stay in the army, and no one in the unit wanted to help me because everyone in the unit thought I was a fuck-up who was not worthy of staying in the army, so I carried out my days pushing paperwork, doing funeral detail, rubbing my swelling tummy, and spending time with James before I left. But there was one last thing, a plea agreement. I would not go to prison for adultery and misconduct if I testified against James.

"Sign it or go to jail."

Captain Apple, the prosecutor in James's court-martial, passed a piece of paper across the desk to me with a Post-It attached that read "sign here," a red arrow pointing to the signature block.

"And if I don't?"

"You go to jail six months pregnant."

He leaned back in his chair.

I signed it.

James had told me over the phone that it was better that only one of us go down for this. He would take the fall. He didn't want me in jail pregnant. He didn't want his babies being born behind bars. He told me that it would only be a day, just like any other, but I knew what it meant—he was sacrificing himself for me and his children. He was giving up his honor, his duty as an officer, his ability to find a decent-paying job for the rest of his life, and he was doing it because he loved me, or at least that's what I thought. Whatever the reason was, he did it all the same, and in a way I am thankful for it even now, but the court-martial, the children, being engaged—it all happened so fast that it strained our relationship. It broke us and we never recovered. Years from this moment, when we are standing in our kitchen in Florida and I am telling him that I know about the affairs, the lying, the cocaine use, and that I could no longer stand him, James will use this day against me and tell me this was the reason why he no longer wanted to be my husband. He will blame it all on me. He will cite the day I sat on the stand and told them he was the father as his excuse to pack his things and leave me for another woman, that this day ruined him and doomed our marriage, but in truth, our relationship was doomed from the get-go. Nothing good survives war, but it still survives in whatever form it left in, and for us, our relationship left Iraq fragile and would continue that way for many years to come.

• • •

I will now read to you the charges which I have been directed to investigate:

The two charges are Charge I in violation of UCMJ, Article 92, Specification 1: In that Captain James R. Haislop,

U.S. Army, did at or near Camp Liberty, Iraq, on diverse occasions between on or about 20 February 2007 and on or about 6 April 2007 violate a lawful general regulation, to wit: Army Regulation 600-20 . . . by having a relationship with Private First Class Brooke King that creates a clearly predictable adverse impact on discipline, authority, and morale of the command, and . . . by dating and wrongfully having sexual contact with PFC Brooke King.

Charge II, a violation of UCMJ, Article 134: In that Captain James R. Haislop, U.S. Army, did at or near Camp Liberty, Iraq, on many occasion wrongfully have sexual intercourse with PFC Brooke King, a married woman, not his wife.

It is my intention, at this time, to call as a witness in this investigation PFC Brooke King.

Q: Please state your full name and rank for the record.

A: Brooke Nicole King, Private First Class.

—Record of Trial of Haislop, James R., Captain, D Co, 299 FSB, 2 Brigade Combat Team, Tried at Conn Barracks, Schweinfurt, Germany, on 7 September 2007

• • •

After the trial that day, we walked into the house, but the silence between us bowed the windows in, a storm of words, a conversation begging to be unleashed. He walked down the hall, his uniform pants swishing in symphonic percussion to the clacking of his combat boots on the tile floor. I sat down on the couch unable to articulate a word, and soon the silence became half-hearted apologies in eyes when they met. It became resentment. It pushed from the inside of my belly, slow-moving feet or hands rubbing churning around with sporadic aggression against my skin. It was three-in-the-morning nightmares, stifled screams into the pillow in the hopes it wouldn't wake him. It sucked the vitamins from my body and stretch rings around my legs, stomach, and back. It nurtured and calmed the air with a faint wind from a stationary fan. It made the tile cold and unfeeling, the water in the shower too hot to bear on my skin. It tightened the band around my finger, swelled my face. It burrowed sunken black bags under his eyes and pulled the thin lines around his smile tight. It became a tattoo gun, a cigarette poised between lips, his fueled cocaine and ecstasy binges in late-night lulls when lovers should be sleeping. It became hatred balled up in fists slammed down on tables and couches, against walls and the hoods of cars. It became emergency room visits, heaving lunch into a toilet bowl, seven pills a day, and the fear that this might not be forever. It became empty *I love you*s and *it'll be okay*s. It swelled the body bloated of sin and wrapped it tight around our hearts. It broke every promise ever made to be true, honest, and loyal. It corrupted values like honor, commitment, self-sacrifice. It tore at your feet when you tried to run away. It brought you back from the brink of slicing wrists and tormented memories. It shushed the staggered breathing between us after we realized that only one of us was going to make it. It slid tape over boxes and labeled them *home*. It instilled determination for things that had not transpired. It soothed and comforted the goodbyes, no *see you later*. And still, as we stood there, my household goods ready to be shipped to the States, the silence became things never imaged. Like faith, and hope, and the promise of a new life together.

But it never became forgiveness. No, never that.

• • • • • • • • • • •

## Outprocessing

Before I left Germany, I sat in a waiting room of the outprocessing medical facility and looked down at the reintegration questionnaire I was to fill out to better help the med board decipher my time in Iraq. Anderson, who had come back from Iraq early to outprocess because she had been granted a compassionate reassignment, sat next to me checking the boxes one after another, sometimes skipping over questions that asked,

Have you seen or been near dead bodies?

Have you incurred any physical trauma while stationed overseas?

Do you feel that you are a danger to you and those around you?

Have you had suicidal thoughts?

She began reading them aloud to me, chuckling every time she came to one that she called a "duh" question. I sat there, legs crossed, staring at the wall, listening to her read the questions. She paused, looked over at me, and asked why I hadn't checked any of the boxes. I looked at her. She saw my disheveled look and knew that no part of me was capable of filling out this form. She grabbed the clipboard from me and began checking boxes. I watched as she checked them all. She handed me the form back, pointed to the line at the bottom, and told me to sign. I looked at her, my tears welling up. She pressed her finger to the form. Sign here.

• • •

It wasn't easy being pregnant, but being a female soldier who was pregnant in rear detachment was even worse. Everyone looked at you like you were a piece of shit. The stares became silent ones, derogatory remarks that read out "blue falcon" or "slut." I tried to hold my head up, tell myself that they didn't know me or what I had been through and that no one could cast judgment on me, but the truth was I secretly hated myself for getting pregnant, a cop-out, a way out of war that didn't get me wounded or killed. But I still felt somewhat like a deserter, an impostor undeserving of the word *soldier*. I couldn't take the suck, and so war spat me out all fucked up and pregnant, a how do you do with a reach around attached to it, but I couldn't complain. I had no place. I was about to be free from all this shit, get away from the suck, and move on with my life. I didn't know at the time if that was even possible, but I had to try; anything was better than doing back-to-back deployments to the sandbox and fuck all the tax-free money; for all I cared, the government, the military, and my unit could take this fucking job and shove it. I was leaving before BOHICA set in, so with separation papers and a one-way ticket home to San Diego, I left and hoped I'd never see this fucking place again.

Inside of the Frankfurt airport, I studied James to gauge his longing, to see the shape of his heart made out on his face. As he said goodbye and told me to keep the boys safe. To keep myself safe. I wanted to tell him that I needed him, that I could not do this without him, that I would waiver, falter, and slip; that this was not for me; that this was just the beginning of the war, not the end; that I doubted myself entirely; that I was not ready; that I was not here; I was still there. But I said nothing except I love you. A hug, a kiss, a wave, and I was gone from sight, leaving him at the bottom of the escalator, tears dropping neatly onto the floor where he stood.

# PART 5

SNAFU

## Shortly Thereafter

I thought I had left the closeness of the war behind when I left Germany, but it followed me home. In truth I could not leave any of it behind. I was the sum total of my suffering made out in the form of a body. And in order to leave any of it behind, I would need to know who I was, but the war had made sure to strip me of that knowledge, and so I was a naked soul, shelled in a body, closed up tight with armor that kept everyone out and trapped me within.

August twenty-eighth, when the plane touched down in San Diego, I was no longer in the army. I was just another civilian, a six-months-pregnant civilian. It was a short walk from the gate to baggage claim. There were people hugging and kissing around me as I waddled to the escalator, my family waiting at the bottom. Formal welcomes were batted off by outstretched arms, ones that wrapped tight and strong as if to say, *you are here, you are home.* There were no words, only toothy smiles and eyes creased in elation. A shuffling of bags off the carousel onto the ground catapulted an echoed thud through the terminal, and it was then that I noticed that, except for the other passengers on my plane and their loved ones, this part of the terminal was all but empty. We walked through the double doors to the parking garage. The air was crisp and cool, tinged with the smell of exhaust from the cab and shuttle line, but it did not reek of shit or smoke and it was not dry or overbearingly insulting to your senses. There was a quiet chaos to the traffic, trucks and cars, limos and shuttle vans driving in sync, following the lines smoothed out on the pavement. There were no holes or dunes of trash littering the road, and it was not for want that I searched for the familiarity of Iraq but for an understanding that this was what home should look like and that I should want that calm and peace, and that it should come easily. I scanned the parking lot, looked at the lines of cars, at my family, turning back every few seconds to make sure I was still there and that I was not a mirage or a ghost, at the people hurrying to some distant destination, a spot on a map placed there by topography and time, and it was then that my heart began to flutter with a dread that this was not home and these people were strangers and that I had no rifle, and the waves of cold air kept cresting until they capsized my expectation and I stopped in midstride to gasp and choke on my newfound freedom. Nobody noticed that I had stopped except for me, and in the silence I came to realize that the world was still the world, I was still breathing in it, and my widening gaze at everything as if I was still at war was only because I could not take a step without suffocating on my own fear.

When my family looked back, I had started to walk again, but the welling of tears spilling over my cheek gave away that my slow, steady gait was not one of comfort or peace but rather the unsure steps of someone who didn't know where they were and was afraid to ask. I looked as though I was a lost tourist in a faraway place, one that was neither familiar nor sympathetic to a frightened person clutching their jacket in the hopes that someone would take pity on them and guide them to a waiting car or taxi to take them back to a place they'd just come from—one where the roads were lined with bombs, where the enemy of our enemy was still a foe, and the air was stagnant and saturated with the smell of shit burning and bodies piling up in black bags next to blown-out trucks. A hand clutched mine and then another wrapped around my shoulder, but a shudder of my shoulders pulled their touches away and I was walking faster now to a car that I didn't remember my family owning. The doors of a small gold Lexus sedan unlocked. I hurled myself into the backseat and shut the door with such force that my grandfather turned around in his seat and told me to take it easy on the car, that it was not new, and that I'd break the window if I wasn't careful. Nana turned in the passenger seat and whacked him slightly. Nana asked me if I wanted to ride home with Dad, to which I nodded my head, and it was then that I realized that everyone was tiptoeing around me and just as unsure of their footing as I was, but this was still not home. This was only the airport.

"Downtown Baghdad looks like the bad part of San Diego. You know, the place we used to live when John and I were little, the one off of Fairmont and El Cajon Boulevard."

"You mean Talmadge? That wasn't the ghetto."

"No, the other one, south of that I guess, Normal Heights area."

"The one off Mountain View Drive?"

"Yeah, that one. Looks just like that."

Dad nodded his head. It wasn't a time in our family's history that my father had been particularly proud of—the years after my parents' divorce were dubbed the "dark ages." I don't recall much of it—too young, I guess, six or seven years old. Dad had been a druggie then, working two jobs and night shifts to keep food on the table and keep his drug use habitual. Most nights I could hear faint music coming through the walls—Jim Morrison's deep melodic voice from "Riders on the Storm" lulling me to sleep. John and I had only survived the dark ages because my grandparents intervened, providing the stable household where I ended up for the rest of my childhood. I looked out the window of my dad's Honda Accord, the faded *Steal Your Face* Grateful Dead sticker covering the sinking California sun.

"That bad, huh?"

"Nah, not too bad, almost like home, except for the people shooting at you and shit blowing up."

Dad fidgeted in his seat, straightening up a little. There was silence in the car, an awkward silence that usually was masked by the radio.

"I mean, it wasn't that bad."

"Right, well, just don't tell Nana about any of it, even if she asks." My dad looked a bit nervous, tense, as though he didn't know what to do or say to me anymore. I wasn't little anymore. I had experienced some of the world and had returned different—at least that's how I saw it.

I wasn't planning on saying anything at all about Iraq. The whole sixteen-hour plane ride from Frankfurt I had thought about what I should and shouldn't talk about, what topics were "safe" for me to discuss, but that was just it—nothing was safe anymore. The word itself was foreign to me, and I found myself wishing I wasn't pregnant so I could be downing as many Jack and Cokes as the flight attendant would've given me for free in an attempt to put Iraq out of my mind. Once I had landed in Atlanta for my connecting flight to San Diego, I had decided that even if I had decided to drink while pregnant, there was no booze sufficient for me to forget or remember not to say anything about Iraq, so I opted for door number three. Fuck it, if I slipped up and said too much at home, I would just sneak off to my room and pretend like nothing happened.

I sat there the whole ride back from the airport staring out the window. The buildings looked the same, nothing had changed, but all of it reminded me of Iraq—the close buildings in downtown as we got onto the I-5, the weaving of Dad's car in and out of rush-hour traffic as he dodged the assholes trying to cut him off. Even the freeway looked like Iraq—the guardrails, the lines, the pavement—everything blurring together in one massive clump of *fuck it all*. The traffic lights, pedestrians, and people walking on crowded sidewalks near San Diego State University—my heart started racing. The horns, traffic helicopters, police sirens, and revving engines—my palms began to sweat. The smell of asphalt, exhaust, and roadkill on the side of the street—I cracked my knuckles and gripped my hands tight. The fast-moving cars, the loud music coming from the vehicle next to us as we waited at a stoplight—the sights, the sounds, my heavy breathing.

"Brooke?"

My dad touched my shoulder. I flinched and shoved him

away, as I quickly grabbed the handle on the car door in an attempt to open it.

"I gotta get out of here. You gotta let me out." Struggling to open the door, I yanked harder and harder on the handle, tears spilling over onto my cheek. "I need to get out, let me out!" I shouted it over and over again until my dad reached over and unlocked the door. I opened it and bolted toward the tree line and canyon on the shoulder of College Avenue. Running frantically, I hit every clump of dirt and shrub in my path, trampling them down as I stumbled over them. I found it harder and harder to breathe the farther I got from my dad's car. I tripped over a rock, stumbled, and fell to the ground, but this time I didn't get up. I turned over and sat down. I tried to catch my breath, but it felt like someone choking the life out of me, strangling my neck, the imaginary fingers gripped around my esophagus.

"I can't. I can't ..."

By now Dad had pulled the car over and was standing by the trunk. He started to walk toward me, but as I looked up, eyes full of tears, he paused. I put my head down, burying it in my arms. Moments later I felt a pair of hands touch my shoulder then wrap around to my back. My dad, for the first time since I had returned from Iraq, was hugging me. I had brushed off his first advance at the airport, but now I welcomed it—anything to ease the panic and overwhelming sadness that I felt. He didn't say anything. He just lifted me up off the ground and gently maneuvered me back to the car. He eased me into the passenger seat and handed me my seat belt. I put it on as he eased the door shut, trying not to slam it as best he could. The rest of the way home we said nothing. He drove and I stared out the window, trying to focus on the world that I was passing by as the car turned into my neighborhood, past my old elementary school, past my best friend's house, and down my street to the place I had called home. Nana, Grandpa, and John were waiting in the driveway, everyone eager for me to see the house for the first time since I had left a year ago.

Dad turned to me. "I won't say anything if you don't."

I nodded, opened the door, and got out. The usual welcoming home that would've taken place at the airport ensued at home—the hugs, kisses, and *let me look at you* turns. Grandpa nodded. He didn't hug me. He knew I didn't want anyone touching me. He had served as a helicopter navigation copilot or something like that—he knew what I'd been through and he was the one who grabbed me by the arm and pulled me away from the welcoming entourage. I walked inside the house, carefully taking one step at a time. Molly, my Alaskan malamute, came running up to me but paused two feet away. She started to bark at me. I advanced her.

"Molly Malone. Come here, girl."

I stretched out my hand and she growled at me. I tried to walk another step and she tried to bite my hand. I recoiled, pulling my hand into my chest.

*What the fuck was that?*

Dad walked past me and grabbed Molly, whose back hair was raised in a ridge line, her teeth gnarled up, her head down low.

"Come on, Molly, dammit. It's just Brooke."

Dad yanked her to the back door until she finally turned and walked with him, her tail between her legs. I stood back up and looked around. Everything looked the same—the same furniture, same scratchy blue carpet, same old, faded cream-colored drapes and squeaky sliding glass door, but somehow it felt different, as though time had changed the old house, as though I had stepped through the looking glass and the house was no longer as big as I had remembered it to be. It was smaller now, more confined. The countertop was not as tall anymore, the cabinets not as hard to reach, the stairs up to the second floor not as long as they used to be. Everything had changed, and yet it hadn't. Was it just me? Had I changed so much that the house I used to live in now seemed like a Tinkertoy space made larger than life by a child's imagination?

I looked around the house as Nana and John walked into the kitchen and past me.

"Don't you want to go upstairs and put your things away?" Nana looked at me.

I still had my green duffel bag on my shoulder. I nodded and walked up the stairs. I pushed open the door. My bed was neatly made, my dresser cleared off, with only a picture of me in my military uniform. I dropped my duffel and picked up the picture. I had been so young then, nineteen when I enlisted. Had I changed that much? I looked at my reflection in the mirror above the dresser, then back down at the picture. I placed it back on the dresser face down and walked over to my closet. All my things had been shoved to one side. Nana's overflow from her closet now resided on one side, my clothes on the other. I turned around and looked at my bed. My leopard print comforter had been replaced with a nice navy blue one, an army throw folded neatly at the foot of the bed, army emblem facing up. I tossed it onto the floor, closed my eyes, and plopped down in the middle of the bed, letting my feet dangle over the side. I opened my eyes, hoping to see the stars on my ceiling, my one constant that kept me going through Iraq, remembering that the sky I was looking at was like the same one I had on my bedroom ceiling at home. They were gone—the plastic sticky stars, the full moon, everything— gone. The ceiling was bare, painted a fresh coat of white. I sat up and looked at the rest of the ceiling in my room. They were all gone. I began to panic and bolted up from the bed into the hallway, where I leaned over the banister and yelled, "What the fuck happened to my room?"

Nana walked over and stood at the bottom of the stairs. "What do you mean?"

"My stars, they're gone, and where's my old comforter?"

"We gave that old comforter away, and as for the stars, well, we took them down and repainted the room."

"Why'd you touch my room?"

"Honey, you were gone. I thought you wouldn't mind. It's just some silly plastic stars."

"This was my room. You had no right to change it without me being here."

"But, Brooke, honey. You were away in Iraq. We had to make your bedroom into the guest room." Nana advanced up the stairs, but I walked over and down before she could get half-way up. I walked into the kitchen.

"Dad, how could you let them do that?"

"Don't look at me. I had nothing to do with it."

"John?"

"I wasn't here. I just found out, same as you."

I turned to Grandpa, who was sitting in his chair. He just shrugged his shoulders.

I looked back at Nana, who was standing at the bottom of the stairs again. "How could you do that? That was my room—my room."

The panic began to come back. The kitchen became smaller, tighter. John standing behind me was starting to make me nervous. A large truck drove past on the street. Its exhaust loud and thundering like the sound of a Bradley tank starting up. Dad motioned for John to step back. I couldn't breathe—the feeling of someone's hands around my neck again—the sharp agony of a pain resonating from my chest. Grandpa stood up from the chair.

"My room—the stars, they're gone." Tears welled up in my eyes and spilled onto my cheeks. "What am I going to do now? They're all gone." My legs grew weak and I crumpled to the floor trying to catch my breath. I mumbled under my breath, "How will I find my way home?"

Grandpa walked toward the kitchen, pushing my dad out of the way. He bent down next to me and hugged me. "It's okay, sweetheart. You cry it out if you have to." He shooed everyone away from the kitchen as I cried uncontrollably in his arms until I felt like I couldn't cry any more. After a while, I lifted my head and said, "Grandpa . . ."

He shushed me. "Don't worry, sweetheart. You'll find you again."

"What if I can't? What if I'm stuck like this?"

"For now, you think you can stand up?"

I nodded my head.

Nana popped her head from around the corner. "Brooke, sweetie, we can get you some new stars if you want, stick them up there on the ceiling again."

I looked up at Grandpa. He nodded. I looked back at Nana. "I'm sorry, Nana. I . . ."

Nana walked in as I was getting up from the floor. She hugged me, interrupting my apology. "I'm just happy you're home."

I looked her in the eyes; tears were filling up the corners. I smiled at her. She moved a piece of hair out of my face and stroked my cheek. "You're home, that's all that matters."

No one spoke at dinner that night—the silence was deafening. Molly lay beside Dad's chair, her eyes on me the entire time. Every move I made put her on alert—ears pinned back, teeth showing. I was a stranger.

A couple of days went on like this—starting out the day avoiding Molly in the morning when the house was empty and everyone was at work, watching TV or sleeping to pass the time, not talking to my dad when he got home in the afternoon, and spending time with Grandpa on the back porch, just sitting and watching the sunset as he drank his three drinks.

"You know, as much as I'm glad you're here," he looked at me, "you ain't doing a whole hell of a lot but sulking." He put his hand on my shoulder. "What's got you strung tighter than a drum?"

"What does that even mean?" I chuckled a little and he smiled.

He shook my shoulder slightly. "Look, you're home now, you're with us. Let things calm down and when you're ready, we'll talk."

"Gramps . . ." I hesitated. "I'm fine."

"You can't bullshit an old bullshitter, Brooke. You need to talk, I'm here."

He got up, kissed me on the head, and walked back inside, shutting the sliding glass door behind him. I looked out over the canyon at the sunset that began to cast a long shadow. It stretched down into Mission Valley, down to Warring Road, where it went flat and covered Jack Murphy Stadium in a dark haze. The sun sank into the oblivion of the horizon, the bed of the world, until everything turned to darkness. I sat there a few moments longer waiting for the night to engulf me, then I stood up and went back inside the house, but before I did, I couldn't help but look at the sun setting one last time. The oranges and yellows set the sky on fire, like the clouds were burning.

Dinner that night was more of the same—utter silence. I excused myself early from the table and went upstairs to my room. Sitting on the edge of my bed, I thought about James as I rubbed my belly. I couldn't be in this room anymore. It wasn't mine.

"What's going on up in that head of yours, girlie?" Gramps asked as he stood in the doorway of my room. When he walked in and sat down beside me on the bed, I shrugged. I didn't know. Truly.

I looked at down at my belly but couldn't bring myself to tell him what had happened in Iraq, even though part of me wanted to. My eyes welled up with tears before I could say anything. Fucking pregnancy hormones.

Gramps just hugged me and said, "I'm here, if you need me."

Before he could get up and walk out, I grabbed his arm. He hesitated and then sat back down. "Gramps, I think I should move into the room downstairs. I can't sleep in this room anymore. Too many memories."

"All right, we'll get you sorted tomorrow, but for tonight, how about you go sleep down on the sleeper sofa in the den."

"Okay."

Gramps patted me on the back.

Rubbing my belly, I said, "I think . . . I think I need to go to the va." I hesitated but knew if I didn't say it now, I probably never would. "I saw too much, Grandpa, too much of everything."

I started to cry, but Gramps hushed me and said, "I've heard all I need to hear." We sat there for a moment, then Gramps got up and started to walk out of my room, but before he left, he paused in the doorway and said, "I'll take you to the VA in the morning."

"What if I can't do it?"

"Well, if it was me, even if I couldn't, I would."

"Gramps, your sayings don't make sense."

"Sure they do," he said, as he walked out of my room. "You just haven't figured them out yet."

A little bit later I walked downstairs and into the den, where Nana was making up the sofa bed. I sat up until midnight thinking about Iraq. I rolled over onto my back and fell asleep to a barren sky above.

The next morning I went upstairs to get dressed and returned downstairs. Everyone was doing their morning ritual. Dad was drinking coffee and reading the *San Diego Tribune*. John was inhaling some sugar-saturated cereal that was in a mixing bowl instead of a regular cereal bowl. He had just shoved another bite into his mouth when he noticed I'd walked into the room. He smiled wide, spilling some of the milk and cereal out of the corner of his mouth and onto the table. Nana was standing next to the kitchen counter, making cinnamon raisin toast, spreading the butter on lightly. The kitchen reeked of burned toast. Under her breath Nana was scolding Gramps for messing with the toaster settings again. Gramps had his back to Nana, trying to ignore her and sneak a shot of bourbon into his coffee before she noticed, but he perked up when he saw me walk in.

"Okay, I think I'm ready."

Gramps smiled, Dad looked confused, John couldn't have care less, but Nana, Nana was concerned and disheartened.

"Ready for what?

"I have to go to the VA." I lowered my head and looked at the floor so I wouldn't start crying. "There's something I have to do."

"It's all right with me," Dad said, folding the newspaper over as he scanned for another article to read. I looked at John.

"Do what you gotta do, sis," he said with his mouth full of Cap'n Crunch.

I looked over at Gramps in the kitchen. He turned around toward the counter, fumbled with something, and turned back holding a pair of car keys and smiling. "I'll drive."

I smirked at him. "Thanks, Gramps."

When I tell the VA counselor that I haven't been raped, that I'm not a victim of sexual assault, she looks at my pregnant belly and then back up at me with a puzzled frown and asks why I checked the boxes related to war trauma. I tell her that I was in combat. Her eyes widen, her frown disappears, and she tells me to hold on as she leaves the room. She doesn't return. Instead a man comes in, asks me to follow him down the hall to the TBI and spinal injury ward. He points to men inside the room, tells me to think long and hard about lying about combat before I tell him anything more. I look at him. I do not tell him the customary *fuck you* that should've come from my lips. I look at him blankly, the thousand-yard stare. He asks me if I have anything to tell him, and it is then that I walk away. Later, when I tell my grandpa what happened at the VA, he tells me to go back, that he'll set him straight, but I tell him that it's okay, that the VA isn't ready to help me, that I don't trust them yet and probably never will.

The VA had been a total failure. We pulled into the driveway, but before we got out, Gramps looked at me. "You know, just because someone doesn't believe you doesn't mean it didn't happen."

"I know, but what the fuck was that?"

"Come on inside. I'll fix me a drink while your grandma nags at you about what happened."

"'Cause you know I'm looking forward to that."

Gramps laughed. "She's just looking out for you."

"She's going to shit a brick when I tell her what they said to me."

"I'll let you take the credit for that one."

We walked toward the front door of the house, but Gramps paused with his hand on the doorknob. "Brooke, can I just ask you one thing. How bad was it over there? I mean, were you in the thick of it or just on the outskirts?"

I looked him in the eye. "I was stuck in the middle like a death trap."

Gramps grabbed the nape of my neck and kissed my forehead. "You know me and Nana are here for you." I gazed up at him. "You survived the war, and when James gets back, you two are going to have a family, live your life, make memories, and have fun."

A tear rolled down my cheek. "Is that even possible?"

"What? Living?"

I nodded, waiting for his answer, but he just smiled and walked into the entryway.

"Why don't you wait till those babies come, and if you still don't know the answer to your question, then you'll know that you didn't really try. Sound like a plan?"

"I hate it when you're right."

"I'm very seldom right, but when I'm right, I'm right."

"What does that even mean?"

"It's grandpa wisdom. Comes from years of experience in the art of bullshit."

I laughed and stepped inside the house. Nana was in the kitchen sautéing mushrooms and onions in a skillet. She turned and looked at us. Gramps looked at me and smiled, but before he had a chance to slink away into the den, I stopped him.

"Hey, Gramps." I opened up the top cupboard, pulled out the Johnny Walker Black, poured him a drink, and handed it to him. "Thanks for today."

He smiled. "Sure thing, kiddo."

"Jake," Nana shouted as he walked away quickly. "Don't you dare."

It was too late; he was out of sight, so she turned her attention to me. "Brookie."

"It's only one drink."

## Warning Signs

The sound of a car alarm: 3:45 a.m. It startled me out of bed. I bolted upright and ran barefoot past the kitchen, out the front door, and to the street in my nightgown. I had set off the house alarm by opening the front door. It blared warnings of an intruder entering or escaping, a variety of sirens set off by a person unaware of the alarm system. The neighbor's Hummer, two houses down, was flashing lights and screeching its horn. I was in the middle of the street, standing there looking at it. The light bar on top flashed in time with the headlights, the flickering of iridescent yellow throwing shadows onto the blacktop. I turned to look at the hedges across the street; a stray cat wandered out of them, sauntering its haunches as it walked off the grass and onto the sidewalk. There was no traffic, no helicopters, no sign of warning beyond the house alarm and the Hummer's lights and sounds set off by ghosts or the wind. I heard my name called from the open door of the house and turned to see that I had woken our household and our neighbor, and soon kitchen lights flickered on in two other houses as I stood in the street trying to find the danger. I turned around in slow circles, looking at every bush and tree and house, but I couldn't find anything that brought me solace, and until someone removed me from my place in the street, I stood there searching, looking for a ghost of the past or maybe just for that fucking cat that walked past me as if I wasn't there at all.

## Definitions

I was the only one in my family besides Gramps who had seen anything remotely close to combat, and it only took a week before we were sitting down at dinner and they asked me what Iraq was like. At first I could not bring the answer to my lips, the question too ambiguous, the answer too convoluted. They wanted a firm answer, something concrete, an answer that would bring justification to the war, so when I did not answer, they were confused. They asked me the question again, as if I hadn't heard it the first time, but when I brought myself to answer, I said this:

Iraq is the shit, the suck, the all-determining factor of things forgotten by time and a displacement of trust. It is the razor-sharp kiss on the end of your tongue that spits blood when you try to speak of peace. It is the bilateral incision on the dagger's tip that slices the Fertile Crescent into almond slivers. Iraq is a wring-dried promise of protection that eludes even the protectors. It is an unfathomable display of fear coagulated by the uncertainty of control. Iraq is Death spelled out I-E-D. It is the trigger-happy complex of soldiers unsure that they will survive. Iraq is civilians used as bombs and collateral damage. It is kicked-in front doors that ask for polite curtsies and afternoon chai tea with scared faces staring back. Iraq is waterboarding and brutality disguised as information-seeking fun. It's concrete walls lined with concertina wire and machine guns. It's tattered American flags lit on fire in protest. It's marketplaces filled with the aroma of saffron and cooking cuts of lamb that will be a blast point for a suicide bomber, his explosives strapped to his chest. Iraq is enemies hidden in doorways, on rooftops, and open windows. It's dogs made into wolves that lap up blood pools and feed on shredded flesh from corpses. Iraq is Saussure's signified mocked and mimicked when the land is left behind. Iraq is dredged-up memories and a conversation that, right now, is better left unsaid. Look me in my eyes and ask me again what Iraq is and I will tell you, Iraq is this. . . .

• • •

Everyone took turns coming to see me. It's best to do it in waves, I had heard my grandmother say. It's best not to talk about the war, she would warn. Each family member would sit down next to me, ask me how I was doing, ask about the babies inside me, make small talk, and say nothing about the war.

My brother came into the house, reeking of cigarette smoke and pot, and with bloodshot hangover eyes. I envied him. He walked over, gave me a hug, and told me what I wanted to hear. *You look fucked.* I was, and for the most part, I wanted to be fucked up, to drink until I could feel again because feeling was better than nothing at all. Nana slapped John for being insensitive, Grandpa frowned, and I smiled at my brother. He knew me best of all, knew pandering to me only pissed me off. Dad stood back for a while, rubbed my shoulder, gave me a shit-eating grin whenever I looked at him, and drank his Johnny Walker and Coke while I sipped on some godawful Lipton Iced Tea that had barely enough sugar to be called sweet. This was the measure of my homecoming: no fancy parades, no barbecue, no celebratory binge drinking, just a living room full of relatives consciously trying to pretend that I didn't look completely gutted and shell shocked.

. . . . . . . . . . . . . . . . . . . .

## Breathe through Your Mouth

"Brookie, honey, is everything okay?"

Sitting in the living room recliner in my grandparents' house, I glanced up from staring at the blue carpeted floor and let the numbing pain in my chest subside before I say, "Yeah, Nana."

I had been back from Iraq for a month now, and it had become a custom since I had returned to tell my grandparents that I was fine each time they asked about my state of mind. The endless maniacal questions that followed any other response to them would be followed by my futile attempt at trying to convince them that I was "better" and that I didn't need a babysitter, at least not until the boys were born. To them I was still their eldest granddaughter, the one they had invested their love in first, and so it was hard for them to watch as I slowly disintegrated from the inside out. Each time I refused to talk about Iraq or go back to the VA, Grandpa would pull out his newspaper clippings from the *San Diego Tribune* and magazine articles from *Newsweek*, in an endeavor to try and comfort me.

"Look here, Brookie, this guy's got the same thing as you, except they gave him one of those service dogs for his PTSD."

"Grandpa, I'm not even close to being as bad as he is. Besides, I don't have PTSD, okay?"

"All right, Brooke," he said, as he walked out of the living room and set the clippings on the kitchen table. "I'll just leave these here for you."

I watched as he poured himself a cup of black coffee, and without raising his head or saying a word he disappeared into the den. I sat in the recliner in the living room, and though Nana sat in the other recliner next to me, I felt utterly alone.

Grandpa was right most of the time, but his valiant efforts at helping me only seemed to push me closer and closer to loneliness, a dark place I had created inside myself where I could cope on my own or wallow in my self-induced misery. I had dodged yet another bullet by deflecting Grandpa's conversation, one that surely would have ended up with everyone in tears. I was not ready to talk about Iraq or myself because I still was not sure how I had made it out alive when I had watched so many others come back in black body bags.

I didn't expect my family to understand immediately all of what I had gone through in Iraq, but I had asked for some distance until I could cope and fully comprehend the extent of how much I had suffered. My grandparents for the most part left me alone. Grandpa gave me what he called "my own space," and Nana only fussed at me when I cursed in front of her.

Having my grandparents there in the first month home while I was still adjusting to civilian life was a comforting reassurance that, if I did decide to talk, I would have two sets of ears that were ready to listen. However, "my own space" only lasted a month, and before long Nana was pestering Grandpa into talking to me again. Grandpa seemed to be more in tune with what I wanted and for the most part kept his word and left me alone, but as any good grandmother would do, Nana felt it was her job to chime in when it came to my health. She was slightly less oblivious to the fact that my repetitive, mono-tone, two-word responses had not changed in a month.

"Brookie, you know you can tell me and Grandpa what's going on. I heard that a lot of soldiers that come back from Iraq have this PTSD thing."

"Grandma's right you know, Brookie. If you want to talk, we're here."

Glancing up from my mechanical drowning of Earl Grey tea with sugar, I said, "I don't have PTSD, so can we drop it."

"Brookie, someday you're going to have to talk about this . . ."

Interrupting Nana, I said, "Yeah, but today is not that day."

Breakfast had slowly turned into another one of their ploys to get me to talk, but having grown up with them under the same roof almost all my life, I knew the best way to dodge a conversation was just to walk away. Getting up from the table, I grabbed my teacup and said, "I've had enough of this." Their longing stares of concern left a burning sensation in my heart, filling me with the awful sense that by not telling them, I was somehow making them suffer instead of myself. Casting my eyes down at the brown patchwork linoleum floor, I said, "I'm just going to go lie down. My back is killing me from carry-ing these two so low."

I rubbed my back and waddled side to side away from the kitchen table and disappeared into the next room. As I walked toward the blue floral print couch in the den and lay down, I tried to think back to a traumatic event that had happened to me during my deployment, but the only thing that I could possibly think of was the time I was blown ten feet back by a mortar round that had come into the motor pool while I was trying to fix a forklift. It was as if I had blocked out my whole deployment and the nightmares were only adding to the frus-tration and anxiety that I was having now that I was home.

The nightmares had started to get worse. Seven months pregnant, I was fed up with not having James there, worn out from being pregnant, and every physical demand that my body endured left me overworked. The encouragement I used to receive from my family about trying to talk about Iraq was now replaced by their dismay at my unwillingness to cooperate in talking about it. I began to fight a battle at home, and it seemed like every week, after the usual Q&A about how I was feeling, Nana would suggest that I return to the clinic. Every sincere effort on her part was met with my hostile resistance.

"Brookie, . . . I'm starting to worry."

Nana would come up to me, sit beside me, rub my back, and try to encourage me to go back to the VA, but it only made me enraged.

"Leave me the fuck alone!"

Slam after slam of my bedroom door; it began to splinter from every even stroke of my arms' strength. I fought as a way to show I was healing, to show how the new me loved another person by not letting them into the horrors of my mind, but each time I showed how much I really loved them by leaving them in the dark, I knew that I was really just extinguishing the memory of the girl I used to be. Each time I slammed my bedroom door, protecting them from the monster I was now, I could hear Nana's quiet sobs inside the kitchen. My hurtful tone and angry words chiseled away again at the love she had for me in her heart. I was no longer the same granddaughter who used to help her form small round meatballs for Great-Grandma Romanolo's famous spaghetti and meatballs or helped her shred the swiss cheese for the quiche lorraine that we had every Tuesday. Each time, I could hear Grandpa's comforting words to her as she sobbed in the kitchen. He knew I would never be the same, but I knew that each time I yelled at her, it broke down her spirit, making her realize that I would never truly be the same again.

"She's got to figure it out on her own, Jackie. You just can't keep reminding her like that. When she's ready, she'll talk to us."

I was there after every nightmare; slouched over, kneeling in the middle of my floor, rocking back and forth, sobbing, smothering my screams with my hands, and shutting my eyes up tight to make the tears go away. I sat there time and again, trying to understand why I was different and why I hated the person I was now. The reeling back of time made it hard for me to translate what it was I was feeling in the present. I knew that from their bedroom, Nana and Grandpa could hear my two-in-the-morning screams of terror, and I didn't want my problems to affect anyone but myself. So I tried to shelter them from my suffering by stifling screams into my pillow, muffling my cries of desperation with my hands, wiping every tear from my eyes with tissues that I would stuff back into the Kleenex box on my nightstand.

What had happened during my deployment had spilled over into my civilian life, ripping it apart like a frayed, loosened seam on a worn-out shirt that was slowly coming unstitched. The only thing I knew for certain was that the nightmares I was having were fragmented, a distortion of the truth, and in them I was scared shitless. In the memories I still have from my deployment, I remember dragging the heavy chains to latch down the Stryker and my messed-up uniform stained with black char smudges and sweat, but I do not remember the blood or the bodies, and in my nightmare that was the most terrifying part.

Into the main cab, I hunch over and climb through the blown-out compartment of the Stryker. My nostrils fill with a putrid smell of iron—like I had just licked the end of a battery. I try to breathe through my mouth, but I can already feel vomit rising in my throat. I spin around to the rear of the cabin, go outside into the early evening light next to the side of the Stryker, puke, and walk back into the Stryker.

Making my way toward the front of the vehicle, something stops me. My right hand strikes something. I stop and sweep the light onto the object. There he is, slumped over. His uniform is blood-soaked and shredded from shrapnel, as if he crawled through barbed wire. There is a thin pool of blood where his left leg should be. A week of Combat Lifesaver training, and the only things I retained were how to give an IV and how to check a pulse. Reaching out to his neck, I gently move the pads of my index and middle finger of my right hand underneath the collar of his gear to the artery in his neck.

Nothing.

For the first time, I point the light onto his head. I stumble backward and slam into the compartment wall behind me. His face is half ripped off his skull. It dangles from his neck, pushed down from the weight of his helmet. A gash on the left side of his face is still dripping blood onto his ACU bottoms. Contorted, mangled, and burned alive, this is his death.

There are two other bodies to account for. I inch farther into the vehicle. I approach the gunner's hatch and find it closed. I turn the handle and open the hatch to get some fresh air circulating into the cabin of the vehicle.

I approach the driver's side.

He is burned alive to his seat. All I can see are both of his black hands, dangling with chunks of flesh, both lying limply, palm up in his lap, turned in as if he had been praying to die quickly. I turn away from the smell of burned rubber and soured blood.

In the passenger seat there is nothing left of the officer, only half a torso. His entrails lay scattered about the seat and on the floor. I try to find something, anything that would give anyone, even myself, comfort in knowing he came back in one piece. I find none. All bodies are accounted for. That is my mission. Now it is complete, and as I turn to leave and walk back into the light of the day, I awake from the nightmare.

Throughout the years after my deployment, each time the nightmare revisited me, it changed, contorting the truth of what happened on my first mission.

Even as I write this now, the truth of what happened on that first mission is lost forever, supplanted by the nightmare's version of that day. I was left with a horrifying reality that I didn't recall happening, and, because of it, I decided that the mission never happened. Yet, the nightmares perverted more than just the mission. They had even made the mundane of the mission terrifyingly painful to remember. I do know that when I returned from my first mission, I took a shower, but I do not remember the sadness, the horrifying look of my own reflection in the mirror staring back at me, or the blood that covered my uniform in wet crimson patches.

I walk past the company building, ignoring everyone who walked in my direction. I stagger to my hooch. All I want to do is get all this gear off me and go to sleep. Fumbling to get the keys out of my pocket, I manage to drop them onto the graveled ground.

"Fuck!"

I yell it loud enough that everyone in a three-hundred-yard radius from where I stand can hear it. Too tired to bend down, I peel off my combat flak vest, helmet, knee and elbow pads, and let each one drop to the ground with a haunting thud. I sit down on the stoop in front of my door. Pulling out my crunched pack of Lucky Strikes, I spark my last one up, take a couple of long drags, sniff myself to see if I need a shower, and reel back from the stench wafting off my body. I look down at my dirt-encrusted hands that are dry-stained with blood and decide it's best that I take a shower. I flick my half-smoked cigarette onto the ground and walk toward the latrine that is catty-corner to my hooch. I ascend the steps with three brisk strides and open the door. A wave of panic hits me. Every single female soldier is staring at me. Ashamed that my appearance must be worse than I thought, I walk to a mirror, my eyes fixated on the speckled-gray linoleum-tiled floor. Halfheartedly, I look up and into the mirror in front of me.

A young woman stares back. I observe her muddled stare, glazed over in front of me. She is so weathered and beaten that her face looks as if she has been fighting life itself. Her face is covered with charred traces of flesh and black smudges. Her hair is tangled and matted with blood. The expression on her face looks unhinged and lost. Her uniform top and bottoms are covered in charred fragments and battered and ripped from use. There are huge voids of cleanliness on her uniform from where her gear was worn, but everywhere else is spattered and soaked with someone else's lifeline. Even I do not know who she is, let alone what happened to her that day, and the woman she was before the day's events unfolded looks as if she is lost forever.

Moved to tears by the young woman in the mirror, I realize

that she is my own reflection. I lurch backward, falling into the toilet stalls behind me. Steadying myself against the cold hard metal wall, I walk toward the shower area and away from the mirror. I walk unsteadily to a shower stall. I look down at my hands and the dried, crusted blood that covers them. I turn them over and over again until the tears begin to well up in the corners of my eyes. They spill over onto my cheeks as I slap my body down on the bench behind me. My silent sobbing is starting to attract attention from the other female soldiers who are in the shower area. Pressing and pushing down on the blood-soaked uniform with my hands, kneading them for comfort like a cat, I sob louder and harder.

I stand up, turn the shower knob to hot, and walk into the lukewarm water with my clothes on. Leaning my hands up against the shower wall to brace my body, I begin to cry even louder. I bend my body under the showerhead and let the water rush over me, cleaning all the blood and charred bits off my face and ACUs. I look down at the water gathering at the bottom of the stall near the drain and watch as it turns from red to black, from black to red, and eventually to clear with every movement of my body underneath the showerhead.

Too overwhelmed by grief and sadness, I fall to the floor of the stall and weep openly. Not caring who sees me or what happens if they do, I cry until I feel as though I can cry no more. No one is bothering to help me. No one is bothering to see if I am okay. They know as much as I do that there is nothing they can do. By the time I am ready to leave the shower stall, I am utterly alone in the latrine and an overwhelming sensation of emptiness washes over me as I sit there in the stall. I begin to panic and hyperventilate. My static short breaths through my mouth force the tears to come again with more grief and pain than I have ever felt before. Shaking from the dampness of my clothes, I close my eyes and lean my head up against the wall of the shower stall. In my fragile state, I hear a familiar voice calling my name.

"Brookie, are you okay?"

I opened my eyes to a nightmare that was over. It had all

been a dream, one horrible fucked up dream that seemed to be another figment of my mind's creation, another painful memory like a hand clasped over my mouth, the one thing that kept me from breathing, but I couldn't breathe with the pain clamped over my mouth, the grip too strong, the ability to breathe through my mouth not strong enough.

· · · · · · · · · · · ·

## Constellations

When I got home from Iraq and stepped into the home I grew up in, I felt like somehow the house had changed, that somehow in my absence they had done something to the house. I walked around for weeks looking and feeling everything, but I couldn't figure it out. Besides the upgrades to the stove and a new coat of paint on the outside, the house was still the same. One night when I couldn't sleep, I went room by room trying to figure out what had changed until I came upon what was once my old room and is now the guest bedroom. I paused in the doorway, almost unable to take a step inside. There were too many memories in this room: eight-year-old tea parties with imaginary friends, the times as a child that I prayed to the moon to take me away from this place whenever my dad went on drug binges, my first kiss (with the neighborhood boy down the street), the first time I had sex in high school (with some skater kid named Nick), the countless times during my childhood and teenage years that I lay awake looking at the plastic stars on the ceiling as I listened to Nana and Grandpa fight with Dad, the first time I did cocaine and meth in college, the night I slept in the room as a soldier before I hopped a plane the next day for Iraq; I remembered them all as I stood there looking into the dark room. I stepped inside, walked over to the window, and put my hand on the window ledge, the marks from where I had dug my teeth into the plaster as a child still there, cutting into the ledge like swiss cheese holes. I rubbed my pregnant belly. The boys were kicking inside, making my back ache. I sat down on the bed and looked out of the window up at the crescent moon that shone just above the tree line. I thought back to childhood, my lame-ass attempt to understand why, even in this room, I still didn't feel as though I was truly here, as though I wasn't really at home.

My eight-year-old self sat on the bed, the oversized tie-dyed shirt hanging well below my knees. I had awakened to the sound of the Grateful Dead softly playing. Jerry Garcia's bluesy voice echoed up the stairs and through my open bedroom door. The melody of his guitar invited me downstairs to the slightly opened sliding glass door of my father's converted patio den, which was a haven for everything controversial in the house. The curtains were drawn, but still the light glinted through as if to beckon me to a place that was usually off limits at night. I opened the sliding glass door a little more, hoping that it was just enough to slip through and step inside. I peeked through the curtain to find my dad bent over a coffee table, his head to the glass surface. I called out to him, but the music was too loud for him to notice my voice. I walked all the way in and stood next to his water bed. I called out to him again. This time his head rose. His eyes, a storm of black irises and wild stares, were fixed in my direction. He got up and walked over to me, grabbing both my arms on either side, picking me up off the ground. My legs dangled. He shouted at me about how I was told never to come in here at night, how this was his time away from me. But, then again, he was always away from me, distant and cut off. The drugs had made it possible to forget me, even now. I tried to say something, but the words were lost as I stared into his eyes. They were bloodshot, and the hazel green around his pupils had all but been swallowed up by black. His grip scared me and I started to cry. He set me down. I can't remember what he said or what I asked him, maybe it was for a cup of water or maybe just a hug, but that is when it happened. He pushed me down to the ground. I remember standing up, crying, and asking something again, but that was met with more yelling. He cursed at me and pointed to the floor, and that is when I realized I had wet myself. He shoved me through the crack in the sliding glass door face first. My shoulders barely made it through before the rest of my body followed. Through the kitchen, past the breakfast counter, and up the stairs I ran to my bedroom. Nana and Grandpa had slept through it. They were better sleepers back then. I slipped back into bed, with wet panties and nightie. I fell asleep that night looking up at the moon that was barely visible through all the clouds that hung around it, like the ears of a cotton plant that has just bloomed.

Other times in my childhood, I can recall looking at the moon outside my window and wishing that it would take me away from all this fighting and bickering. Grandpa and Dad fought constantly, mostly because Dad disagreed with Nana on how he should raise John and me. The bickering always turned into a shouting match, one I would listen to while holed up in my room, the one I shared with my brother until I was in high school.

I remember crying next to the window in elementary school, my head poked through the curtains so that the light wouldn't wake John. I remember praying to the man in the moon, asking him to help my dad. I knew there was something wrong with him. I had heard Nana say it over and over again. I asked her if I could help him, but Nana just replied that Dad needed to want help before he would ever take it. The yelling stopped. The front door slammed shut. I heard the fan belt on Dad's vw Jetta squeak to life, the exhaust sputtering fuel out of the tailpipe. The headlights turned on. I duck my head down and lie back down on my pillow and stare up at the ceiling fan turning around and around as my dad pulled away quickly down Lancaster Drive. Nana and Grandpa didn't talk about the fight or the fact that my dad had left, and when John asked where Dad had gone, they just told him that he had gone out of town and that he would be back as soon as he could. Grandpa slowly began to box up Dad's things. I knew what it meant. I had seen Dad do it to Mom's things when she left. It meant he might not be coming back, but, unlike Mom, Dad came back for us a week later, not just for his boxed-up things. He took us away from Nana and Grandpa's house. I didn't set foot back in the room until I was in middle school, and even then Dad, John, and I didn't stay long before we left again. After some years John ran away and went back to Nana and Grandpa's, and then was forced to leave and go to a Baptist boarding school in Missouri. Dad said it was for his own good. I knew better. John had fucked up, run away from home, done too many drugs, gotten into too much trouble, and now he was paying the price for his youthful indiscretions. After middle school I didn't return to my old room until college, but even then I didn't think the room had changed.

Freshman year of college I lay on the bed and looked up at the ceiling. The stars that I had plastered all over it in elementary school were still there. I had bought a new red couch, a coffee table, and a mini fridge. It looked like a dorm room, one that came free of rent and roaches. It wasn't long before I was in with the wrong crowd, like John had been. I got mixed up with drugs and bad people, and before I knew it I was ditching class and spending my tuition money on blow, crystal, and booze. Weeknights I spent getting thwacked out of my mind and drunk, stumbling down a street in Lemon Grove, screeching punk rock songs, my Lower Class Brats T-shirt stained with puke and possibly someone else's blood. Tattooed and rebellious with a loop ring hanging out of my nose, I thought I was unstoppable. Sitting on the red couch in my room doing lines of coke off the coffee table, playing my music at 2:00 a.m., not giving a fuck if I woke up Nana or Gramps, just that I was high and lying on my bed staring up at the plastic stars that were mashed onto the ceiling and glowing softly from the blacklight bulb I had installed in the ceiling fan. Fuck, life was good.

A few weeks after my second semester of college, Nana told me they were going to kick me out. Their eldest granddaughter, I was the one they had invested the time in. I had become a letdown. Their hopes for a prosperous adulthood were dashed by my foolish need to rebel from my family's expectations. All I wanted to do was throw a big *fuck you* in everyone's face, but in doing so I had become a "reckless young lady," one that they were no longer willing to fund or help. I had, in short, become my father, and I was ashamed. I had sworn as a child never to become like him, but the truth is, as my dad always put it, we become the very thing we seek to avoid. When I told my dad what had happened, he asked me what I was going to do. I mentioned that Tony, my childhood best friend from down the street, was getting clean too and that he was joining the army. I had already gone with him to the recruiting station, and I had made up my mind to join as well. Dad was silent for a while and then asked if, when the time came to take me to the airport, he could drive me. I told him that when the time came, it would be harder to leave if everyone was there and especially if he was there.

A month went by before it was time for me to leave, but I had one last night in my room before I left. I sat on the bed and looked around. Boxes lined the wall closest to the door. The closet, dresser, and nightstands were empty. All my things packaged up. A large black duffel with my things for basic training was packed and lying next to the door. There was nothing left in the room but the red couch, my bed, and the stars on the ceiling. When I went to lie down that night, I didn't draw the curtains shut. I left them open. The moon wasn't out. The sky was black, covered with a layer of thick gray clouds that blanketed any chance at a nice night. I looked up at the stars on my ceiling and hoped that the room would be the same when I returned, just like every other time I had come back to it, but as I lay there, I knew that this might be my last night in this room.

Now older, war torn, I looked out at the moon again as I sat on the bed. The room was still the same shape, same color. My red couch was still next to the window. The curtains had been replaced, but they were still the same soft blue color. The walls, freshly painted, were the same low tone of blue. The dresser had been replaced; so had the bed. I lay down and looked up at the bare ceiling where the stars used to be, and just like that, I realized that my childhood was behind me. This room was no longer mine, and the one thing missing that made this house my constant home was now a memory. I got up from the bed and walked to the door. I no longer needed the room. I had been afraid to let go, afraid to let the pain in. I thought if I clung to what I used to be then Iraq wouldn't swallow me whole. But that's just it, isn't it? Sometimes you have to let the pain in so you never ignore it again. I rubbed my belly as I looked at the room one last time. One of the boys kicked at my hand from inside my pregnant stomach, and I knew it was time to go. I walked out of the room, leaving the door wide open.

· · · · · · · · ·

## James (#5)

James had pleaded guilty, a plea agreement struck so that he could get out of Mannheim military prison before the boys were born. The names were picked out—Bowen Gabriel and Zachary Michael—but the nursery wasn't nearly complete and I was a walking catastrophe of pregnant woman rage and PTSD. The crib lay in a shambled mess, the changing table half-assembled, and the rocking chair put together in between pee breaks and vomit sessions with the downstairs toilet. Before he left, I sent him a sonogram picture, one he said he would put in his Bible and look at it every day. It would be his only comfort. He was allowed to receive letters. I wrote him daily.

Hi James!     September 20, 2007

Well, the boys are getting big. The left baby is aa and he is 2lbs 2 ounces. The right one is bb and he is 2lbs 1 ounce. Both of them are facing the same direction now. The doctor said they're both breech, which means they are both facing feet down by my cervix and head up near my stomach. The right one is giving me hell and just will not stop kicking, punching, and moving around. Last night he grabbed hold of his umbilical cord and just started yanking on it. Lord did that hurt!! I think he gets it from you. Well, other than that they are doing great and we all miss you and want you to come home soon. Stay safe, babe.

Love you with all my heart,
Brooke and the boys

James,        September 23, 2007

Every day I wake up hoping to see you next to me. But I open my eyes and roll over and realize that you aren't there. I feel the boys inside me and know that even though you aren't here physically, you're here in spirit. . . . We are both about to become parents. . . . I'm scared about giving birth without you here . . . and I guess what I'm trying to say is don't be late. . . .

Your loving wife,
Brooke

A large black stamp reads, "Soldier letter," and the paper, now eight years old, still holds the smudge marks from where the tears fell on it the day I wrote it.

Dear James,   Oct 17, 2007

Sunday: I went to church and saw the cutest thing! a set of twin boys! Oh, they were so cute! There's a new priest. He's Irish, accent and all. I said a prayer for you. I say one every day, praying for your safe return. Me and Nana are going on Tuesday to pick out the car seats and stroller.

Monday: Well, I went to the VA today. I'm enrolled now. They're letting me pick my own doctor for the delivery. They gave me some spiel about not enrolling the kids until they're born, blah blah blah. Oh, they diagnosed me with PTSD and some brain disorder due to combat stress, whatever that means. These people are so full of shit. Fuck this place. Anyway, the boys are fine and I'm getting huge!!! I mean Aretha Franklin huge. I don't even fit into my overalls. We started moving everything from the upstairs to the downstairs. By the end of the week the nursery should be done. It's so silly. By the time you get this letter, you might already be here. I'm so proud of you, James. Anyway, take care of yourself and keep reading that Bible!

Love always,
Brookie

Hi Baby,    October 1, 2007

I know it's been a very long time since I talked to you last, but I wanted you to know that I'm still here thinking of you and loving you just the same. Ever since I had to say goodbye, I've felt like there's this big cloud over my head. Like nothing I do makes me happy anymore and nothing I do can keep me from my own thoughts, or the nightmares. I don't sleep anymore, not without you there to comfort me.

James, why does my heart feel so empty without you here? It's like there's a big void where you used to be. I don't trust anyone anymore. Please hurry home. All I want to do is hold you again and have you whisper into my ear that everything will be ok, that the nightmares will stop, that this hurt will go away. Just get home to me, James, as fast as you can.

With all the love I possess,
Brooke

Weeks go by with no response. I began to question if he was getting my letters or if they confiscated them. Did he still love me? But when hopes of a response began to wane, a letter arrived with a stamped logo of Army Europe Post Office and my name on it:

James Haislop
Unit 29723
Box LL
APO AE 09028–9723

My Beloved Brooke,    October 2007

I received your letter today. It was good to get one. Can't wait to see the latest picture of the boys. And of course you. Of what you said about missing me and can't wait to be back in my arms; I think of you all the time, baby. You just need to hang in there a little bit longer. I have 14 days left. By the time you read this I'll have roughly a week left in here and I can call you all the time. Brooke, I can't wait to get back in your arms and hold you, kiss you and make sweet passionate love again. I have not been the same since you left, but I know I will see you soon and hold your hand while Bowen and Zachary enter this world. I can't wait to be a father and start a family with such a wonderful thoughtful woman as you. You are my everything.

With love,

James

There were tears, a longing, and a sigh of relief, but it was short-lived. It had only been a week since the letter came, and already I was lost again in my own thoughts, nightmares, and unrest. I opened the letter again and again, reading the words scribbled in chicken scratch writing, trying to give myself hope, a reason to keep fighting back against the sadness, a reason to fight at all.

· · · · · · · · · ·

## Ghosts (#2)

He walked in front of me, but after our brief encounter in Iraq and the fact that I was pregnant, I thought for sure he wouldn't recognize me. The time apart had put age around his eyes, burying them in crow's feet and covering them with a furrow at his brow. A weary face, downtrodden from so many years of worrying, and still it seemed as though his eyes were still the same shade of cobalt blue. He saw me. Our eyes met. He looked away, sure that he had seen a ghost, a memory from the past that couldn't possibly be in front of him begging for him to feel the same again. But he looked back again, and it was then that I said his name. Kyle. He smiled and began to walk up to me, but he stopped short. He saw my belly— pregnant. It wasn't his, and so he naturally assumed I was married. I wasn't. Not yet anyway, and so I reached out for a hug, parting the distance between us with a friendly gesture I was sure he would accept. We hugged, exchanged small chitchat about our lives now, but it was when I told him that I was engaged to be married, still waiting on my divorce to be finalized, that he gave me a look of disapproval, not as though I was wrong for falling in love with another man while married but that it wasn't him and these children weren't his. He told me that I should've waited, for him, for us, for all sorts of things that timing and place would've reconciled in the end. I nodded. I knew he was right, but that had always been our thing, timing. And though looking at him, with all the feelings rising within me, I couldn't bring myself to run away with him. We walked to the nearest bar, sat down, and talked in code that only lovers would know, the slow, steady remembering of touches, lost memories, and things forgotten by age. I told him that I'm not the same person anymore, that the war had changed me. He told me he knew but that he could've brought me back. He was right. Of all the men in my life, he was probably the only one I could've emptied Iraq onto and who would still have loved me the same, as though not a day had gone by. Still, I shielded him, told him half-truths, fuzzing the edges around what I had done in Iraq, gave short answers that amounted to more questions than answers. When I told him that I couldn't really articulate what it was like being there for so long, I mention our encounter in Iraq, hoping that I had imagined it somehow. He nodded his head yes and gulped some of his beer. I tried to explain what that day had done to me, almost as a way of apologizing for the present, but he stopped me and said, "You know, there's nothing we can do about the present, but the past is something to hold on to. You remember me, the times we had while dating, that shitty apartment, the sex. God, the sex. And, me, well, I remember you always writing. Sitting there in my room on my bed scribbling away in your notebook. One day, you need to write all this down, the good, the bad, the horrible, and the amazing, but don't forget that there is a world beyond Iraq. We're here for you. I'm here for you."

I looked down at the table unable to stare into his eyes because I knew he was right. Fuck him. He was right. I had been trying to do all of this on my own, but I didn't need to. So I opened up to him. He was the only person I trusted enough. I told him about Iraq, James, Rob, the missions, good and bad, the nightmares I'd been having, all of it. When I finished, all he said was, "Fuck me, you've had it rough." I smiled at his honesty, but when he insisted on driving me home that night, I didn't say no. I should have. When he walked me to the door, I didn't hesitate. I should have. And when he kissed me good-night, I should have resisted, but I couldn't. I had let the war beat me down until I had no fight left in me to give, and so I let Kyle kiss me goodnight, give me a hug, and walk to his truck. I had needed that kiss. I needed to know that someone who wasn't my family was still capable of loving me. Even though Kyle hadn't gotten a full glimpse of what I was like now, it was enough for me that he cared, that he genuinely wanted what was best in my life, and that he hoped James would be it. I watched the headlights turn on and roll down the street until his truck turned the corner. That was the last time I saw Kyle, and though I still talk to him from time to time, the what-ifs of that night become glaring. I should've talked to him more, let him in the house, or anything really that would have made him stay, but I didn't and I'm not sure I will ever forgive myself for letting him drive away. Or maybe it was the right thing to do. Either way, he was gone, another ghost created.

· · · · · · · · · · ·

## Preparations

Seven months pregnant. The nursery was finished. The blobs on the ultrasound now looked like mini human beings. The house still didn't feel like home. And when I walked in each time, I still touched things to make sure I wasn't still in Iraq. The soft linen fabric of the old blue couch that was worn with ass indentations. The chip in the corner tile of the breakfast bar that I had created when I slammed my skateboard into it as a teenager. Each time I walked into the house, it took me twenty minutes to figure out that I was home. Nana would watch me go from one room to the other as she sat in her recliner reading her book. Open and close the french doors. Sit on the piano bench in the den. Walk up the brown carpeted steps to the second floor. Sit at the top landing. Walk back down. I wanted to tell Nana why I did this but still couldn't find the words. But that was just it, I had no words. There were times I carried out the routine and the silence that fell in between my task and hers made it easy to realize that words were too much. It was what made what had happened to me in Iraq a perfect understanding between us, the simple moments of just being in the house; it was all we needed it to be. And so each time I sat back down in the living room in the recliner next to hers, we said nothing, content with the stillness to just be.

· · · · · · · · · ·

## Childhood

I remember little things about growing up with my dad. Thirty-six packs of Natural Ice were cheaper than Budweiser. When trimming pot, make sure you cut the stems at an angle. The best way to make a fire was by stacking the wood in a square, putting the kindling at the bottom. The words of Shakespeare were to be savored, not flipped through lightly. Never eat the marshmallows at a Grateful Dead show.

It is early June. 1994. Cal Expo in Sacramento. The Grateful Dead are playing a three-show series, and my dad scored tickets in the recording section. I am nine.

It is the second day. It is hot, the sun beating down on the unshaded section we are standing in. Dad laid down the Kodak blanket, the bright-colored yellow, orange, and red star emblazoned on its face. I watch as Dad sets up the microphone, the tape cassette, and the plastic milk carton crate that covered the contraption so that no one stepped on it while dancing. I hold the tape, waiting for Dad to put his hand out again for another piece. The crowd is filing in. Hippies in bright-colored tie-dyed shirts, patchwork pants, and some just naked walking around. Dad had made me a sweater or bought it, I couldn't remember. It had a red heart with tie-dyed rings surrounding its shape. I wore my plaid Converse sneakers. Dad was in his tie-dyed *Steal Your Face* shirt, jeans, and brown Birks. The sun was starting to set, the lights coming on in the stadium where fans lit up sticks, glow-in-the-dark necklaces and bracelets, and when the music came on, camera flickers lit up the sky like stars twinkling in iridescent glimmers of faces melting together smiles and *fuck yeahs*. Dad and I danced to the music, and I remember asking for food. Dad smiled and handed me a bag of Twizzlers and a bottle of water. I was still hungry. What happened next was nothing short of a child's misunderstanding about adult music shows and a variety of misguided concepts about free food. The crowd had gotten louder. "Sugar Mag" was playing, the melody rhythmic, the swaying hips of the dancers in the standing-room section. Everyone singing along, the words as clear and gargled through the microphone Jerry was singing into. His guitar electric, the crowd wild with the anticipation of the break-off jam session coming after the chorus, and the band kept playing on, waiting for their cue to solo.

In the midst of the chaos a concert-goer had begun to fling marshmallows into the crowd. One hit me in the head. I picked it up. A dancing bear in green ink was stamped on its face. Without permission, I went around the perimeter of our blanket gathering as many as I could find, using my skirt as a basket. When I had collected enough to be a smorgasbord of sugar, I plopped down on the blanket. I ingest the first one with ease, but before I can consume another, Dad snatches my arm, smacks the sugar treat from my hand, and asks where I got them. I point and tell him that they are all over the place. Free food. I smiled, but Dad did not. He lifted me up, grabbed one of the marshmallows, and ran me to the med tent. Inside they asked me questions like how many did I eat, did I feel funny. They asked my dad if he wanted my stomach pumped, to go to the hospital, but before he could reply, I told him I was fine.

I don't feel weird, just happy. Dad smiled. I had taken a hit of acid at nine and was handling it better than most of the adults in the tent. The medic suggested that we leave, go to the hospital, but when I started screaming, saying that I didn't want to leave the music, the medic and Dad decided the best thing to do was to just let me be, keep an eye on my progress, and if I got worse to come back. I smiled. Dad looked concerned and the medic was deeply upset. I refused to stay in the tent. So Dad took me back outside to the lights, the music, and the people. I don't remember much after that, but I do remember being up on my dad's shoulders the rest of the time, seeing a dancing bear in lights spinning in circles and dancing to the music, seeing the stage, the band, and the people. I'll never forget dancing among the Deadheads.

Some people wouldn't call my childhood conventional, but then again none of my life has been conventional. What bothered me now at the age of twenty-one was how I would move past this point in my life. It had taken me years to come to terms with my childhood, to accept that my father had done the best he could; that my mother, with all her massive faults, didn't want me and still doesn't; that my grandparents tried as best they could to help me, my brother, and my dad; but the truth was, the three of us were the outcasts of the family, seen as failures in part because of my dad. Now I had come back from war changed even more. How was I going to resolve this part of my life? How can anyone come back from war and walk through the rest of their life without feeling as though they haven't really left the war behind?

When I came back from Iraq, I asked Dad if he remembered that night at the Grateful Dead concert. He told me no with a smile. He asked me if I remembered what Iraq was really like, and I told him that it was like when you crack your back and a drop of spinal fluid pops out a dose of leftover acid and you trip for days, forgetting time and space, the reality molded together with the past, a blend of symphonic melodies merging into pastel watercolors that drip from a painting on the wall that is in reality just another memory of a mangled corpse that you forgot you put into a body bag. Dad looked at me, not with sympathy but with horror as he leaned back in his chair, trying to hold back the tears as he said, "What have they done to you, Brooke?"

· · · · · · · · · ·

## At a Glance

At nights when I was awake, the war followed me around the sleeping house, making victims of the darkness. I paced the floors of the kitchen, and living room, and around the rim of the pool while thinking about the stillness of the palm trees, the fog that was seeping in from the beaches inland and up the canyon. The hedgerow was tall enough now that I couldn't see over it. I stood on the diving board, my feet barely lingering over the edge, and looked out past the canyon, past I-8 toward San Diego State University. Several of the dorm lights were on. I imagined what they were doing. Some studying. Others drinking their faces off, trying to make memories of a time when there wasn't trouble or any bills to pay, just the promise of a good time and a bad hangover. I zoomed out. Looked at the rest of the world around me. Americans going about their lives, but I let my mind trickle off until my imagination took over and I stood there at that very moment, wondering if there wasn't somewhere in Iraq a young man preparing for the afternoon.

He looks out through his bedroom window, at the vast wasteland that has become his home, and tries to remember what his life used to be before the war, before violence knocked at his door begging him to take notice of the landscape, of what his country had become. And maybe he does this because there is a deep need to understand that the world around him has changed, has grown accustomed to hatred and the promise of bullets. And as he stands there looking out past his car, beyond where the horizon melts into the land, maybe he does this to breach the meaning of war, to emerge fully from the cocooned existence of his home to the street where he will drive his car a few moments later, where he descends into a maddening state of rage that he must feel in order to commit himself fully to steering toward the tank that awaits him by the overpass. Maybe he must do this to gain what little destiny he can control. But as he drives down the road, does he think about the roads lined with bombs, or the mother who will soon be left childless, both her children taken by this war? Does he wonder what life would be like in America, what a young man his age would be doing if his life did not revolve around chaos and the uncertainty of living through to the next day? Does he wish for just another night's rest? Will he think of the finality of it all when the bullets come piercing through the grille and into the radiator, penetrating the cab of the car? Will he think of the certainty of his death just before his car crashes into the ditch, a flying piece of metal made shrapnel splitting the side of his skull open, exposing his brain tissue to the tan interior of the headrest? Will he contemplate the end as his breathing labors and gives way to a deepening of his eyelids as soldiers rush toward the car, a medic trying to work on his injury as he slowly closes his mind to the violence of it all?

I thought of all these things and more as I stood hovering above the covered pool, forcing back the urge to step off and let the waves of blue plastic take me under.

• • •

What happens when the war follows you home? How do you break apart those moments, divide them into categories of living, and continue with your life as though those moments never happened at all?

• • •

I got a phone call the other day, the voice on the end of the line barely recognizable. James. He told me he was leaving Mannheim soon, that he was getting out early for good behavior, that soon he would be in San Diego. He must have heard the panic in my voice when I told him to hurry because he cut the conversation short, with an *I love you* and a *see you soon*.

## Household Goods

My stuff from Germany arrived on an unmarked truck, the boxes stacked halfway up to the ceiling in my room. I opened the first box. Nana was there to help. Grandpa stood off to the side, waiting for it. Inside on the top were uniforms; one by one Nana pulled them out and set them aside until she got to the last one. It was mangled, charred, and blood-splotched stains covered it in patches. I could hear Nana gasp as she looked up at me. The tears were already spilling over my cheeks as she got up and left the room. I got up too, walked past Gramps, and went into the living room, where Nana was sitting in her blue chair, her hands covering her face. I sat on the armrest, put my arms around her, and told her that it was okay, that I was fine, that I had made it back alive and in one piece. I told her lies.

• • •

James made it to San Diego a few weeks later, and when he arrived at the airport, I stood there and held him in my arms and cried. I still don't remember why I did it. Perhaps out of grief, or longing, or time spent apart, or maybe because now I finally had someone in the house who understood what had happened to me or at least had a vague inkling of the aftermath.

The checkups at the doctor were going fine. The boys were getting bigger. I was getting bigger, but there was not enough of me to contain the war inside.

• • •

I was standing in the car seat aisle of Babies R Us staring at a dark blue- and tan-covered matching car seat and stroller combo. The pattern looked checkered or maybe digital. James walked up behind me and put his hand on my shoulder. When I jumped from his touch, he wrapped his arms around me and held my stomach, putting one hand on each side of the boys. I told him that I couldn't decide which car seat combo

I liked the best, which pattern I wanted to buy. He laughed at me and said that if this was the least of my worries now, then I should be fine with everything else that was going on. I knew what he was talking about, but my indecision on car seats infuriated me, and soon I turned to practicality. I tried to pull the stroller out, but it was stuck. James lent a hand, pulled it out, and pushed it toward me, telling me that the tandem style was a bit big, that it might not fit in the Camry. I held on to the handle, pushing it back and forth along the tile floor. James was smiling. I asked him about it and he replied that I had changed. His comment made me nervous. I let go of the stroller and walked away, telling him that this one will work, to get a sales guy to help him, and that I'd be in the car.

• • •

I could no longer sleep. Between the heartburn, acid reflux, and too much baby, I could barely lie down. I tried to sleep sitting up, but most nights I sat awake, looking at James as he slept.

• • •

I remembered him asking me once if I had gone to the VA yet. I told him yes. And then he asked it: "So did they tell you you're crazy because of the war?"

# PART 6

In shaa Allah

• • • • • • • • • • • • • • • •

## Just before You Die

It was November 25, 2007. A few days after my birthday. Almost
Thanksgiving. We were sitting in the living room watching
the news when a story about a bombing in Baghdad came on.
Grandpa turned to James and asked if it was anywhere near
where we were stationed. I tried to get up from the couch,
but I fell back down into the pillow-entrenched seat cushion.
James answered him with a polite yes, that it was about four
minutes away from where our base was. My heart started to
race. I had to get up. I had to get out of the room, but I couldn't
get out of the couch. I tried harder and harder to rise up from
the cushions, but the panic was pushing me back down into
place. Nana told Grandpa to shut up, and everyone looked at
me. I couldn't breathe. I sucked in air as fast as I could, but
it felt as though my esophagus was closing in on itself. James
got up and lifted me from the couch, but I stumbled and fell to
the carpet. On all fours, I knelt, panicked, unable to breathe.
Was it anyone I knew? If I had been there, could it have been
me? The thoughts raced and raced until the panic was overwhelming. Tears spilled onto the carpet and I could not catch
my breath. The place, the timing, the people, the waves and
waves of grief and shame crest over, bashing my body against
the pain of remembering. An ocean of survivor's guilt built up
into a hurricane, the waves breaking too high over my head,
swallowing me up into the carpet. My body drifting swiftly
out to sea, the rip current too much pull for my body to handle. And then it came, a pain in my stomach, the churning of
a sharp ache like shrapnel ripping through your flesh, searing
the skin as it passed. I screamed in pain. James did not know

what to do. Nana said the boys were coming, but I could not bring myself to my feet. It was too early. They were too early. It was only thirty-five weeks.

At the hospital, my doctor came in, told me that they had to give me a series of injections to make the babies' lungs develop enough to give them a chance at survival after the birth. I was in tears. James was upset. Nana and Grandpa sat in the wings. Nana was asking questions. They said I could go home in the morning, that they had stopped the labor; the contractions had subsided, but I didn't feel any different. I knew something was wrong still, but I didn't know anything about giving birth, let alone doctorly things like lung development or contractions. I had skipped those mommy-to-be classes, and now I was kicking myself because I wished I knew what the hell they were talking about. I wish I had asked more questions.

Even though it was the next day and they said that I might be released, I had not left the hospital. There was pain, sharp and unrelenting, that went on for minutes, but sometimes only seconds. The night before, I had asked one of the nurses what contractions were and what they felt like. She laughed at me. She must have thought I was joking, but I wasn't. She stopped laughing and said, "Honey, when you start getting contractions before birth, you'll know what they are." This had to be what a contraction was, because it hurt like hell, like one big "fuck you" from the inside of my body to me, compliments of the two little babies who were about to come pouring out of me at any minute. What I hadn't known at the time was that during the night one of the boys had turned sideways, pushing the other baby toward my cervix, but as the anesthesiologist gave me my first epidural the next morning and laid me back down onto the bed, the baby that was shoved down near my cervix began to go into distress. At some point after the first epidural, he pinched my foot and asked if I felt that, to which I replied, "Ya," and "Aren't I not supposed to feel anything below the waist?" He looked perplexed and told me that he would be back again in a few minutes to check and see if the epidural had kicked in yet. But before the anesthesiologist had made it back to my room, the needle on the fetal monitor that I was hooked up to began spiking all over the place; one baby's heart rate was too high. At the sound of the fetal monitor chiming loudly, a nurse came running in. She asked me if I could feel my legs. I told her yes. The anesthesiologist was paged, but when my doctor walked in and looked at the fetal monitor, he told the nurse that there was no time for another epidural. The anesthesiologist would have to try again once I was inside the operating room. Once in the operating room, the anesthesiologist gave me another epidural, about ten minutes after the first one, but it did not work either. Apparently, I had too high a tolerance for pain. It was too late to try anything else; they would have to give me local anesthetic. If they waited any longer, we might lose one of the boys. They took James away to scrub down. A curtain was put up so I couldn't see what they were doing. The doctor told me that he was giving me local anesthesia. He began cutting me open. It didn't work. I felt the scalpel tearing into my flesh. I screamed loudly. James could hear it from the other room. The doctor asked me if I could feel it, and when I screamed yes, they decided to wait a second to see if it would kick in, but I was bleeding too much. As James came in, he rushed to me and asked what was wrong. I told him in half shouted screams that I could feel them cutting me open, that the pain was too much. The anesthesiologist came in, upped my dosage of pain killers, but it still was not enough. They couldn't wait any longer. They had to deliver the babies, so I lied and told the doctor I couldn't feel any pain, but the truth was, I could feel the scalpel cut into my skin again. James was there, and because he was scared, I bit my lip and held back the screams and the scared look from my face. I could feel them digging into my abdomen and then I saw him—the first baby came out. Bowen. Then a minute later another tug and pull into my abdomen and Zachary came in to the world. I have a picture of all four of us right after they were born, but I don't remember the moment the picture depicts. By the time the boys were cleaned up and the doctor was sewing me shut, I had lost consciousness, the pain too much for me to bear any longer.

· · · · · · · · · · · ·

## Battle Fatigue

They said I died.

He stood above me with both newborns in his hands. The blood still fresh on the surgical tools. My eyes still open as he looked at me.

They said I died when my heart gave out.

The reflex to keep fighting waned from my body. Each boy's face pulled up, shown over the curtain, and taken away. Seduced by the feeling of completion, the utterance of some deathly man's voice breaking open the creases of my lips, beckoning me to take one last breath, taunting me with glimpses of that hero's death, as he traced the outline of his finger around the serrated flesh resting on my abdomen and drew up the line toward my heart until the tip of relief pressed firmly on my heart and then released.

A tear drew down my cheek in a translucent stream, as I realized the consequence of my submitting to open abdominal surgery with no muscle paralysis to calm the pain of the metal meeting flesh, the burrowing sensation of steel splaying open my insides, the warm blood seeping down from all sides as the doctors perform magic with carefully placed hands inside what was once a sacred vessel. Here, death was no longer a dream or a hope. There was only the agony of real pain with no hushed words of comfort, no hands held tight. There were scared faces that drew back from the curtain and looked at you as though this, this was the last of you. This was the measure of your sacrifice. For those who were left in the room, this would've been their last memory of me.

They said I died when my heart gave out right after the boys were born.

And after he left the OR to take both newborn boys to the NICU, after they sewed the abdomen back together with sutures and staples, after working on my body with paddles for three minutes, after two shots of epinephrine and chest compressions, after they called time of death, 7:32 a.m., my body refused to die. Hours later in the recovery room when the doctor told me that in all his years of being an OB/GYN, he'd never seen someone come back to life, I replied back through morphine gurgles, "Can't kill me. I'm already dead. Did it in Iraq. Six bullets in a fifteen-year-old boy's chest."

They said I died when my heart gave out.

· · · · · · · · · · · · · · · · · · · · · ·

## The Boys Come into the House

I set it aside. The war. I pushed it away. Locked out the memories as best I could. When I came out of the hospital five days later, America was still there. Each person walked around, blinders on, their head down toward brightly lit screen texting coded messages to friends, and family, and lovers. Cars drive past down the freeways toward their houses, apartments, jobs, or malls. Consumers swipe credit cards, paying for material things like clothes, shoes, cookie-cutter furniture from Ikea that they couldn't hope to assemble even with well-written instructions. They borrowed money they didn't have. Drove cars they couldn't possibly afford. Went to college they knew someday they'd have to pay for once they got a job that barely paid enough to cover all the other things they couldn't afford. Americans being Americans, shielded from the violence in the streets in Iraq, the hate that rolled off lips in foreign languages indecipherable to those pointing the weapons, the anger made out in vests that exploded the truth behind the rage, the misunderstanding of the Qur'an and what it meant to be Muslim, and fists balled up in protest for their country, the one we invaded, destroyed, disassembled on false pretenses. And still, America sat there at Starbucks and drank hypocrisy in a cup while shaking their heads at the headlines in the *New York Times* as they said, "What a shame it is for those poor people in Iraq, what a shame it is to be a country at war."

· · · · · · · · · ·

## Traditions

When a child is born into the Islamic faith, they are welcomed into the world with a celebration, the tradition of Aqiqah, which consists of the father, on the seventh day after the child's birth, slaughtering a goat or sheep to mark the occasion. The prophet Muhammad used to perform the ritual when he was bestowed with a newborn child. It is used to announce the birth to family, friends, and neighbors. It is a celebration of life and the bestowing of great honor by the Creator. Before the goat is slaughtered, the child's hair is shaved and weighed to determine how much money is to be given out to the poor; an offering of alms must be made. It is suggested that the father sacrifice a healthy goat humanely while the child's head is being shaved. While the slaughter is taking place the *dua* must be said:

> In the Name of Allah and through Allah, this is the ʿaqīqa of . . . [name of the boy], son of . . . [name of the father]: its flesh for his flesh blood, its bone for his bone, its hair for his hair, its skin for his skin. O Allah, let it be a protection of the family of Muhammad, peace and blessings of Allah be upon him and his family.
>
> O gathering, I am free from what you associate; I turn my face to Him who split the heavens and the earth, a true believer and a Muslim, and not one of the polytheists. My prayer, my piety, my living, and my dying are for Allah, the Lord of the Words. O Allah, from You and to You, in the Name of Allah; Allah is greater. O Allah, bless Muhammad, and accept [this] from . . . [name of the child].
>
> Son of . . . [name of the father].

After this rite of passage, the child, if male, is circumcised. It is customary that before the circumcision a prayer is said:

In shaa Allah

O Allah, this is Your practice and the practice of Your Prophet (peace and blessings of Allah be upon him), Your blessings be upon him and his family; obeying Your ideal and Your books is the result of Your volition, and Your will and judgment you decreed, a rule You executed. So take away from him the pain of the knife in his circumcision and his scarification through a command —You are more knowing of it than I, O Allah. And cleanse him of sins, prolong his life for me, drive away injury and pain from his body, increase him in wealth, and fend off poverty from him; for You know and we do not.

These traditions are followed to ward off evil spirits from the newborn and the mother, as well as to protect and celebrate the coming of new life. The ceremony is performed in front of the village, everyone partaking in the festivities as a way of welcoming the child into the world, upholding the practices of Islam, and thanking the Creator for the bringing of new life.

We did not slaughter a goat. But we prayed. We thanked God. We celebrated their birth. We counted our blessings. We shared the birth with our friends, and family, and neighbors. We took pictures, cleansed them of afterbirth, and named them five days later. We circumcised them. We cherished them as a gift from God.

· · · · · · · ·

## Alive Day

There was a lull in the excitement; the bloody battle zone of birth was over. There was a coming home ritual, the bringing of the children into the house. I stepped across the threshold.

Maybe it wasn't so hard to come home, but the home had felt incomplete when I came back from Iraq, the longing for more than the house was before. Somehow, the children and James had completed it, rendered it full.

I felt for the first time as though I was finally home, that the war might be behind me, left in the dust and sand of a world that I no longer inhabited, one that was across mountains, and deserts, and oceans, one that was starting to fade slowly out of the memories, replaced, supplanted by the two things swaddled tightly in hospital blankets, a place washed clean from my existence, the absence of time lapsed over, the faces blurring, the wind brushing my footprints clean, the roots of date trees branching over shell casings as they were absorbed into the earth to rust for eternity in the dirt of the Fertile Crescent. And maybe one day I would look back at Iraq, remember the faces, the landscape, the roads, and sunsets, and consume it all into my soul, committing the memories to a softer place in my locker full of hurt, but for now I was home, and I could not think of those things.

· · · · · · · · · · · · · · · · · · · ·

## Burying the Coffin of War

It has been days since I have slept more than three hours. It has been months since I have thought of Iraq. Years since I have been able to laugh.

· · ·

James was changing a poopy diaper on Zachary. The stench was foul, and he moaned when I told him it was his turn for diaper duty. We were talking about moving to Florida. The subject was too harsh to speak of in front of my grandparents, so we whispered, taking half breaths, pulling away from the smell of feces. I told him that I didn't want to leave, that I finally felt at home, that moving would change all that; I would have to start over. I didn't want to start over. I held Bowen. It was his turn next. The diaper was off and in the poop receptacle, which was supposed to keep the smell in but didn't. James laughed at the stench; I was not fazed. I knew smells that were worse than baby poo: burning trash, port-o-shitters on a hot day, flesh rotting from sweat, socks after brigade runs, charred flesh, blood that has been sitting in a blown-out truck too long and had soured, tires when they catch fire, petrol on the skin, a dead body baking in heat with its innards gutted out onto the ground. All these things were worse than a child's shit.

There was the sound of water trickling. James was still talking to me of moving. We were lost in conversation, but the sound of water stopped us both. James turned around to Zachary. He was peeing an arched stream over James shoulder onto the carpet. James put his hand up to stop the pee, but it deflected into his mouth. James was screaming, trying to cover Zachary's penis. I was holding Bowen, laughing. James was spitting piss onto the carpet. Zach was crying because James was yelling obscenities as loud as he could. Bowen was crying because my laughter startled him. Nana and Grandpa ran in. They started laughing too when James told them what had happened. I could not help myself. I laughed and laughed, and I did it until tears of happiness, of joy, of repressed years of not laughing spilled over. I let it happen. James was the only one not laughing, but he turned to me and saw I could not stand up straight because I was laughing so hard. He stopped cursing. He turned to me and smiled, on his mouth the still lingering smell of piss as he kissed me on the forehead. It was the first step, letting the laughter in, but as time went on, the next laugh became easier and easier until I remembered what it was like to laugh again.

But the bombs did not stop falling on Baghdad. The death toll, beyond the count of grief.

• • •

As a child, I remembered the sirens outside my window from the nearby fire station waking me up at night. I would run to the window in my bedroom, pull back the curtains, and watch as the red lights reflected off the tops of the trees down toward the highway. I would pray for the people who needed help. Ask God to watch over those who tended to them. To keep all those in need alive.

In Iraq, the sirens were the same, the lights the same, but the ambulances different. The Humvees barreled down the main drag of Camp Liberty during the night, sirens blaring loud enough so that you couldn't hear the soldier dying in the back. I would run out to the road every time, watch the Humvee bear down on the road, tires screeching around corners to the CASH, the lights flickering red and white in circles, pinging reflections of the dying onto the barriers, trucks, and buildings. I would pray for the soldier inside. Ask God to make it a quick death. I would pray that the doctors do what they could to make the soldier comfortable, that the chaplain would hear the siren too and make it in time for last rites. But I never prayed for survival; it was a fate worse than death.

• • •

I was walking the floor with Zachary tucked neatly into the crevices of my arms. His eyes were slowly fading down to sleep. My heartbeat comforted his fragile body. His eyes finally closed, and it was then that I watched him sleeping and envisioned him much older, around my age, standing next to me, asking me about the war. I imagine that after all these years, I cannot bring myself to answer the question in full honesty. I tell him instead about the Jericho rose, the resurrection flower. I tell him that the desert flower survives by lying dormant, curled up in a state of limbo for many years before opening up and turning green once again. That in the desert, if there is no water, the rose will tumble for miles, picked up by the wind until it is placed near a water source. When it opens, in the middle, a small lilac-colored rose blooms, a rare desert flower that I found once while walking in Iraq.

• • • • • •

## Legacy

I sat on the back porch next to Grandpa. He was on his second drink. I was finishing my first. And even though the children were only a few months old and I was still trying to breastfeed, I brought the Johnny Walker to my mouth once more, considered the scotch, the ice cubes, and the three-drink rule. I looked

In shaa Allah

out over the canyon wall toward the VA hospital that loomed in the distance of Mission Valley and thought of another Iraq veteran bringing whiskey, or rum, or vodka to their mouth. They do so to drown the pain, the pills, or maybe the memories of the soldier who once stood next to them. And after the drink is done, they walk away from the bar and wander down the street, stepping out onto the ledge of the bridge, letting gravity take away the weight of silence. And somewhere across the country, another is setting the glass in the kitchen sink, kissing his children and wife goodnight before he steps outside to the bitter cold night with his service revolver shaking in his hand and wraps his teeth around the cold steel, bearing down on whiskey lullabies. It is like this all over the country and in parts of the world that time has forgotten. England, Vietnam, Germany, Poland, Iraq, Sudan, Nigeria, Japan, and countless more. They take it all in.

And I sat there, clinked the ice cubes in my empty glass, and remembered. Three drinks. Three drinks to fall asleep.

Sometimes I was in the kitchen. Other times I was standing in the backyard. I was sleepwalking through my nightmares. I was sleepwalking through my life.

James stood next to me. Never touching me. He would call my name. Tell me I was here, but in my mind, I was somewhere in Iraq standing next to a blown-up vehicle. The bodies inside burned alive. There was no more backyard, no hedgerow to peer over, no silent house, and no freeway noise; there was only shrapnel, and dismembered bodies, a mission, a consistent line to toe that deepened moments of humanity into unfathomable despair. He leaned in close to my ear and said, "Let's go home." He knew where I was. He saw it in my eyes when he looked at me; the unfolded body bags on the ground, unzipped, and waiting for their occupants. He noticed the shaking of my hands, the impossibility of his statement, and yet I turned and walked into the house. And though I was still nursing, I took one of Nana's sedatives. Two, maybe three that night. Each night was different. I washed it down with Johnny Walker. Only one drink this night. I sat on the edge of the bed unable to forget. In a few moments, once the sedatives had kicked in, I would lie down, close my eyes, and though they were closed, I knew James would stay up watching me, watching for the jitters, the shakes, the moans that turned to screams, the sweat trickling down my brow that braced the pillow before the unforgotten memories broke the seams and busted open the insides. He would stay up and watch all of this because he knew in moments, I would be in front of a Stryker burned out and blown up and staring at a hatch where three bodies lay inside. He knew I would be covered in char and flesh, that my hands would stain blood into my cuticles, creasing it into the cracks. He knew that the stench of iron would fill my nostrils, push me past the point of gagging, that I would not keep the contents of my stomach down. He knew that I would feel the brush of bullets ricocheting off buildings, feel around bits of bodies lying scattered on the bottom edges of Humvees as I looked for dog tags, treaded gently around pools of blood baked and soured brown by heat, that Iraq would be inside me again, if only in my sleep.

• • •

When the soldiers came home from Vietnam, there were no parades, no clapping, no thank-yous or handshakes. There was no reintegration. No pills. No VA forms to fill out.

There was booze. A rattling of the brain. The violent, jostled thoughts that synced together in waves of remembering. There was a truth to their submission, their reason for surrender. There was hostility, and shame breathed embers into raging fires that seared down on their souls. When they walked the streets, they saw their victims' faces in the reflections of windows, buses, and street shops. They saw their comrades, they saw the Viet Cong, the women raped and murdered, the children holding guns, and the distant glow of jungles burned black by napalm. They felt the heat on their tongues when they tried to speak of it to anyone who would listen. But the words were harsh, unflinching, the confessions of fear and repercussions. They felt the stares of a country that despised their existence, their questions made out like blame. Why did you go to war? Others at home asked where their sense of morality went, their ability to keep living with the atrocities, but the soldiers see only one-sided conversation that heaped guilt on like a military-issue woolen blanket, scratching at their words as though it were held tight against their mouth. They burned their brains full of answers unspoken, but still America demanded to know. And the vets, they stayed silent because the present was hard enough without having to look back and question their actions, beliefs, and their cause for suffering.

When their silence became intolerable, when America pressed them even further for an answer, and when they could not produce a single syllable when asked, they stared blankly into their eyes as though they were children looking into the sun wondering why it burns the eyes to see. I am nothing, they would say. I am the fault of my government, my father. I am plagued with nothing but lies. I did what I was told. I did what you would've done. I am here standing when the dust settled, even though I am not living.

And when America asked them to come back, to care, to be a part of society again, they said, "Someday I will be back from the dead."

. . . . . . . . . . . . . . . . . . . . . . .

## Breathe through Your Mouth (#2)

I was in Florida now, standing in my own home. I had been married to James for two years. The boys were almost three. I was a junior at Saint Leo University. I was studying literature. The nightmares had spilled over into my waking life.

"Brooke, you awake?"

I turned and looked at my husband, who had just walked into our bedroom. He walked over to his side of our king-size bed, plugged his iPhone into the charger on the wall, and turned to face me.

"I took the trash out and checked on the boys; they're sound asleep."

Sitting there in bed, I must have looked off because James gave me a look of concern. His cobalt blue eyes stared inquisitively at me, as if to judge the extent of how concerned he should be. I narrowed my eyes and furrowed my brow in order to keep from crying.

"What's that look for?"

I frowned. "What look?"

Insistent that there was something wrong, he said, "That look you just gave me. You okay?"

Hesitant about telling him what had just happened, I said, "I'm fine. What about the boys?"

"No, you look like you're about to cry. What's going on?"

I thought to myself, *Why did I have to marry the one guy who actually gives a shit?*

When James got back from Iraq, he didn't have PTSD or anything resembling it. He had been an ordnance officer, and while he did go out the gate a lot during his first deployment, in 2004, his last deployment had been a desk job. Though we had shared a deployment together in the same battalion, living only five hooches away from each other, we did not share the same experience. Yet, even though he supported me through the tough times during our deployment, bringing me dinner and spending nights in his hooch holding me after a hard day, his hardest challenge was helping me now. There had been times in the beginning when he first came to California that I woke up hyperventilating from a nightmare and wished that he could have shared my pain, but I know now that I would not wish this struggle on anyone else. To have done so would have been to witness two trains heading toward each other on the same track, a wreck on a wreck. I could not imagine a family where both parents have PTSD. For our family it would have been like living in a house where no one survived. The children would have been collateral damage to the horrific pain of a marriage forced apart by war and words unspoken.

"I had a nightmare."

With one eyebrow raised, he questioned me: "I thought

those stopped a while after the boys were born. How long has it been since your last one?"

"A couple of months."

"A couple of months? How come you didn't tell me?"

"Would you have listened? Besides, they haven't been bad enough that I've needed to talk, and to be honest, I'm not really sure why I just had one."

"You gonna be okay?"

"Yeah," I said, as I thought about how different this nightmare was from the rest. It had been more emotional, like so many others lately. Yet it felt more real than the other nightmares I'd had in the past few years. Struggling with what the change meant, I decided it was time to tell James that the nightmares had changed.

"This one was different. It was less graphic, less scary in a way."

"Hmm . . . maybe that means you're getting better."

"I don't know, it could've just been a fluke."

"So you're sure you're okay?"

"Yeah, I'll be fine."

James had processed out of the army in Germany and had come to California for the boys' birth, but I had made Nana and Grandpa promise not to tell him about what was going on with me at the time because I just wanted him to focus on the babies. They had kept their promise because it wasn't until after the boys were six months old and we had already moved to Florida to be closer to his family that I woke up one night screaming. He had found out about my nightmares in the worst possible way. After some very long conversations and several futile attempts by James to make me go to the VA, we made it a point to avoid the words that should be spoken about my nightmares. We thought of them as my silently understood struggles that most of the time I blocked out as if they didn't exist. It was just as well, because I never really wanted to talk about them and he never really wanted to listen—a match made in denial heaven. Most of the time I didn't tell James because he had a habit of ruining moments, moments where we could connect as a normal couple, but James and I weren't a normal couple. We never talked about politics or war; instead we exchanged stories and laughed at how ridiculous our day had been, and somehow by laughing our lives away, it kept both of us from crying about the pain.

Instead of James's usual goofiness that he used to ease the tension, he divvied out an asshole remark as he walked toward the bathroom, "You're not gonna start crying when I leave the room are you?"

"No, jackass, I'm not, but if you don't leave," I said, picking up a nearby decorative pillow on the bed, "I'm gonna throw this at you."

"So, I can go take a shower?"

I threw the pillow at him. Catching it, he jumped onto the bed, wrestled with me, and then paused to kiss me before he crawled off the bed and walked into the bathroom, leaving the door cracked slightly. Over the years, James had learned how to tell when I needed him and when I just needed to be left alone. Most of the time, though, I had to give him some sort of an emotional cue to let him know I needed him, but tonight he could tell that I just wanted to be left alone.

After the boys were born in November 2007, the nightmares had become less severe and less frequent. I had come to the conclusion that it was my pregnancy that had heightened their severity, but even now they were still happening. Yet, they had changed slightly. Instead of them being morbidly graphic, like a battle scene from *Saving Private Ryan*, they had become emotionally jarring. Yet, I had changed too. I had become a more emotional creature because I was a mother, but the added stress of being a full-time student in my junior year at Saint Leo University and a part-time worker made the emotionally charged nightmares just as gruesome and painful. The stress of all my obligations left me stretched thin and worn out again, and it seemed that as my stress level went up, the nightmares became more prevalent, but sometimes I also had flashbacks that came without warning and were triggered by my daily life.

A month prior to the nightmare I had in my bedroom, I had

just come home from picking up the boys from daycare and from a long, exhausting day at school. The end-of-the-day ritual began with the boys unpacking their backpacks and tossing their shoes off, letting each one remain wherever it had landed. In the kitchen I had started dinner, frying potatoes in a skillet. The sizzle of the bacon grease hissed in the pan and wafted the smell into the air.

My kitchen was small and modest, befitting the house James had secretly bought for me as a peace offering for dragging me from my family in California to his family in Florida. After we moved in, I made the house my own but could never get over the vaulted ceilings in the kitchen and living room that made the house echo like a cave, vast and deep. The living room was more like a great room, which I nicknamed my "lovely room of death" because it was where James hung the mounted kills from his hunting excursions. In the living room a large wood entertainment center housed the flat-screen plasma TV that the boys flipped on every day when they came home from daycare.

That day in the kitchen when I heard loud suppressive gunfire coming from the living room, I instinctively slammed my body to the floor. Sprawled in a low prone position on the wood floor, my heart thumped hard, like a loud drumming in my chest. As I crawled to my feet and walked toward the living room, a swell of anxiety rose in my body and quickened my pulse. I had hit the floor with my black plastic spatula in hand and still had a death grip on it when I walked around the corner past the fridge and into the living room, where my three-year-olds were inadvertently watching the movie *Iron Man*. I hastily snatched the remote from the coffee table with my free hand and turned the channel to Nick Jr. Doing an about-face, I whipped around and walked back into the kitchen. I could hear my kids complaining about how I had changed the channel away from the superhero movie, but I tuned it out.

Returning to my place at the stove, I gave in to the overwhelming sensation of sadness that swelled inside me. The stress of the day coupled with a flashback of being in Iraq brought tears welling in the corners of my eyes. Setting the spatula down, I gripped the rounded edges of the stove, bent over at the waist, closed my eyes, and pointed my head at the floor. The swell of sadness crept over me like a hot flash flare that had ignited in a burst of unbridled burning. Unable to control the feeling any longer, I began to sob, muffling the sound of my weeping with my hands over my mouth. One after another, each tear came rolling down my cheek and plummeting to the floor below like a steady-dripping faucet. Overwhelmed with a deep misery, I stepped back and fell into a corner of the kitchen, butting my body in between the sink and the pots and pans cabinet. I tucked my knees to my chest, folded my arms, buried my head in the voided space between, and cried uncontrollably.

From inside the kitchen I could hear the echoing argument of the boys as they fought in the living room over who got to sit on which couch. Realizing that the fight was not going to stop and that being a mother right now outweighed my own despair, I raised my head, wiped the tears from my face, and used the countertop to stand up.

"Boys, stop fighting," I said, letting my shaky voice reverberate off the ceiling. "Don't make me come in there . . ."

The fighting continued in the living room while I tried to wipe away my tears and snot with my hands, rubbing each swipe from my face onto my denim jeans. I tried to compose myself but found that the only thing I could do was cry. A relentless stream of tears rolled down my cheeks and dripped onto my embroidered white blouse. The screaming from the living room had become louder, but I was powerless as a mother to do anything but cry in the kitchen. I could hear Bowen, my oldest twin boy, screaming for me.

"Mommy! Mommy! Mommy!"

I could not move. It felt as though if I took a step, the floor would swallow me whole. Bowen's screaming got closer and closer to the kitchen. In panic, I tried to compose myself, but before I could wipe away the tears he had reached where I stood.

"Mommy, I'm hungry and Zachary won't stop kicking me. He keeps . . . he keeps kicking me off the couch, Mommy."

I stood there, wrecked with sadness as tears ran down my face. Bowen stood in front of me, begging me to be his mother, but I could not even function as me, let alone as a parent. I turned from him, so that I could wipe the rest of the tears off my face and collect myself.

"Mommy . . . Mommy . . . Mommy . . . Mommy, I'm hungry . . . Mommy, I want a snack."

Bowen's shouting coupled with the flashback made the sadness turn into rage, a compound feeling of fullness in my chest. The sensation flooded every emotion out of my body like a tsunami wave, inflicting it upon the closest thing to me, my son. I spun around and quickly grabbed Bowen by his shoulders. Shaking him violently, I shoved my face three inches from his and in a half-shouted scream said, "Get the fuck out of the kitchen!"

I crumpled to my knees, surrendering to my moment of emotional deterioration and broken failure as a mother. It was Bowen's first step into my world of suffering. Frightened for what I might have seen, I hesitated to look up at my child from my shattered expression of grief on the floor. Bowen's face was glazed over with a mixed look of terror and surprise, as if he had truly seen my nightmares. His lips quivered as he started to cry. Tears welled up in the corner of his deep blue eyes, spilling the salty tears over onto his cheeks. Taken aback by what I had just done to my own child, I covered my mouth, stood up, and stepped back from Bowen. Remorse and regret swelled in my heart, supplanting my sadness and pain. He stood there in the middle of the kitchen crying.

In an attempt to soothe him, I stretched out my arm and moved forward to hold him. He stepped back from me and pulled his hands to his face, trying to shield himself from me like a wounded animal sheltering itself from a vicious predator. I put my hands over my mouth again to cover up the shock and dismay on my face. Sobbing and breathing through my hands, I watched as my own child cowered away from me, recoiling backward into the wall behind him. Paused in that moment, transfixed on his frightened face, I thought, "I'm a monster."

I wiped the tears from my eyes, knelt on the floor, stretched out my arms again, and pleaded, "Bowen . . . please, baby . . . I'm sorry. Mommy didn't mean to yell at you like that. . . . Come here, please."

Bowen hesitated for a couple of seconds, then slowly lowered his hands from his face, and walked cautiously into my outstretched arms. As his tiny frame wrapped around mine, I held him in my arms warmly and gently, as though it was the first time he had ever been hurt. "I'm sorry, baby," was all I could say, over and over again into his ear as I held him to my chest. I pulled him back and, staring straight into his eyes, I said, "I love you so much, honey. You know I love you, right?"

"You scared me, Mommy."

"I know, honey, and I'm sorry."

I wiped the tears off his cheeks, brushed his shaggy blond hair from his forehead, and cupped his face with my hands. "Now, what did you come in here to ask me?"

"I'm hungry, Mommy."

"Dinner's in an hour, honey."

He gave me a look of disenchantment that drowned me in a downpour of mother's guilt. Out of shame for what I had done, I gave in to him. Getting up from my kneeling position on the floor, I said, "Okay, you can have a small snack." I pointed to the pantry and said, "Go ahead and go find something."

As I stood there and watched him slide open the white pantry door and stare up at the tiered shelves full of food, I wiped my own tears from my face and collected myself enough to walk over and help him grab the goldfish crackers off the third shelf. I opened up the box, filled a bowl for him, and watched as he walked out of the kitchen as if nothing had happened. As we walked into the living room, it was hard to tell if Bowen had imprinted that moment into his memory, but somehow I knew that he had. As I stood at the stove again, looking down at the burning potatoes in the skillet, I tried to make sense of what had just happened. I picked up the spatula and flipped the potatoes over, but the only thing I could think of was my own self-reproach.

The guilt of that day weighed heavy in my mind, even a month later as I sat there in bed wondering if I should double-check the boys while James was in the bathroom, but the sound of the water turning on in the bathroom quickened my pulse and made me think back to the nightmare, to the sound of the shower water running in the stall. I decided that the nightmare was still too fresh in my mind and that I was in no condition to deal with my kids. I leaned back on the decorative pillows behind me and pushed back the tears that were starting to form in the corners of my hazel-brown eyes. Trying to keep my composure, I told James the good news of the day: "I got a B-plus on my Early Brit Lit paper."

From inside the bathroom, trying to shout over the sound of running water, he said, "That's great, honey . . . proud of you." He swung wide the bathroom door, sauntered out in his boxer briefs, stood in the middle in of the doorway, and said, "You wanna take a shower with me?"

"The last time you said that to me, we ended up with twins. Can we please just chill out on the baby-making factory for a while before you try to double-stuff me like an Oreo again?"

We both laughed a little at our luck when it came to having kids, but after the moment passed, James walked back into the bathroom and started the shower. A twinge of pain grasped at my heart as I heard the shower. I looked down at my hands, turning them over and over again, noticing that there really wasn't much to notice about them anymore. They were my hands, the hands of a mother and a wife.

Papers from the study packet for the junior-level oral exams were sprawled out over the bed next to various books on famous dead white guys. I must have fallen asleep while studying. I stacked the books and papers into a neat pile and set them on my nightstand. After throwing the decorative pillows off my side of the bed, I peeled back the sand-colored comforter and wafted the lavender smell of softener from the sheets. I curled up in the indentation on my side of the bed, closed my eyes, and began to let the haphazard memory of my deployment fade from my mind, but before I could doze off to sleep again I heard Zachary's voice: "Mommy."

Opening my eyes, I peered at the cracked bedroom door. There stood Zachary with tears in his eyes.

"What's the matter, baby? Why are you crying?"

Sobbing and walking toward me, he said, "I had a bad dream."

As Zachary climbed up onto the bed and under the covers next to me, I sat up and stretched out my arms so that he could snuggle into them as if he were a newborn baby. Comforting him with my warmed embrace, I thought to myself, "Like mother, like son." He started to cry again, shutting his eyes up tightly. I couldn't help but be moved by the visible pain on his face and the pain I felt inside from my own nightmare. As salty tears started to form in the corner of my eyes, I held him closer to my chest, kissed his forehead, and began to rock him slowly back and forth as I softly said, "It was just a dream, it never hap . . . you'll be okay. You'll be okay."

You'll be okay.

The words hit the back of my throat, tore down my esophagus, and shredded my stomach as I spoke them. I remember the context and the time; they were words that I said to myself in the mirror as I got ready for another day. They ate at me, melting away the sun-weathered skin around my eyes, the crow's feet lines stretched thin and crisp. The words scraped off the tan from the hours, days, months spent in the sun. They rubbed down the brown in my irises until the green returned. They took turns circling patterns of skin, malleable to the touch, forming and shaping it into a younger version of myself. The mold was worn, beaten, and bent in at the edges, but it was still usable. I resurrected myself every day with the words, bearing my body down deep into the casting, moving my limbs farther until the flesh was pressing up against the rims perfectly. The words trimmed away the excess, which must be put aside and saved for next day when the words must strip away the war and make me new again.

· · · · · · · · · · ·
## Suicide Watch

James was in Puerto Rico—a bachelor party. I was home with the boys; they were five.

At first I didn't know what to make of the feeling in my chest—the hardening of my heart, the cracking of my mind—but I couldn't stop the feeling. I couldn't stop the pain, and so I went to the safe, pulled out the 9mm pistol, and wrapped my mouth around the steel.

My hand was shaking. The boys were pounding on the door of our bedroom, but I switched the safety off. I knelt on the floor. There was no coming back from this, but the war inside this bedroom was loud and hateful, and full of shame. The boys called me, but my hand did not stop shaking. I pulled the pistol from my mouth, told them I would be right there, and rested the front sight of the pistol on my forehead. I heard them run into the living room as I called James on the phone. I called and called and called, but I got no answer. The phone, his voice, it was a lifeline that I would have gladly gripped instead of this string of death my hand was wrapped around now. He did not pick up. He did not answer, and it was then that I knew I could not leave without hearing his voice. The voicemail was not enough. I left desperate messages, begged him to call me. I told him I was worried, that I needed to talk to him, that there was something wrong, but I did not get a reply phone call, and soon the ringing on the other end was going straight to voicemail. I was beginning to lose my determination to hold out for his call. I could not control the tears, the pain, or my willingness to pull the fucking trigger, and when I went to put the pistol in my mouth again, the phone rang. It was him. I remembered having a mixture of relief and pain when he answered with an unsteady hello. The conversation was concern muffled with the grogginess of a man who was half drunk, half high, and in need of sleep, but I was on the other end begging for him to listen, and he had to explain to everyone in his hotel room as his hand muffled phone that I was crazy, that I was this way because of the war, that he had to take the call and would be down at the bar as soon as he got my crazy ass to calm down. I heard the shuffling of feet and a door slam before he spoke. "What's up, Brooke?"

"I'm having problems."

He sighed, which I learned years later was his way of telling me he didn't give a fuck, that he would keep up the conversation, but that he had already turned off his give-a-fuck ears.

"What sort of problems?"

He listened intently, answered my questions, and tried to console me, and when I told him I had the pistol, that I had broken the lamp, as well as the blinds, and there was a hole in the wall, he asked me where the kids were and I told him they were fine.

"Bullshit, Brooke. I know you. Fine isn't in your vocabulary."

It was true. For all the "fine" that I was, I could hold a jumbo jet full of "fuck off" as well. "They're in the living room watching TV."

When he asked again, the tone was less sensitive. He warned me to put the gun back, to get my shit together, to stop this while he was gone, but I heard jumbled words as I focused on my static short inhales.

"This has to fucking stop, Brooke. Get your shit together or that's it."

At the sound of his threatening voice coming through the phone receiver, I started to cry.

"Or what? You'll leave me?"

"Fucking stop this or I'm hanging up."

"You hang up and I'll blow brains all over the wall."

"Fuck, that's it. You put that fucking gun back and get fucking help for this shit or I'm divorcing you."

"Go ahead. You never loved me anyway. This whole fucking marriage is a fucking lie."

"What the fuck are you talking about?"

"Your mom told me on our wedding day that the only reason why you were marrying me was because you knocked me up."

"That's not true."

"You never loved me and you never will."

"Come on, Brooke."

I sobbed uncontrollably; a sharp pain stabbed into my heart. I knew now what heartbreak felt like. I could hear it in his voice when he said my name. It was true. His mom had been right; he never loved me and this fragile marriage that we had was close to crumbling.

"Please stop this, Brooke. Put the gun away . . . is this what you really want? You want to leave me with these kids all by myself? You want to do that to our boys?"

I sobbed into the phone, the tears collecting down my chin, coagulating with the snot that oozed over my upper lip. I tried to compose myself.

"You need help, dammit, and there's nothing I can do from here. Can you at least put the gun away and when I get home, we'll talk. Can you do that for me?"

At the sound of the syllables bringing together the resonance of losing everything, knowing that there might be another way to get rid of the pain in my chest, the nightmares, and flash-backs, and all the sadness, I answered with a shaky and sob-bing *okay*.

He said he was going to go get dinner, that he would call me before he went to bed, and to go put the gun away. I switched the safety back on. The storm had subsided. James had talked me off the ledge, pulled the pistol away from my head. Still to this day I don't know why I pull back from the darkness, why I feel as though I must walk alone in this darkness, the never-ending circling of pain, fear, and the remembering of who I was when the world stopped at my feet and I truly felt for the first time. All the shame of pulling the trigger on my M4, the sorrow for the lives I took, the pain from the shrap-nel slicing into skin, the smell of the body's blood rotting in the cab as I walk toward the truck that is only in my dreams, the sadness I feel when I realize that those soldiers, the ones I put in the bags so many years ago, are all but buried some-where in the United States in a six-foot grave that only took two days to dig, but me, the lowly mother, the soldier, the person who feels the need to wrap my lips around steel, she feels the survivor's guilt, the shame of living instead of committing myself to the six-foot grave those many years ago in Iraq. And every time that feeling comes up after flashbacks or nightmares, triggers that spurt from anywhere my body roams, I push them back down into the locker full of hurt and shut it up tight, but lockers are also meant to be opened, and that urge to pull the trigger will come again, and next time there may be no stopping it.

$$\cdots$$

There were times when I was younger that the silence in my house on Underwood Street was punctuated by the aftermath of violence, booze binges, and attempted suicides stopped by my childhood voice begging my father to live.

I watched Dad walk around in circles in the kitchen, dangling a bottle of liquor in his hand, the masquerading dance of a man whose sanity was no better here in northern California than it had been in San Diego. The only thing that had changed was that he had traded heroin and cocaine for marijuana and booze. His stumbled dance of intoxication reminded me that this type of binging was better than that of a year ago in San Diego, where, instead of taking us for ice cream like he promised, he had taken John and me to a crack house and left us in the garage so he could go hit the vein and trace trails for hours. My ten-year-old self couldn't comprehend that this new situation, our life now, was Dad's recovery, that he was trying to get clean for us, and that the more sober he became, the more the pain of losing my mother to another man, his failures as a student in college, and the repercussions of youthful recklessness came flooding back, as well as the urge to kill himself. What I could comprehend was that I was far away from my grandparents, living in a house that smelled like mold with my dad barely able to keep a job and put food on the table, but I tolerated the surroundings, the booze-fueled binges, and the attempted suicides because Dad was getting clean of hard drugs and this small fishing town

In shaa Allah

of Trinidad, California, though beautiful and friendly, was his last-ditch effort.

He stumbled to the living room and looked through the sliding glass door. The rain was coming down sideways, slicing through your skin, shaving a man clean if he stepped into the wind just right. It was getting dark. We hadn't eaten dinner yet and probably wouldn't if I didn't attempt to make it myself. Dad had used the last bit of money to buy a bottle of whiskey. He leaned his head on the sliding glass door and stared out at the rain.

"It's really coming down."

I walked into the kitchen, looked in the cupboards. A can of refried beans. Some rice. Pasta. What was left over from the food bank line had been mostly consumed by week one of the tropical storm that had knocked out the power. The fridge wasn't to be opened or the milk would spoil, but my stomached growled, John whined, and Dad stood there drunk. At half past six I knew that I would have to make dinner, that Dad was not fit to be Dad, and that the fire had to be lit in the stove soon or we would freeze tonight, the house too cold to sleep in, our bodies jittering and shaking as we clung to one another while lying on the floor near the potbelly stove.

Outside I chunked the wood using Dad's ax that was too heavy for me to wield, but I did it as best I could. John picked up the pieces of kindling and logs and carried them inside, as I continued splitting a log with the wood wedge. Inside Dad continued to drink, lying on the couch, eyes half cast. When the cutting and splitting were done, I went in, stacked and layered the kindling, alternating wood with newspaper. I lit the fire with the lighter I found in Dad's pants pocket next to his crunched pack of Camel nonfilters. The fire was started in the potbelly stove, so I went to work pouring water into a pan and measuring the amount of rice needed. Behind me, I could hear John carrying on about hating rice, about wanting pizza, but he knew as well as I did that we couldn't afford pizza and that the only food we could ever afford was the free food that Dad went to get in between working his construction job and getting drunk or high. I groaned at his whining as I set the pot of water on the stove and watched the smoke rise up from under it, creep up the sides, and waft up into the air. Dad turned over, looked at me, smiled, and sat up.

"Making dinner?"

I nodded.

"What would I do without you?"

I wanted to say *die*, but I curbed my tongue. I told him I needed to open the fridge and get the milk.

He responded in a gurgled low tone, "Drink water."

With a drunken sway, he got up from the couch and walked outside. I walked to the window and watched as he pulled out his pack of smokes and pressed his pockets for his lighter. I turned to look at the stove. I had forgotten to put it back. From the opened front door, I heard his yelling.

"Where the fuck's my lighter?"

I walked over and handed it to him. He patted me on the head and shoved me back inside, shutting the door behind him.

I walked back over to the stove and watched the water boil. I had put the rice in and begun stirring it when John came out from our room and asked what Dad was doing. I looked out to see him stumbling down the street in the rain, falling every five feet onto the ground and struggling to get back up. John watched him as he made it past the church, down the hill, and to the stop sign. I stirred the rice. Dinner was more important. I was used to this. The drunkenness. The lonely stumbling walks of a man who is barely living. The sad disillusionment of his thoughts when they wander to our mother, how she had left him for another man, how it had driven him to drugs. I didn't have to look over and watch him wander down the street. I knew he turned the thoughts around in his head as he got back up from the pavement again, each fall making him more determined to get to the end of the street. I stirred the rice. John asked if Dad was okay. I looked down the street. He had made it past the lamppost and was almost to the stop sign. On most nights like this he stopped at the sign, looked back at the house, and turned around. Most nights. I took the

In shaa Allah

rice off the potbelly stove and placed it in the sink. I had started dumping the rice into a bowl when John yelled for me to look. Dad had wandered past the stop sign and into the adjoining street, the one next to the cliff. He was across the street and at the cliff's edge before I realized that he was not coming back. I yelled at John to stay put, to stay in the house, that I'd be right back, to start eating without me. I dropped the bowl of rice on the kitchen table and ran out the door into the rain.

The wind beat the rain against my face, slapping my hair like plaster across my eyes, but I kept running. Past the church. Past the field. Past the lamppost. Past the stop sign. Across the street. I ran until I caught Dad, his balance at the cliff too precarious. He had lost his courage. His will. His strength. It had been swallowed down his throat. I yelled at him to come home as I held onto the back of his tie-dyed shirt. He swatted at me. Told me to leave him alone. I held tighter, pulling back as best I could, but he only swatted harder.

"Go away, Brooke. Get out of here. Go back up to the house."

I yelled back at him that I wasn't leaving without him.

Behind me, I heard John yell to Dad. He asked what he was doing. I grabbed Dad by the arm and tried pulling him back from the cliff. The wind had shifted directions, moving up off the sides, pushing his body toward me and away from the edge. Dad slammed into me, knocking us both over. We toppled back, away from the grassy edge, past the curb, and into the street. The rain was coming down harder now, in fat droplets that banged against the tops of our heads as we lay prostrate on the pavement. I sat up and looked at Dad. He was staring at me. I couldn't tell if the water running down his face was tears or rain, but his face was upturned in a grimace, eyes squinted open enough for me to see the irises, his mouth open, exposing his yellow, tar-stained teeth. And though I knew what he was going to say, I stayed his speech, grabbing his shirt as I tried to raise him off the ground. I turned to John, told him to get out of the street, to go back up to the house, that we would follow in a minute. John whined about not wanting to leave, but I yelled for him to go, and so he left, trudging with sopping shoes up the hill toward the house. I helped Dad to his feet with an uneasiness that worsened when the wind lifted up from the cliff and swirled around us. It knocked us to the ground again. I turned to look and saw that John had barely made it halfway up the hill before he stopped and sought shelter at the steps of the church. Dad looked at him as well.

"We have to go. The storm's getting worse."

He nodded.

"The rice will be cold."

He nodded.

"Dad, now."

He looked out at the ocean beyond the cliff. "Brooke, look."

The swells had risen higher since this morning. Now the waves crested over the fifty-foot rock in the harbor. Boats anchored down now drifted out to sea. The lights on the tops blinking in the chaos of the rain until finally the current swept the fishing boats under, dragging them to the depths of the black unknown. I prayed no sailors were on the boats, but I knew that most of them lived in town and were no doubt standing on their porches watching their livelihood being taken under by the storm, the harsh life of a seaman taking its toll on their mind as the waves crest again, smashing the debris up against the outer rock formations of the harbor. The lighthouse's beacon cast out horizontally with the wind, marking land to those who did not make it to shore before the storm broke suddenly on Monday. Dad and I watched from the cliff as the sky gave no measure of hope.

"Dad, you can't go yet."

I had shouted it before thinking, but it made as much sense now as it did then. Dad looked at me.

"You can't go until John is taken care of."

"That's why you're here."

"I can't, Dad. I'm just a kid."

I shouted through the rain and wind my plea for him to keep living, so I could be a kid, have a childhood, but his response was always the same each time we came to this point, each time I brought him back from killing himself. He would smile at me, tell me he loved me, that I had an old soul and a good heart that cared for everyone I met, that he was proud of me, even though I knew I hadn't accomplished anything yet, that I should take care of John because he couldn't anymore. And each time we got to this point, I would begin to cry, tell him that I could not do it alone, that I'm just a girl, I'm not an adult.

That day on the cliff, Dad looked at me, said nothing, and nodded his head when I said that I was just a kid. Instead of arguing his willingness to die, he got up from the cliff. We walked past the stop sign, past the streetlight, found John hunkered down at the church, and as a family, we walked into the house on Underwood Street and ate lukewarm rice.

That day at the cliff is the last memory I have of saving my dad from committing suicide, and I wonder now whether or not my children will remember any of my attempts, whether they will know how many times they stepped into my childhood shoes and saved me from the same failed fate as my father. And just maybe, one day, they will pull me back from the cliff and it will be the last time I try to step off into the darkness alone.

· · · · · · · · ·

## Diagnosis

"I think I'm crazy."

The VA psychologist looked at me. "Define crazy."

"Like, bat-shit crazy."

She pulled away from her notepad. Told me to be more specific. Buried her head back into the yellow pad in front of her.

So, I told her.

The kind of crazy that dreads Fourth of July, New Year's Eve, and Memorial Day. The kind of crazy that avoids military funerals. The kind of crazy that hits the dirt at the sound of loud noises. The kind of crazy that runs outside to check every helicopter or plane that flies over the house. The kind of crazy that carries two knives in her purse. The kind of crazy that backs the car a ways down the driveway and looks underneath it, just in case. The kind of crazy that checks the locks and secures doors over and over again every night. The kind of crazy that downs a bottle of wine or a half bottle of scotch just to fall asleep. The kind of crazy that has nightmares about dead bodies that rip your flesh and drag you to hell. The kind of crazy that screams violently while sleeping. The kind of crazy that wakes up in the middle of the night drenched in sweat. The kind of crazy that gets up every morning and reaches for an invisible rifle. The kind of crazy that still has a full kit of TA-50 loaded to the teeth with ammo. The kind of crazy that shouldn't have married a soldier. The kind of crazy that uses her kids as a distraction from the truth.

She stopped writing notes on her pad of paper and looked at me with a stare that let me know that now she was listening.

So, I continued.

The kind of crazy I am forces me to live a life in secret agony. The kind of crazy I am leaves me weak and burdened. The kind of crazy I am shouldn't have come back from Iraq. The kind of crazy I am should have died right the first time from a mortar round. My kind of crazy only has one outcome, and I can tell you, lady, it ain't living.

I leaned back in my chair. "Write that shit in your notebook."

• • •

I was sitting in the chair across the desk from my new shrink. She was looking at me, saying nothing, just looking.

"I'm not sure what I'm doing here."

I started to peel away the cuticle skin from the inside of my thumb with my index finger, a nervous tic.

"Why do you think you are here?"

"I don't know—because my husband and that other doc think I'm crazy."

"Are you crazy?"

I shrugged my shoulders and mumbled an unintelligible, "I dunno, but if I don't fix whatever's wrong with me, my husband says he'll divorce me."

"Do you know what PTSD is?"

"Yeah. It's that thing soldiers get when they see too much shit. Shell shock."

"Do you think you have it?"

"No."

She turned around, walked to her bookshelf, and pulled out a book. The cover read *Diagnostic and Statistical Manual of Mental Disorders, Fourth Edition*. She sat back down, opened the book, searching for the right page. She found it and put her finger on one of the pages, tapping it in place.

"What's that?"

"It's the definition of PTSD."

She continued to tap her finger on the page.

"And?"

"It's funny."

"What is?"

"Your name's not under the definition and neither is the word *crazy*. You must not have PTSD."

"This bullshit psychotherapy thing you're doing. It's not working, so cut the cute shit."

She smiled.

"Okay. Fair enough. You want to hear the definition of PTSD?"

"Sure, why the fuck not."

So she began to read.

"The person has been exposed to a traumatic event in which both of the following have been present: The person experienced, witnessed, or was confronted with an event or events that involved actual or threatened death or serious injury, or a threat to the physical integrity of self or others. The person's response involved intense fear, helplessness, or horror."

I began to fidget in my chair, crossing and uncrossing my legs. I thought back to Iraq, my first mission, the bodies, the shredded metal, and all the fucking blood.

"The traumatic event is persistently reexperienced in one (or more) of the following ways: recurrent and intrusive distressing recollections of the event, including images, thoughts, or perceptions."

I thought of driving over the overpass near my house, down

the highway to school, or to the park with the kids, looking at every pile of trash and debris on the side of the road, every culvert pipe and crack in the road, every person walking by on the path, uneven ground, roadkill, the heaviness in my chest when I was in traffic and I could not find an alternate route out of the cluster fuck that was rush-hour traffic.

"Recurrent distressing dreams of the event. Acting or feeling as if the traumatic event were recurring (includes a sense of reliving the experience, illusions, hallucinations, and dissociative flashback episodes, including those that occur upon awakening or when intoxicated)."

I thought about how many times I had awakened every night for the past four years wondering why it was that I couldn't dream of anything else but Iraq. I thought about how James was ashamed to take me to parties because he knew I would drink to forget that I was surrounded by people, then be too drunk, and begin thinking about Iraq, begin crying or get angry, and then eventually, he knew, I would lose my shit completely. I thought about how he regretted taking me because of the apologies he had to make for me, my inability to function because of my hangover in the morning, and the fact that his wife was crazy. I lowered my head onto the desk, pressing my forehead up against the laminated wood surface.

My shrink stopped talking.

I looked up, but when my eyes meet hers, the pain in my chest came and I could not control the tear that fell down my cheek.

She grabbed the tissue box, pushed it toward me, and continued to read.

"Intense psychological distress at exposure to internal or external cues that symbolize or resemble an aspect of the traumatic event. Physiological reactivity on exposure to internal or external cues that symbolize or resemble an aspect of the traumatic event."

I thought about the times I had been riding my bike in the hills and come across roadkill—the bloated body of the animal swollen at the stomach, waiting to be poked open by buz-

In shaa Allah

zards, picked apart, and devoured until there is nothing left but bones. I thought about how many times the body cavity was opened, the smell of death lingering in the air, how many times I had to hold my breath, try not to look at the body, close my eyes to avoid thinking about body bags, the smell of souring blood, and the pieces of soldiers that used to spatter the roadways instead.

The tears were uncontrollable and fell with more persistence. I could not silence the sobbing that came when she began to read my life on the pages as though she had been there with me each time the memories, dreams, and triggers smashed the locker open, spilling the hurt onto my head and down my body.

"Persistent avoidance of stimuli associated with the trauma and numbing of general responsiveness (not present before the trauma). Efforts to avoid thoughts, feelings, or conversations associated with the trauma. Efforts to avoid activities, places, or people that arouse recollections of the trauma. Inability to recall an important aspect of the trauma."

I thought about the missed July Fourths, concerts, bars, lazy beach days, and movie theaters. I thought about how many conversations I stopped from happening, how I pushed away everyone who wanted to talk to me. And now, I could not stop the tears or the pain in my chest, and it was then that I raised my head from my the desk and looked at my shrink, as if I was silently begging her to stop, but she continued.

"Persistent symptoms of increased arousal (not present before the trauma)."

I buried my head back down, pressing it against my knees.

"Difficulty falling or staying asleep. Irritability or outbursts of anger. Difficulty concentrating. Hypervigilance. Exaggerated startle response."

I could not take it anymore.

"Stop."

She closes the book gently and looks at me.

I was a pile of flesh with a leaky faucet. My fingers were searching through my hair for a comforting place to rest, but the pent-up memories, and feelings, and years of forgetting stretch past them, pulling each fingertip off my head, forcing me to look up.

I looked at her.

She half smiled.

I pulled a bunch of tissues out of the box and wiped away the snot and tears that were drawing streaks of translucent phlegm down my face.

"I think I have PTSD."

She nodded.

"Your brain's broken, but the good news is, your brain can heal and so can you."

"So you can fix me?"

"PTSD is a disorder, not a disease."

I threw a handful of tissues in the trash can and pulled a few more from the box, holding them in my hand, scrunching them into a ball.

"So how are you going to fix me, Doc?"

"I'm going to elect that you go through CPT."

All this shit was new to me, so I was confused at the terminology already, and soon I looked at her as though I was a blind man in a strip joint with an outstretched hand waiting to be led, instead of being shown the way.

"Cognitive processing therapy. We are going to have you relive, in your mind, the traumatic events again from your deployment and see if we can't reprogram your brain to process them differently."

"Sounds painful."

"The pain is part of the healing process, but I know you can do it."

"This is going to fucking suck, isn't it?"

"Yep."

She handed me my first assignment.

"I want you to write down every trigger you've ever had. Then, I want you to start writing the traumatic event down. Take your time. Don't try to do it all in one day. You're a writer, so I know you know how to take your time writing a story.

Think of this as a story. Let the words come when they can. Don't force it out. Then, next week, we'll sit down and you can read me what you wrote."

"I have to do this on my own."

"Yes. It's your version of the events as you see them. Try to focus on the most traumatic one first."

"So the Stryker?"

"Yes. That would be a good one to start with."

I grabbed the worksheet packet and stood up to leave, but I stopped at the door before she stood up and came to the door to walk me out to the waiting room.

"So, I'm not crazy?"

"No, not crazy—just human."

· · · · · · · · ·

## Treatment

In my dreams the war looked like blurred faces, burned piles of trash and debris, and body bags laid out longer than I stood tall, but the glint of the mirrors still reflected the sun into my eyes the same, making the war a sum total of things felt rather than instances remembered years later. And while sitting in the waiting room of the VA PTSD clinic a week later, I looked nervously at the door that kept opening and shutting, the disheveled veterans who sat waiting too, all of them much older and grayer than I, their war much longer fought than the one I was fighting, but I stared at the door instead, waiting for my psychologist to produce herself, call my name, and usher me back to a room that was cold and bare except for a desk, a few chairs, and her diplomas masquerading as confidence hanging on the walls. But as every veteran was called, shuffled in, and produced back out the door more unevenly keeled than before, I began to realize that war, at its simplest, was a machine without feeling, that it was the people involved who gave it meaning, who brought hope and fear together like the frayed split ends of a paintbrush smoothed clean when dipped gently and rolled into a glob of saffron red acrylic paint.

I watched a Korean War vet in his motorized wheelchair roll past me, one of his tires half inflated, his legs frail, no muscle definition left, the skin around his eyes drooping, covering the look of unchanged disenchantment for his forgotten war, and I looked down at my worksheet. The letters on the page spelled out my fears in paragraph form, with comma splices, run-ons, and fragmented sentences smeared with ink from the countless times I touched the words and sentences, wondering if that was exactly how the body rested in the cab of the truck, if the teeth protruding from the mouth of the driver were slightly covered with his lips or if his upper lip was burned away, leaving only his teeth exposed, as though he were locked in a deathly scream. I read the words over again, wondering if I had gotten every detail right, if I had completed the assignment correctly. I did not write about the sound the blood made when it sloshed in the body bag. Or the taste of my half-eaten breakfast coming back up as I vomited next to the burned Stryker. Or the way the texture of torn flesh feels like a raw chicken breast with its wing still attached. The way it slimmed in your hand and slipped if you didn't sink your nails into the tougher part of the muscle. Or the way shrapnel rips through face tissue and skull as though it were shredding cheese off a new block, the pieces falling from it with more ease with every downward force. I did not write any of this. I read my worksheet out loud, my psychologist sitting there listening. When I was finished reading, I passed the worksheet to her on the desk. She picked it up and, without looking, ripped it into pieces and threw it into the trash. She opened her desk drawer, pulled out another worksheet, and pushed it across the desk.

"Now that you've written down what happened, write what really happened, but this time, don't treat it like it's something you have to regurgitate to someone in the army. What do you call those?"

"After action reports."

"Yes. Write this one as though you are trying to tell some-

In shaa Allah

one in your family what really happened that day, how you felt, what you saw, how it makes you feel now to think of it."

"I have to do this all over again?"

She nods her head.

"Fuck that. You know how hard it was to write that in the first place? I'm not doing it again."

"Do you want to heal or do you want to keep living the way you have been?"

I grabbed the worksheet off the desk. "Is that it?"

"Yep."

She stood, walked to the door, opened it, and ushered me back out to the waiting room, but before I walked away, she told me, "Remember, this time with feeling."

I mumbled under my breath, "Fuck your feeling bullshit."

Months passed, CPT was almost finished, and I felt as though I might have made some sort of progress. I started to write down what happened in Iraq, formed words together into what looked like poems, and shared them with some of my professors at Saint Leo University. They gave me encouraging words, told me to keep writing, that after graduation I should look into going to a master's program for creative writing, but I did not feel confident in the words or my remembering of Iraq, so I began to write it all down, so I did not forget, so that I remembered, so that a part of me, however small and insignificant, could learn to live again.

. . . . . . . . . . . . .

## Survivor's Guilt

I didn't know his name or even where he was from, but I watched the young Iraqi boy topple over the two-story building and hit the ground in front of my Humvee. Maybe I shot him. Maybe I didn't. Either way, I was there, and because I was there, because he had tried to kill me, I didn't care that he died, just that he was dead and I was not. Now I see my noncompliance with mourning, caring, or even remorse for his death as my admission of guilt. I didn't kill him. I didn't shoot, but I was there and that was proof enough of my guilt. I was present the moment he plummeted from the top of the building, and that was enough to imprint his death in my head, enough to make me remember him, even now.

So I wear a black bracelet on my right wrist that reads "Don't Fuck Up" in big bold capital letters. I look at it every time I think about Iraq. It reminds me that the war was boredom punctuated by violence and that, at any given moment, fucking up could lead to my death. I look at it now, and though I am no longer in a war zone, the bracelet still gleams the same meaning.

· · · · · · · · ·

## Mementos

At my desk I was flipping through pictures of Camp Liberty on Google, trying to find maps, locations, and areas where I was once stationed, when I came across a picture of a woman standing next to a burned-out Humvee. At first I did not recognize the area or even the route where the Humvee was hit. I clicked on the photo. On the right side of the computer screen the caption bar reads, "2006 IED attack. Three dead." I saved the photo. Opening it up in Photoshop, I enlarged it. Then I saw it. The pixilated face of the woman standing there was me. My memory came back. I looked at the photo and remembered.

The next day, I Facebook messaged my battle buddy Anderson, asked her if she had any photos of me in Iraq, or maybe just of Iraq. She sent me a reply.

"If you go to Facebook, I put a bunch up of our deployment. You're there."

I went to her page, looked through the photos, and found more than what I was looking for; I found the fifteen-year-old boy, my old gun truck, the base, friends, places that I thought I had left behind, and as easily as it was for me to open the webpage, I clicked on the X in the top right-hand corner of my computer screen.

I went back to Google. I searched through the photos again, looking for what Camp Liberty looks like now, and it was then that I found an aerial photo of the base. I stared at the photo, trying to visualize where the DFAC used to be, where my hooch was, the front gate, the clearing barrels, Mortuary Affairs, everything, but it was gone. The trees had disappeared; the place looked like a concrete wasteland, stripped of everything but the hooches that lined the camp like gravestones, marking where refugees now lived in deplorable conditions.

And in a sense I was looking on at a body postmortem with the lividity fixed and rigor mortis setting in, the limbs now stiff and crooked, unmovable. In a way it was unsettling and pleasing at the same time. The world making use of what was left behind, and yet the decomposition still forced a cringe when looked at too long. Years from now, when the violence of Iraq settles down, I may be able to venture back to this spot where my life once circled around in busy successions of simple tasks carried out day after day with no end in sight. For now, the camp looked as though it was in its final stages of death, the earth ready to bury the concrete blockades, buildings, and barbed wire under its heavy soil, to have this place forgotten, a picture placed on the internet that soldiers go to when they have lost the ability to recall where it was that the war took place, or maybe it will be in a textbook under the all-encompassing title "Iraq War" and perhaps then there will be a paragraph that accompanies it and speaks of the camp and how it was one of the major footholds in Baghdad during the war.

But then again, the war, this camp, it has a way of living on through the ages, as so many things do after they are forgotten. And like those that have been left and displaced through time, patience is their friend. The camp will wait through it all and be there again, if only for those who seek it out.

I stared at a screen that flickers flocculent light onto my face while I sat in a dark room in front of my computer and reimagine a place that time had made me forget. The photo, meanwhile, through no admission of its own, had dismantled the memory of the camp and the luster it once held.

# PART 7

Homeland

········· · · ·

## Eyes Cast Down

But maybe going home isn't as difficult as I thought. Maybe it is that the home isn't strong enough to hold back the war and everything that comes with it. Maybe it isn't where home is that matters but that I have brought the war home with me.

Iraq is in everything that I do, and it is this vast expanse of land that swirls up into a sandstorm and creeps into everything that I touch. Maybe this is what I must do—travel back to Iraq and leave for home again, except this time, leave Iraq, leave the war, leave PFC Brooke King behind and return home Brooke. Just Brooke.

• • •

At one point in my academic career, I tried to go to law school. I wanted to write, but I still felt a sense of civic duty. I still to this day do not know what possessed me to try my hand at the worst profession for a short-fused Iraq vet to dabble in, but I studied, took the LSAT, and got a decent passing score, one that would get me into a mid-tier law school with reasonable bar-passing rates, but sometime during the last semester of my undergrad I had a crisis. I didn't know what I wanted to do. It was mid-March, just before St. Patrick's Day, and my mom was driving me, Courtney, Ashley, John, and my stepdad, Fred, through South Lake Tahoe. I looked out the window and noticed a college. I thought how cool it would have been to go to school there. I had always wanted to be a writer but knew that with two kids it might not ever be possible. I guess I did law school to make something of myself or prove that I could do something else of worth. It didn't last. I found out that a poet I admired was opening up an MFA program, and I decided to go for it instead, to be a writer. I thought, *What was the worst that could happen?* I certainly couldn't die or be in a position to be threatened with death. I applied, got accepted, and went to get my MFA in creative writing.

My first residency in and I was doing fine. My PTSD was manageable, but my writing was attracting attention. No one had really seen a female vet try to write about Iraq, not in an MFA at least. Some said I was doing great. Others wondered why I was trying to write fiction when I should be writing nonfiction. Others let me be, let me write, and became drinking buddies, but something struck me. A professor kept asking me, bugging me, pushing me every time she asked it: Why was I writing fiction when clearly I had enough to write nonfiction? When I was attending the MFA, I bounced the question off my shoulders, avoiding it by simply saying I knew how to write nonfiction and that I wanted to learn something new, but the truth was that I was scared to write nonfiction. I hadn't processed enough of my deployment to handle writing it all down and sharing it with anyone. I confided in the director of the program, a vet and mentor of sorts, and he seemed to give me sound advice. Write where your heart takes you, and when you find that place, live in it until there is another place that seems worth going to next. So I wrote fiction, but as I began to write the story of a young female soldier, I started to realize that the soldier wasn't fictional; she was me, and the harder I tried to write away from myself, the closer I came to the truth until finally, when it came time to turn in my thesis and graduate, the story I had unfurled onto the page was almost completely true. But what was truth in the eyes of war? Was my somewhat semifictional account of a female soldier's struggle so different from mine? Or was I simply applying my demons to the page until I had the courage to write about myself? None of it made sense and all of it confused me, but the point I am trying to make is that it was okay that I didn't know at the time; I did later on and that was what made the story truthful and real even though it was nonfiction written in the guise of a novel. I had found out about my pain, unleashed it on the page, and realized for the first time in my life that it was okay to hurt while writing, that the best part of a story is when the writing leans into the pain on the page instead of leaning away. It didn't matter if I was writing fiction or nonfiction; writing was helping me deal with the war, gain perspective about what had happened to me, and broaden my sense of the world around me and the people I was affecting. In a sense, I was molting my war skin and becoming something entirely different. I was leaving behind Private King and becoming Brooke with every story I committed to my MFA thesis.

. . . . . . . . . . . . . . .

## Neurosis Therapy

My son told me a joke once.

Why did the RPG cross the road?

To hit the Humvee on the other side.

It was a harmless joke by my son. When pressed hard enough about where he'd heard it, he said he made it up, but why did it enrage me? Then make me sad? I realized he was right, that there was a truth to the punch line, a joke that could have easily come from my mouth or that of another soldier during deployment. I would've probably laughed at it, shaken my head, and passed it on, telling the next soldier I knew would laugh too. So why did it affect me so much now that I was out? Was it because I know now how a joke parodies reality? Surely it couldn't be that. The joke was as true today as it would've been almost a decade ago in Iraq. So why did it bother me? Had the war changed me that much? It must have been because the joke is no longer funny.

## The Professor

It was winter. I was at Lake Tahoe in my second MFA residency. The snow was falling down outside the window of my dorm room, but I was asleep. The quiet tribulation of each snowflake clinging to the glass because of heat radiating from inside seared the impact with warmth on its surface, liquefying its insides, forcing it down the windowpane in droplets of cascading water.

Across the campus, a girl was screaming in pain or ecstasy, no one knew, but she was screaming all the same. Her screams woke one of my professors from her sleep, made her bolt upright in bed, and the first thing she thought of was whether or not the screams were mine. She contemplated trying to find me as she listened to the screams intensifying. Soon she worked up the nerve to get out of her warm bed, slip her tennis shoes on, and roam the second- and third-floor hallways in her bathrobe, listening for the room where the screams were resonating. She did this thinking of me, remembering that I was a veteran, that I had PTSD, and that I had nightmares; my poetry had told her this much. Soon the screams subsided, the urge to look for me dying with them. She went back to her room frazzled, wondering still if she should go see if I was okay, if she could be of any comfort to me, but I was fast asleep. The dreams had been kept at bay that night. The next morning she came up to me at breakfast, asked if I was okay, and I looked at her, puzzled. She gripped me on the shoulder and, holding firmly, she recounted the previous night, told me about the screaming, how she thought it was me, and how frantic she was about whether or not she should come find me. I smiled at her as I drowned honey in a cup of Earl Grey and told her that I was okay, but it was a lie. I was not okay, and I knew very well that the girl screaming could've been me and might be me that very night.

## Walking with the Dead

In Galway, Ireland, the day of my MFA graduation, I stood in a graveyard looking at a bronze plaque. It read as follows:

> This Plaque . . . erected in memory of more than 300 sailors of the Spanish Armada who, having been washed ashore in 1588, were arrested by the English Authorities, brought to Galway and executed. The people of Galway who took pity on their plight laid them to rest in this graveyard.

> Ar dheis Dé go raibh a n-anamacha
> Que descansen en paz

For a long while I stared at the marker in Forthill Graveyard. I walked the unstable paved path of stepping stones that grass, roots, and flowers had overgrown; the years had taken away from the beauty of the stones that constituted the path. I looked for the sailors. Walked every inch trying to find them, but after an hour of searching without result, I left. For a while I wandered the streets of Galway looking for them. Past the Hall of the Red Earl. Past the King's Head Pub. Past endless side streets and through crowds of people meandering, carrying shopping bags filled with souvenirs. I wandered alone looking for them, the souls of those who were lost. I wandered into Charlie Byrne's Bookshop, skimmed the pages of countless war books looking for them. I ran my fingers over lines, words, pictures. I sat in a heap on the carpeted floor, creasing the pages of Joyce and Yeats. I searched in the bargain books, gently used paperbacks, and ceiling-high stacks. I ran into friends I now call family who asked what I was searching for, but when I replied the souls of the dead, only one of my friends, a vet as well as a poet, replied back as he left the bookstore that the souls of the dead are inside of us, not in books. Though I knew he was right, I told him that I needed proof. He handed me a book of poetry, *100 Years of War*. I told him that this was not the proof I needed. He smiled, told me to read it, to see what shakes loose. I bought the book, wandered out of the bookstore, bought a bottle of Jameson, and sat on a bench waiting for the sun to go down.

The words spilled over in my hands and fell down the pages in splashes of black that wrapped the thin paper with swaying forms of loss, pain, and suffering. I followed the lines until they stopped the pages from turning. In my drunkenness, I had found my answer. The dead were buried there in the cemetery. I had been walking along their path of eternal sleep.

The hillside blushed, soaked in our broken wave.

They buried us without shroud or coffin
And in August . . . the barley grew up out of our grave.

—SEAMUS HEANEY, *Requiem for the Croppies*

The next morning, I walked the streets with my head hung low. I knew where the dead loomed, where the ghosts of the past cast their shadows on the living, but as I passed High Street Gallery, Gordon Harris's *Battling Demons* stared out from the shop's window. The two warriors stood apart, clashing against metal, their swords and shields giving their due attention to the irrevocable calling toward victory. Blood dripped the metal clean of peace; the two men had brought their lives to the battlefield, breathing the odds of failure with every strike of the blade against their opponent. And as I looked on, the pane of glass separating our bout in history, I still understood the need to thrash the metal, wield it through the air, and bring it down upon the earth. I remembered the need to pit the dirt in tiny shells and break open the flesh like the strokes of bright vermilion red splattering outward from uneven stippling over the canvas, the brush swiveling upward, leaving the painting with bristle indentations carved out in the pigment and etched in the lines where the red hues splayed on the metal met the dark desert brown dirt. The war had done its work on the living, claiming the motions of fear in a single swipe of the sword.

And I remember now—the ghosts of the sailors wandered

the streets of Galway, some gathering down by the King's Head Pub, some dangling their legs over the seawall near the Spanish Arch, others laid supine in Eyre Square on the grass staring up at the sky, waiting for the stars to appear and break open the mystery of celestial navigation and the route home to Spain, where their loved ones lay fixed in white marble in orchards that bear nothing but bones.

I stood there outside of High Street Gallery, staring at the painting in the window that, in different light, reflected the bloody scene as abstract beauty. And while the three hundred dead wandered around me looking for peace, I wondered if people would pause momentarily on any given day to remember that year after year, the bones of the dead sink deeper into the earth, drifting farther away from the land of the living— breaking under the weight of soil until the marrow is stretched thin and turned into mineral and rock, burying itself back into the dirt, where all manner of life begins and ends.

· · · · · ·

## FUBAR

It had been five years, seven months, twenty-two days, and some odd hours since I had been at war. And the one thing I can recall with certainty was that my war was different than Vietnam or Desert Storm or, hell, even World War II. Every war was different, and yet, they were all the same. Just different places, faces, and enemies. We fought them all for different reasons. But for the Iraq vets, it was hard for us to pinpoint what it was we were fighting for, so we started to question why we were fighting. For some of us, we never stopped to question why we walked with the rifle; we just carried until we realized that we had walked with it for so many years that when the war was over for us, we didn't know how to walk without it. For some of us, including myself, we still carry the rifle as we walk because for us, we are still in the desert, waiting for the sun to rise, for the darkness to end. We are still in that good forsaken desert because we are still waiting to come home.

And whenever I told someone I was a veteran of the Iraq War, they always responded with the same question: What do you think about the war? Usually my response was that I didn't have a readily available opinion and that the topic was best left undiscussed. Exercising my right to be silent on the subject usually raised eyebrows, but I did have a response to that question and it wasn't one most of the general public liked to hear. War was a machine that kills without rhyme or reason, that has no feeling toward you either way, that stole from us the very best and the very worst of who we were with no particular plan for who might be next. It took away all that we were, all that we were not, all that we might've become, and at the end of the day, they stacked us neatly next to one another because among the dead there were no survivors, only the remnants of who we used to be and would never be again.

· · · · · · · · · ·

## The Fallout

We don't play hide and seek.

We don't scare Mommy.

We don't play war.

We don't talk in the car when Mommy's driving.

We don't shout in the living room because the ceilings echo.

We don't pretend to have a gun in our hand.

We don't pretend like we're dying when we play fight.

We leave Mommy alone when she's upset.

We make sure, when we go out to eat, that Mommy gets to sit in the corner.

We don't talk about dying or killing anyone.

We don't point at amputees when Mommy has to take us to the VA.

We don't touch the knives in Mommy's purse.

We don't talk about people being crazy.

We respect the dead on Memorial Day.

We say *Roger that* and know the signal for mount up and rally point.

We use them often.

We don't pretend to be a normal family because this is our normal.

··········
## Ghosts (#3)

Sometimes I wonder what would've happened if I had conversed with the Iraqi girl I saw in the market years ago, the one standing there with her mother next to one of our trucks and waiting to get water and supplies. I imagine it would be the way a camel spider stares down its prey before injecting venom. Silent. Unmoved. I sometimes imagine that she is not dead and has grown up like I have, getting married, raising kids, kissing them every night before she goes to lie down next to her husband like I do now, and thinking of how much the war has taken from her.

And sometimes, at night, early morning, o-dark-thirty, I look out the back sliding glass door at the outside world and imagine where she would be now, somewhere off in the desert in a small village, far from the city, but not yet on the outskirts of a town, nowhere near a checkpoint or weapons, somewhere in Iraq where the war cannot reach her now. She is looking out of her window, staring out at the stars, the vast desert, the oblivion beyond the horizon where she knows the war is still fighting against peace, where the new age technology of a first world country is giving the war a shot of adrenaline that has been begging for years to be used. She contemplates what the dunes would look like if they were scattered with bodies like the marketplace had been eight years ago, when she lost her father and mother instead of dying herself.

The concussive blast. The women and children, elderly, and herds of goats caught out in open land, the blast radius already certain of its killing capacity. She thinks of the shockwave, the debris, of what the dirt would look like when the blood soaked through it to make brown mud. And of the retaliation of men with vehicles bearing explosives that puncture the human barriers of crowded streets where families become separated and loved ones, shrapnel fodder.

Maybe as she stands there like I do, she thinks of all of this too. Maybe she thinks of her family who still grieves the loss, or the countless other children the blast orphaned that day. Or maybe if she were alive, she would think of me and trick her mind into thinking that her inaction, her unspoken words, her inability to help that day were not the mind's way of seeing itself as evil but rather the cyclical way that prey and predator need each other in order to survive the world bent on chaos and ruin.

$$\cdot \; \cdot \; \cdot$$

## IED

"I don't know why I did it, but I told him."

I looked up at the veteran sitting next to me. He pointed to one of my poems, the acronym IED, improvised explosive device. He said it has a different meaning now. I was puzzled at what he meant, so I listened as he began to tell me his story.

"I was sitting in my new counselor's office, talking to him about an incident that happened to me over the weekend. I was at Home Depot standing in the lumber aisle when all of a sudden I couldn't remember what I needed or why I was there. Frustrated, I punched the piece of sheet plywood in front of me. Like boom. Just punched it. I don't why I did it, but I did. So, when I tell the story to my counselor, the guy types up something on a piece of paper, prints it out, and hands it to me. It was a new diagnosis. I had been there not even five minutes and this guy hears one story I told him and diagnoses me all over again with something new. So I get upset at the guy, tell him there is no way that he could've diagnosed me by hearing only one story I told him."

The vet turned and looked at me. "You know what he diagnosed me as having?"

I shook my head.

"Intermittent explosive disorder. IED. All that time in Iraq and I've been labeled the same thing that tried to kill me. Can you believe that shit?"

I shook my head in disagreement, but the sad truth was that I could imagine being killed by an IED at war and at home.

· · · · · · · · ·
# NUMB3RS

"How many have you killed?"

The old man asked me when I told him I was a .50 cal gunner. The other questions he had asked when I mentioned I was a vet while we waited for a nurse to call our names at the front desk of the doctor's office no longer mattered, my answers forgotten. All the old man saw now was a killing machine that had a number, this quantifiable proof that I, not just the weapon I used, was capable of killing. Giving him the number would confirm it. And yet, to me, saying it aloud was an admission of guilt, a point of reference that someone could put their finger on and say, "See here, there is your proof. She's not capable of compassion." To me, the number was something that could be held against me or dangled over my head, as if anything that I happen to do later in life that's questionable, that number can be pointed to and used as evidence of my inability to care about life. I've told people the number before, mostly vets, Nam vets. But all they saw after I told them was the number of kills, not the invisible number of times I did not pull the trigger, the number of times I spared a life rather than taking it. No one seems to care about that number, and so it is never seen, but it holds just as much weight. So much so that I made sure I would never forget it. I tattooed the proof on my back: a large cross with a skull and crossbones screaming, a bullet hole in the center of the forehead. I carry it there as if to say, "Here is your proof. Here is what you need to see. This is the measure of who I am." It takes a lot of courage to pull the trigger, to take a life, but it takes even more courage to find a reason not to, to give life in a place where only death is created day in and day out. But there are other numbers as well. That's all that war is—a quantity that is added to or subtracted from.

Every day I was deployed in Iraq, I counted, measured, kept tallies and tabs on all sorts of things:

The body bags in the back of the truck after my first mission—3

The seconds that pass just before an incoming mortar round hits—4.1

How many in the unit have been killed—5

The number of times I wanted to call home but didn't—9

The months I waited until I saw my family again—10

The total number of gauze pads that fit into a grenade pouch—17

The pages I had left until I finished *The Sun Also Rises*—22

The number of birthdays and holidays I missed—29

The number of bullets in an M4 magazine—30

The number of hot meals I'd eaten at the DFAC—46

How many times I woke up from a nightmare screaming—too many

The number of tears shed over body bags filled with soldiers I didn't know—not enough

And yet none of these numbers made a difference to those at home, and the old man sitting next to me in the doctor's waiting room couldn't have cared less about any of them except the one—the number of people I've killed.

For me, this wasn't the measure of glory or honor but that of a job done too well. So, I give out the only number that gives weight or meaning to my time at war—the number of lives I chose to spare—and it is this number that I gave the old man when he asked me how many people I've killed: 250. I told him 250. He replied that the number seemed a bit high and did I really kill that many, but I replied that the number represented not how many I killed but how many I chose to let live. He looked at me strangely. Ashamed of the lowball number, I looked down at my black Converse sneakers as I told the old man that the number was not nearly high enough. He lifted an eyebrow at me and then nodded his head. The nurse called his name. He stood up and slapped me on the shoulder, which startled me. I flinched a little. The old man stepped back, thanked me for my service, and told me to take care. I looked at him bewildered. No smile. No handshake. I told him that I was just doing what they told me to do. He nodded his head and thanked me anyway before disappearing with the nurse through the double doors.

Years later I was driving my kids to school when I realized there was something in the road. It had been eight years since Iraq, but still my training, instinct, muscle memory, or maybe just my PTSD made me stop ten feet short of the object. It moved. I clinched the steering wheel. Was it worth getting out of the Jeep to investigate? I contemplated turning around until one of my boys in the backseat pointed to the object.

"Look, Mom, a duck."

Duck.

Duck.

I thought it over and over again until it registered that the duck was the quacking, flapping kind.

"Is he hurt?"

I looked closer, leaning over the steering wheel. There was blood on the pavement; the duck had been hit by a car, no doubt from some asshole driving too fast while texting on their phone. I knew I couldn't leave it there to die, and the voices in the backseat insisted that I help. I put on my flashers, got out of the Jeep, and walked toward it. It tried to get up, making me jump. Startled by its attempt to get away, I moved back, not wanting to injure it further, but I couldn't assess its injuries from far away. I slowly inched closer. By this time, two cars are backed up behind my Jeep, all interested as to why my vehicle had stopped in the middle of the road. A man walking his dog came up on the sidewalk.

"Is it hurt?"

I gave him my stupid face and told him, no, it's just sleeping.

The man muttered "fuck you" under his breath and handed me a section of his newspaper.

I gave him the stupid face again as I looked down at the newspaper section, at an advertisement from Ashley Furniture about a china cabinet and dinner set marked down for a heinously low price for the Presidents' Day sale. "Sunday, Sunday, Sunday" scrolled across the top of the ad in canary yellow bold lettering.

"To pick him up with," the man said.

"Why me? Because I stopped to see if it was all right or because my Jeep has an Iraq vet sticker plastered on the back window?"

"Both," he said, as he handed me an extra leaflet. "Just in case," he said, as he walked away with his dog in tow.

No chivalry these days, I guess.

The lady stopped directly behind my Jeep ran out, asked me if it was okay, and if there was a vet nearby. I almost gave her my stupid face, but then it occurred to me that New Tampa Animal Hospital was on the corner right before the school. I gave her my stupid face for good measure. I replied back to her that there's a vet down the street and to give it a call while I tend to the duck. She called. I stared at the duck the way my father, with no plumbing skills, used to stare at the kitchen sink when it was broken, trying to figure out the best way to fix it without fucking it up even more. I had been a Combat Lifesaver in Iraq, knew how to stitch a wound, stop bleeding, and check for fractures on a human. I guessed that a duck would be no different. I bent down to look at the duck, to see how bad it was. I felt its rib-cage. Nothing but mush. I shook my head and looked back at the lady calling on the phone.

"Don't bother."

She hung up and asked what I was going to do.

"The only right thing to do. Kill it."

The lady looked back at her car. Her son was in the back-seat playing on some gaming device. I looked over at the Jeep. The back window was rolled down; both boys had their heads out it, looking at me.

"Do me a favor," I said, nodding in the direction of the Jeep. "Keep them occupied."

She nodded at me, walked over to the Jeep on the other side, and asked the boys to roll up the window and come talk to her.

I heard one of my boys yell, "Stranger danger!"

I laughed and said it was okay that they talk to her.

With the boys occupied, I used the newspaper to pick the duck up. Walking over to the side of the road near a hedge, I set the duck down. Its mouth was open, panting; its tongue sticking out. I looked into its eyes. The brown surrounding its irises faded as its pupils got bigger. I sighed. Now or never. I put my hands around its neck. I hesitated. I tightened my grip around its neck harder. I froze.

The only other time I could remember freezing like that was a few months after I had gotten to Iraq. After a recovery run, on our way back to base with a 5-ton on the HET semitruck trailer, the fire that we had put out in the bed of the 5-ton broke out again. We pulled over on the side of Route Irish five minutes from Camp Liberty, got out, climbed on top of the trailer. Sergeant Lippert handed me up water bottles as I stood on one of the 5-ton truck tires and started dousing the flames. I was halfway into the third bottle of water when a bullet whizzed past my head and ricocheted off the quarter panel next to me. Sergeant Lippert hit the dirt and scooted underneath the HET trailer. I jumped off the 5-ton and onto the trailer bed, scooting underneath the axle and behind the tire I had just been standing on. In a low, prone position, I waited. With no weapon and the backup security a half mile down the road, I heard Sergeant Lippert tell me to get off the trailer and get to the ground. I went to move. Another bullet pinged off metal. And then again and again. Seconds of enemy fire turned into minutes until our convoy security came back for us. They laid down suppressive fire. I ran for it, jumping from the rig and toward the cab of the HET. I grabbed my M4 and jumped down next to Sergeant Lippert, who had only his side pistol. I started laying it down thick in the direction everyone else was shooting. Then it happened; an insurgent lifted his head just enough for me to get a shot at him. I was sure one of the .50 cal gunners from the security detail would pick him off, but he went back down. Then lifted his head again. Through my front sight, I could tell I had a clean shot. Sergeant Lippert spotted him.

"Shoot him."

I looked through my front sight again, gripped down on the front plastic handle of my M4, and waited for him to pop back up. He did seconds later, with an AK in his hand, shooting wildly in the direction of our convoy security. Sergeant Lippert looked at me and yelled in my ear to shoot him.

I gripped harder down on the plastic handle, lowered my head down to see through the front sight, and waited for him to show his head. He did. I froze again, but this time I watched through the front sight as his head snapped back, the bullet entered his forehead, and he disappeared entirely.

Looking down at the duck now, it was the same feeling—that out of everyone present, this job had fallen on me. I was the only one there in the right position who was qualified to do it. This time I did not freeze. I gripped down on the duck's neck harder. Snap. The body flapped a bit and then went limp, but I didn't let go until the panting stopped. Setting it down on the grass, I saw feathers fly out of my hands from where I had squeezed down too hard on its neck. I went over to the nearby retention pond and washed my hands of the blood and remaining feathers. As I stood up and walked back toward the Jeep, I nodded at the lady. She mouthed a "thank you." I half smiled. I opened the Jeep door, hopped in, put on my seat belt, turned off the flashers, and put the truck in drive. On the road again headed toward school, and the boys finally worked up the nerve to ask me what happened to the duck. I told them I killed it. From my rearview mirror, I watched as their eyes widened. I had said the wrong thing. The mother in me was kicking myself, but the soldier in me knew it was the right thing to say. A barrage of questions followed: *Why did you kill it? What will happen to it now? Will it go to heaven? Can ducks go to heaven?*

I listened to the questions all the way to the school drop-off line. I answered them all like a mother should, which meant that I lied: *It was for the best. Yes, it will go to heaven. Yes, ducks can go to heaven.* Up next for drop-off, I said my good-byes, told them I loved them, listened to the door slam shut, and watched them scurry away before I drove off. I left the school and drove down the road toward where the duck lay, but as I got closer I thought about what I should have told the children about the duck instead of my blatant, motherly lies. I wanted to answer them with the truth: *I put it out of its misery. It was better to have a quick death than a long painful one, like a sunken bullet wound to the chest that makes your lungs fill with blood until you choke to death. The duck will most likely decompose, rotting from the inside out until its bowels swell with gas and the internal organs putrefy enough that the smell attracts the vultures, a process that of course will take several hours, depending on how hot it is in the sun. Then the vultures will take their time picking the carcass apart, fighting over the best organs, the scraps with the most meat on them, until the duck's body is nothing but a pile of leftover flesh, sinew, and bone that will continue to rot, splayed out in the grass until the rest of the beasts and bugs devour it. And no, dear, it is not going to heaven.*

As I passed the duck's carcass on the side of the road, a blur of feathers and blood, I thought about my number, the number of lives I chose to save in Iraq. I thought about how my number hadn't changed since I left, but now, after today, it had. And though I wasn't in Iraq anymore and the duck was not human, I decided to subtract one. 249.

· · · · · · · · · · · · · · · · · ·

## A Message in the Sand

It seems as though every soldier is handcuffed to history, their lives made into the pages of a history textbook that years from now will mark the occasion of the invasion by a timeline, a ticker running off to the side reading, "Operation Iraqi Freedom and Operation Enduring Freedom," with the beginning date and a dash that is followed by nothing. There is no permanent death toll, no paragraph that tells the strategic battle plans that led to the end of the war, and no picture with a face that is labeled as the clear victor.

The war is still raging on.

The bombs still dropping.

The bullets still firing.

The people on both sides still dying.

. . . . . . . . . . . .

## The Boy I Killed

When the boys were seven, they asked me if I had killed anyone. The responsible mother that I was, I answered with "of course not." Then I asked them why they thought I had killed someone. They told me that they knew I had been a soldier, that I had gone to war, and that it must be the reason why I get so upset, start crying, and turn off the TV whenever a war movie is on and someone gets killed. It was a rational explanation from two very curious small children, and for the most part they were right. I wanted so badly to tell them the truth, to let them know how spot on they were about me, about the war, about why I acted a certain way, but I knew they weren't ready. And yet, I hope someday they will ask again, so that I can tell them this:

On most days I sped past the dead, watching, shooting, or observing the bodies turn to corpses, their chest cavities rippled backwards from bullet impacts, their bodies hitting the pavement or dirt with a dull thud that absorbed the blood, which seeped out of their chest or head or limbs as though it were a sprung leak in a hose line, easily patched up with a piece of cloth, if only our convoy would've stopped or paused a moment to aid them. I sat there and listened to the last words they spoke, which mumbled inaudibly the request for family, or sometimes they rambled on about the afterlife. Some asked for a final kiss or cigarette. Some just wanted one last sip of water. Either way, I sat there perched in the turret or behind a steering wheel as their bodies heaved and seized from the loss of blood, a death rattle that shook the bones clean of sin and broke open their mouths as they inhaled their last breath and let their soul slither out from the creases of their lips.

Or maybe this:

On a good day outside the wire, through the back gate, and away from the FOB, no one would die. The mission would go according to plan, a straight shot, no fancy business, just there and back. On bad days, when the ravens circled overhead as the convoy moved slowly down narrow streets and through throngs of people, the hairs on the back of my neck would stand at attention, my eyes tracing the outlines of building tops and side streets. And on really bad days, the body count exceeded the number of body bags we had brought with us.

But there's no relative distinction between any of these days, except for one, and it is this one that I will tell my children when they ask again:

He stood above me, two stories up on the edge of a building, with an AK-47 in his hand. Lightly, his finger pressed the trigger. He closed his eyes. *Blat. Blat. Blat.* The bullets whizzed past my head and into the concrete wall of the building behind me. He had missed shooting me in the head, the only part sticking out of the Humvee turret. I swiveled the turret around, pointing my .50 caliber machine gun to the right, glancing quickly from the sidewalk all the way up the building until my eyes met his—his weapon still pointed at me. The fear of uncertainty flickered in his eyes as we stared at each other. I couldn't shoot, but everything inside, from my heart slamming against my chest to the ringing in my ears, made the adrenaline course through my veins harder, beating my pulse into my fingertips, which longed to pull the trigger.

Visual contact. Rooftop. Three o'clock. A deep inhale and slow exhale. Waiting for the natural pause before the inhale again, I aimed in his direction and found him standing there trying to fix a weapons malfunction. Putting my gun at center mass, I wanted to mash the butterfly trigger down, let loose my fear, my anger, my will to live.

I don't remember now if he jumped or fell or even if I had shot him or someone else in the convoy had; those details are gone, lost by time and a well placed TBI. But he was shot, he flew through the air, he hit the ground, and I watched all of it. Of that much I am certain; the memory of his body is all I have left of that day.

A few seconds passed before I watched his body topple over the edge. A hollow thud is the only thing that accompanied the sound of bones being splintered and broken from the impact of his body hitting the street.

The boy lay dead on the ground five feet in front of me with six M2 Ball (706.7 grain) bullets from a .50 cal machine gun in his chest—the blood thin and shiny around the holes. The wounds gaping open resembled thrown-up hamburger meat— chunks of flesh resting on his abdomen. His neck was snapped sideways from his two-story swan dive from the roof where he'd stood with the AK-47, his finger mashed down on the trig- ger. He had missed his kill shot by fractions of a centimeter— his aim a little too left of center. His head was kinked up to the sky, his eyes open. His jawbone was touching his shoul- der. His mouth lay shoved open from the weight of his head pushing against his shoulder. Crimson blood dripped off his tongue as it lay halfway out of his mouth, bit in half on one side with pieces of a broken tooth stained tar-brown lodged into the soft tissue. His forehead was covered by nappy black hair that swept sideways across it, and his cheeks were thin—his face square-shaped. The young boy's arms were gangly—he had barely hit puberty. His brown flannel shirt had the top two buttons undone, exposing the bones of his clavicle. The blood from his chest drew a line down to his belly button, where it separated and trickled off his body onto the dust-covered ground. A congealed pool formed at the small of his back. He lay face up, arms twisted, legs canted off to each side, bro- ken—a mangled pile of flesh, sinew, and bone dead on the side of the street next to a pothole filled with raw sewage. A frail

young boy, he wore dark brown linen-type pants and hajji sandals and a muj talisman around his neck—Muhammad, the
prophet, stamped on its face and some Arabic writing that was
too faded to read, even if I could've deciphered it. His sandals
had fallen off midair on his way down. One lay next to him,
the other a few feet from his head. There were no thoughts
about killing or how it happened, only the body that was left
on the ground after the bullets stopped firing.

He could have been born Jahir, but he could've just as easily been born a girl, Amira. Maybe he was the only son of
Raheem Saeed Azar, a well-known businessman. Did Jahir,
after school, go to his father's warehouse to help pack and
load large wooden crates full of produce bound for various
Baghdad marketplaces? The scent of leeks, Zahdi dates, red
onions, and Persian limes wafted from the open doors each
time he stepped inside. What did the warehouse look like?
Maybe it was a large warehouse that had been in Jahir's family for several generations. Was his father proud like mine?
Did he hound Jahir about needing to do something with his
life? Or did his father have it all planned out for him already?
I know my father had plans for me. College. PhD perhaps, a
cushy job at one of the family friends' companies. A position
not too far up to be considered nepotism. I guess going to
war ruined all that for him. My father always reminded me of
what I gave up before I left for Iraq. Did his father walk him
around the warehouse floor once a month, reminding him
that someday the warehouse would be Jahir's to run? When
Saddam Hussein fell from power, had Jahir's family stayed
neutral? Maybe not taking sides was better for business. At
least, that's what my father would've done—not get involved
with politics; too many hurt feelings, he would've said. Jahir
didn't look like the soldier type or even close to being a patriot
for his religion, but maybe he had found that as the war in his
country moved on with time, his religion forced on him a tradition of sacrifice for Allah. I imagined his father too proud to
take sides like mine but behind closed doors to be a proclaimer
of faith and country. It is the Shi'a way, he could have over-

heard his father say from the kitchen as he spoke to Jahir's mother and grandmother. *Every boy must learn the ways of Muhammad.* Did Jahir want to be religious? Did he think his father was right, that in order to come of age he would have to serve? Our upbringing and our arrival in this place, was it so different? My father had pressured me constantly about getting into Stanford. I could imagine Jahir sitting on his bed as his father talked to him. We all endured the sacrifice for our families, his father could've said, but what sacrifice did his father mean and did it eat at Jahir when he dwelled on it too long, like college had for me? I bet it was hard for him to ignore the traditions of his religion. Three times a day it rang from the mosque loudspeaker—the *adhān* probably echoing off the warehouse floor, through the paper-thin walls of his father's house, through the alleyways and marketplace streets of Baghdad. The call to prayer backed by zithers and a stern voice chanting. Did it beckon him to take his place among the ranks? Maybe Jahir had been taught as a child that a man's honor lies in his family. His duty was to protect them. Did Jahir spend his days at the warehouse contemplating the war like I had done when I worked at a video store? Did he slip out the back door near his father's office at lunchtime to sit down and smoke? He wore a talisman around his neck—the inscription on the face worn. I wonder if he looked down at the talisman around his neck and questioned if his father was right. Did he think about the duty he had to his family, to his religion, as I had thought about my duty to my country? Was he resigned to telling his father that he would become a man of faith until he had reserved the right to take over his father's business? Did his voice waver like mine did when had I worked up the courage to tell my family my decision? Yet being a man of business didn't suit Jahir, and I wondered if this was why his pious stance was strong enough to kill another human being. Did he do it because he felt the urge to bring honor to his family or was he just as scared as I was to pull the trigger?

The late afternoon sun beat down, wafting waves of heat up from the ground like asphalt being freshly laid. The blood pool around the body had begun to sour, sending a putrid smell of iron and excrement into the air, like burning trash or raw sewage. The corpse of the young boy, fifteen at best, still lay twisted in the position he had landed in, his head in the shade of an apartment awning where a tomato plant in a hanging planter dangled precariously on a metal hook. The wounds on his chest had pools of blood around each frayed piece of flesh—his chest cavity sunken in. Both his eyes were wide as if his eyelids had been glued open.

The holes in the building in front of me were spread apart, with a crack in the concrete running down to the sidewalk where the boy lay dead. This street must have seen another firefight. The hanging plant twirled in a circle from the wind that had started to pick up. The late afternoons always brought wind, as well as the occasional sandstorm. The building was nothing special, a rundown merchant shop with apartments above the store and a staircase that led up to the roof. *Why'd he jump?* I looked down at the boy.

Frail and skinny, Jahir was not suited to a life of hard work in a warehouse, but maybe that's why piety was something Jahir was sure to be good at. He probably came from a good family that didn't care for him being a soldier of war the way mine had, but maybe anything was better than his family's constant nagging about getting his life together. That's why I left.

I wondered if the war followed him around to every produce delivery like it did to me in this country—the sound of far-off gunfire, soldiers in Humvees and tanks rolling around the highways and streets, patrols of military men stomping down the same sidewalk he had grown up strolling down, a soccer ball tucked underneath his arm. I wonder if he had spent as little time learning my language as I had his. Or maybe he was forced to spend four years in school, like I had, learning a foreign language that wasn't spoken in his country.

Maybe he was like me, a daydreamer. I imagined him drifting off for a moment in a daze, only to be snapped out of it by a merchant who was trying to hand back the signed delivery slip. Had the other boys in school teased him for always having his head in the clouds, like the girls in my eighth-grade class had? Did they tell him that the real world was out there and that he should start living in it? Did the boys chant that he lived in the clouds, looking for Muhammad, the prophet, instead of fighting for him? Did they shove Jahir to the ground, slap the books out of his hand, and make fun of his inability to fight back, like girls had done to me? Did Jahir think about fighting back, like I had, but couldn't bring himself to do it? Sitting in the cab of the delivery truck, did he wonder how he would he be able to fight in the name of Allah and bring honor to his family if he couldn't even fight back against the boys at school? He must have fired at me to prove them wrong. Or did he fight for his family or to survive in his country? Would he have been able to move on if it was me lying dead and not him?

The sun sank below the apartment building's roof, a shade of soft oleander formed behind the stratus clouds, and it seemed as though they streaked the sky in lines of pink. We had been there too long; the mission had taken longer than the typical drive-by shootings that took place when our Humvees rolled down the streets in the marketplace. The young boy's head was slanted just enough that his head was toward the oleander clouds, his eyes still fixated, open, staring up as though he were deep in thought. The blood from his mouth had clotted in a rim around it. The stain on his shirt was still wet, as though he had just been shot, but the blood was brown, aged from oxidation.

The young boy's limbs were frail and long—barely any muscle definition to be considered an athlete, but maybe it was because he was a bookworm. Maybe he was like me, destined for a future with nothing particularly amazing about it beyond what he was already doing. Our paths crossed here, and despite being on opposite sides of the gun, the young boy I killed no longer had a future—of that I was certain.

Was Jahir a believer in the possibilities of what could be or had he, despite his father's persistence that he take over the family business, continued to feed his curiosity about his religion? Maybe there were parts of the Qur'an he had not yet figured out. Did he go against his father's wishes like I had, taken up a life that my father was certain I was not destined for? Did he quit his daydreaming when he realized that it would get him killed if he didn't learn how to fight properly? Was he like me, sneaking up to the roof at night when everyone else was sleeping, our footsteps as gentle as we could manage? Did he sit looking out over the city, the vast unknown of his country, like I had before I left for Iraq, and just watch the lights of the city twinkle? Did he pray, like I did every night, for God to give the strength, the courage to serve, to lead him down a path different than this?

The corpse was entirely in the shade now, the awning covering him. The shadow of night was creeping in. The flies jumped from one side of his body to the next, the wounds on his chest festering as the insects buzzed. No one had come to claim the body or cover him up. He lay half in the street, face pointed up at the growing night sky. The star-shaped wounds were like a constellation on his chest, the ladle end of the Little Dipper. I looked at the talisman around the boy's neck. I pulled out my dog tags, another sort of talisman. Maybe he and I weren't so different after all. Maybe we were fated to meet and one of us was fated to die. I put my dog tags away, looked down at the boy, and wondered, What if it had been me? Would I look the same lying on the ground? He lay face up, arms twisted, legs canted off to each side, broken from the fall from the two-story building. He had tried to kill an infidel in the name of Muhammad, but did he fail?

I imagined what Jahir must have thought about as soon as he pulled the trigger and I swiveled around in the gunner's turret. Did he think he could've survived or did he know that he was as good as dead? When the six bullets pierced the flesh of his chest, did he panic? Did he look down at the ground, at the line of military trucks in the middle of the street, and envision a better ending than this one?

As Jahir leaped, I heard him wail "Allahu Akbar" over and over again and watched as he fell through the air, down toward the ground, his limbs limp and dangling.

Even now I haven't quite figured everything out, but on most days Jahir forgives me and on some days I can barely forgive myself. As I go about the usual routine of the day, doing laundry, picking up pieces of Legos I see stranded underneath furniture as I vacuum, I try not to think about it. I occupy myself with the living. But on rare occasions, when I am out and about, waiting for a car to pull out of a spot at the grocery store or dropping the boys off for football practice, I see Jahir walking, shuffling his sandals as he sways back and forth with his hands in the pockets of his torn linen pants. I watch him as he crosses my path without looking at me. I say nothing but watch as he keeps going, turns a corner, or disappears in the sea of cars. And as soon as Jahir trails off in the distance and is gone, I hear the honk of the car behind me or my boys shouting as they jump out of the Jeep with their football bags dangling around their shoulders, and I forget Jahir and that day until I see him again. Maybe next time, I will work up the courage to apologize.

· · · · · · · · · ·

## Playing War

The boys were playing in the backyard. I had consented to let them play with their Nerf guns. Bowen was running around chasing Zachary. The bullets whizzed out on automatic fire. Bowen's finger was mashed down on the trigger. Zachary was running frantically, side to side, trying to dodge the foam bullets. They bounced off his back and neck. One deflected off the Murcott tree. Bowen kept firing, every once in a while missing Zachary completely, and it wasn't long until Bowen's magazine of foam bullets was empty. Realizing this, Zachary spun around, unhurt by Bowen's rear assault. Zachary had a full magazine of ammo and was running toward Bowen. Bowen was now running away in a sprint screaming, "Don't shoot! I'm out of ammo!"

Zachary unleashed the bullets from his Nerf gun, one after another. Bowen scrambled to get away. He yelled as he ran toward me, "Mom's base." He wrapped his arms around me.

"I can't die because Mom is base. You can't kill me because Mom is base."

Zach got upset. Threw his Nerf gun on the ground and screamed, "No fair. You can't make Mom base."

"Yes, I can."

They argued back and forth, but I stood there stunned. Unsure of what to say to them, I held onto Bowen tightly.

"You can't use Mom as base."

"Yes, I can. Mom came back from war and didn't get hurt. She's like a superhero."

Zach was visibly upset at Bowen's rational explanation.

"Just because Mom has a force field of not dying doesn't mean she's base."

"Ya-huh, if I hold her, I can't die." Bowen looked up at me. "Right, Mom?"

• • • • • • • • • • • • • • • • • • • • • • • • • • •

## The Weight of War Takes Us Under

No one knew when the war had started. Some thought that the war began a long time ago; others believed that it has been there since the beginning of human history, but either way, it existed. Back home, they searched for reasons, the *whys* and *whodunits*, because they wanted to believe we had gone for a noble cause, that there could be an end result, a time when there was no more war, a time for it to end. But they were wrong. The war came out of a desire, a petty need to further one's reach or gaze, and like so many before them who remembered the memory of the great wars and what glory of victory had once felt like when they claimed it, they let us go to war until it followed us, the distance of the past creeping up on our bodies like a five o'clock shadow. Like our grandfathers and fathers, the war would follow us, their sons and daughters, and it would live on after us, if only to see another war take its place.

At times, when we felt the war closing in on us, we tried to shut it out with more violence, but it crept into every vein pulsing with the need to kill against our skin as though it were trying to escape, but no sooner had the urge to tap the vein subsided once more than we were hurled back into the violence as though our addiction were an absence that could be measured in bullets and weighed in body bags.

And though we did not know when the war started, what name to give it, how or when it might end, or what place we should give it in our lives once we left the battlefield, we knew it well and still do, as though it is a battle buddy that we still depend on to watch our back. And what we still do not know is peace, the manner in which it is found, or how to leave such a constant friend behind because the necessary training that helped us survive the war also taught us that no one is to be left behind, and so we carry the war with us, a friendship formed through the mutual understanding that our survival is based on how violent one human can be toward another when given the bullets and the means with which to use them.

It is now more than a decade later, and still there is no peace because the war has not ended and surely never will because there is no real end to war, only the absence of it, a lull in the fighting, a time during which another generation is born for the kill.

And yet, I pray that someday this world might give us a war
and no one will come.

# EPILOGUE

## Present Arms

The ceremony could be on Camp Liberty. Or maybe even in San Diego. Everyone from Bravo Company 299th FSB will be there. ACUS. No dress greens. There will be a picture printout. Or a nice framed one perhaps. There will be a pair of boots, a rifle, dog tags, and helmet. They will all be stacked up in front of the formation representing a soldier's death. A kind of fucked-up irony. There will be no body on display, just the pile of things left behind.

First Sergeant will stand in front of formation and shout, "Company, atten-tion!"

Bravo Company will come to the position of attention.

First Sergeant will call out, "Sergeant Crump."

"Here, First Sergeant."

"PFC Taft."

"Here, First Sergeant."

"Specialist Kennedy."

"Here, First Sergeant."

"PFC King."

There will be no reply. Silence.

First Sergeant's voice might waver as he says it again.

"Private First Class King."

And as if no response has pissed him off, as if I had been caught fucking up again, he will say it louder with inflection and anger, a sort of controlled rage that bounces off of each syllable.

"Private First Class Brooke Nicole King."

The air will be still as the silence of the formation stands rigid. Some will hold back tears. Others will bend their knees slightly to keep them from buckling under the weight of their own body telling them to fall to the ground and grieve.

"Taps" will play long and slow, dragging the battlefield's lullaby in B flat. The formation will stand there and wait for it to end, each soldier acutely aware that some day, it will be them that the trumpet player purses his lips to when the mouthpiece comes close enough to echo the sound of mourning. But for now, they will stand in formation, stare at a picture of who I once was, and think about how lucky I was to have gotten out alive.

# SOURCE ACKNOWLEDGMENTS

I wish to thank several publications for their support of my work.

"Redeployment Packing Checklist" appeared in *It's My Country Too: Women's Military Stories from the American Revolution to Afghanistan*, edited by Jerri Bell and Tracy Crow (Lincoln: Potomac Books, an imprint of the University of Nebraska Press, 2017).

"Redeployment Packing Checklist" appeared in *Incoming: Veteran Writers on Returning Home*, edited by Justin Hudnall, Julia Dixon Evans, and Rolf Yngve (San Diego: So Say We All Press, 2015).

"Redeployment Packing Checklist" appeared in *War Portfolio*, edited by Brian Turner, in *Prairie Schooner* 87, no. 4 (Winter 2013).

"NUMB3RS" originally appeared in *Retire the Colors: Veterans and Civilians on Iraq and Afghanistan*, edited by Dario DiBattista (Albany NY: Hudson Whitman/Excelsior College Press, 2016).

"Dog Tags" originally appeared in *War, Literature, and the Arts* 27 (2015).

"Breathe through Your Mouth" originally appeared in *Red, White, and True: Stories from Veterans and Families, World War II to Present*, edited by Tracy Crow (Lincoln: Potomac Books, an imprint of the University of Nebraska Press, 2014).

CPSIA information can be obtained
at www.ICGtesting.com
Printed in the USA
LVHW100905170822
726161LV00001B/108